Painted From Memories

Barbara Forte Abate

Halcyon Moon Books

Halcyon Moon Books

ISBN: **978-0692209349**

This book is a work of fiction. Places, events, and situations in this book are purely fictional and any resemblance to actual persons, living or dead, is coincidental.

Printed in the United States of America

Original cover design created by Caitlin L. Abate

For Jimmy

Also by Barbara Forte Abate

The Secret of Lies

Asleep Without Dreaming

ACKNOWLEDGEMENTS

There are no words to adequately convey how truly appreciative I am of you who take my books into your hands and travel through my stories. You are a treasure to this writer's heart.

And to those of you who so graciously continue to rally my efforts to the moon and back—you know who you are and I love you most dearly.

A sincere debt of gratitude and appreciation to Karen Sanderson, "The Word Shark," for reading and polishing my pages as a consummate professional and then staying to become a friend.

Viva Cristo Rey!

One

She considers telling him the truth—that she isn't the person he thinks she is—but in the end she doesn't. To say something is to potentially say everything. And it is simply too late now.

They are married by a justice of the peace in Columbus, Georgia; joined together, in a spare ceremony quickly concluded. She senses an urgency to gather every detail, whether whole or fragmented, tucking them away to be saved forever after; scenes strung together in a reel of vaguely scribbled portraits barely familiar even as they are unfolding.

A young woman in borrowed wedding attire. A sweetly uncomplicated dress—gauzy white cotton lightly sprinkled with a pattern of tiny blue flowers—plain white pumps that pinch her toes as much from unfamiliarity as imperfect fit.

It's as if a million hours have passed since morning, when she'd tried, but miserably failed, to replicate the hairstyle torn from the pages of a discarded magazine she'd picked-up from a sticky plastic seat in the laundromat; thumbing the pages as she waited for her jeans and tee shirts to tumble dry. What she'd imagined would be effortless was anything but, and her frustration took a steady climb with each clumsy attempt to coax her unruly mass into a passable semblance of the glossy model's sleek and tidy chignon. In the end surrendering, leaving her heavy, wheat-colored hair in its accustomed state—tumbling down her back in unfurled waves forever determined to manage themselves. The impossible-to-attain image balled and pitched at the waste can beneath the bathroom sink.

Distracting points of nervous apprehension peck away at the lining of her stomach like a snarl of peevish birds as she stands beside Gray in the colorless room, helmed by a stiff and unsmiling justice of the peace, startled by the sound of her own voice reciting the solemn promise of forever vows.

… and do you, Catherine, take Grayson …

She focuses, listens, waits, and still she fails to catch the passing echo of her own certain response. But maybe it doesn't matter. Her reply is *yes.* It will always be *yes.*

Despite the wavering mirage she holds of herself, her recall of Gray holds sharp and clear; the steady light and surety of his presence a stark contrast to the pallid backdrop of the room. Even as she stares at the disinterested man standing before them—watching the sharp line of his mouth as he speaks, hearing his words without listening—her focus never leaves Gray standing at her side, firmly rooted, steady as a rising oak. *Her Gray,* like some eternal shining prince in his neat dark suit, each of her stolen sideways glances bringing a surge of warmth flooding her insides, trailing along her thighs, pooling at the backs of her knees.

She is so wildly, crazy in love. So altogether lost to him. The sort of feelings, which before Gray, were as impossible to conjure as stone birds taking flight. A delicious madness that allows her to overlook, even forget, the inherent dangers of such all-out surrender.

Fear, uncertainty, danger—they have been the flavors of her life until now, when the impossible collides with an unshakable sense of wonderment-laced disbelief, shattering her long-held conviction that such a person as Grayson Barnett cannot possibly exist. The sort of miracle desperately longed for, but never quite believed, should it actually arrive. Blink too hard, too fast, and it's gone. A mirage so fleeting as to never fully form.

For the first time in forever, Cat dares just enough to believe that the past is ended. A book slammed shut on the final chapter, at last clear to lock the door and lower the sash against the wrecked and hideous memories of her long-ago existence. With one defining sweep, Gray has unknowingly erased the careless scribbles colored outside the lines, allowing Cat to relinquish all things undesirable, ugly, and poisonous—her entire life until now.

The constant sense of dread barely concealed beneath the veneer of her uncertain smile is steadily fading. She has stepped into the role of a lifetime, a nameless wanderer plotted into a shimmering fairytale. The press of things threatening to split wide open at any instant, now steadily spinning off into the distance.

And she very nearly forgets for a time, the truth that she is as much an impostor as she is a liar.

Two

It isn't as though he's the first man to tell her he loves her. He's just the first one she's believed. The first she's ever longed to hear say it.

And there are times when simply looking at him breaks her heart. Not in a sad way. It's the other kind of heartbreak. The kind that clenches the insides upon discovery of something particularly beautiful or altogether implausible.

There have been passing moments when she considers telling him. Not all of it, just enough to allow herself to feel honest. But how? How does she go about unclasping her fingers from around a secret she's held as tightly as sin, caged within her fist with the hope it will eventually suffocate?

She knows so little about relationships—about love, sharing, unveiling. Considerations of full disclosure begin and end the same. She wrestles with herself through several rounds of uncertainty, and when the bell rings she finds herself unable to break from the corner.

Maybe if he hadn't asked her to marry him, maybe then it wouldn't be so hard. But a proposal changes everything. The boldness of unvarnished honesty feels all at once uncertain. Even dangerous. If he knew, would Gray still feel the same way about her? Could he?

She isn't altogether sure what she believes. Whether it is possible or even sustainable to separate a person from their past, because maybe the truth is that personal history is something of a predetermined grafting which cannot be undone, regardless of assiduous attempts to disown it.

In the months preceding their flurried wedding ceremony, it was far too easy for Cat to sidetrack her thoughts, pretend, and ignore, and now it is too late. They are already connected. Contracted. Promised. Vowed for life.

And yet, what does it really matter? For whatever the reason, it appears she has won a free pass to trust her instincts and hold to the conviction the odorous mess of her childhood has no place or purpose aligned with the brilliant promises awaiting her future as Mrs. Catherine Barnett.

That Gray has only alluded to, but never pursued entry into the carefully sequestered compartments of her past, make her omissions all the more effortless. His inquires, when they come, are simple and ordinary, asking where she is from (Memphis she says, because she likes the sound of it), places she's been (nowhere really), her family (mother, father, sisters—though in fact there is only Leafie—Leafie her baby sister, gone for years, Cat doesn't know where). Safe, uncomplicated questions that fail to stir the ancient dust.

She is far too relieved by his lack of appetite for details of her history and missing family to consider his apathy at all curious or otherwise lacking. It simply makes caution that much easier, allowing her ease in giving him only those things she deems it favorable for him to hear—nice, safe little bits of nothing. Lies which feel more and more like truth every time she is called upon to repeat them.

Just as she swallows the temptation to ask for particulars of Gray's own history, limiting her questions to the uncomplicated variety least likely to elicit in-kind queries, even as she longs to know everything about him—every bump, bruise, and trophy that have melded together to form the man.

Thankfully, miraculously, Gray accepts her penchant for brevity without resistance, as if he finds nothing especially curious in her simple responses and careful omissions; her strong deliberate strokes into safer currents. Regardless of his reasoning, Cat gratefully accepts his undeclared agreement that past things are simply that—the prologue which doesn't require reading before paging into the future.

It is a gift Cat grasps with the gratitude of someone spared a deadly blow. And for the first time in her life she believes it wholly possible that she might successfully conceal the litter of ancient corpses, secure in the assurance they will remain where they've been entombed.

It hardly appears necessary to continually strive to hide things her new husband has little interest in seeing.

"I don't know … I've just always been alone," he says.

They sit together on a wooden bench at the bus stop downtown, although they are not waiting to go anywhere. The final handful of passengers have long boarded and gone, leaving Gray and Cat alone in the deepening twilight.

The heat of the day has turned their rented room impossibly airless and hot, the sounds and smells of neighbors too close to pretend away, and they look forward to the solitude of this quiet place where no one cares to come afterhours.

"Well, not always … just for a really long time. There was a family once," he adds, and she is uncertain where the statement has come from. What question he is answering, or even if one has been asked.

Once? She glances away quickly from the crux of what he has said, startled by the recognition of a statement that might just as easily have been her own.

"It was a fire in the middle of the night," he says, pausing, as if reaching for something—some thought or necessary word which will enable him to continue. "Everyone was asleep," he speaks so quietly Cat must lean forward to catch his words. "Completely unaware," he says, of the blaze sweeping through the house on a merciless tear, smoke and flames smothering his entire family in their beds. Not a single one spared. All gone before the first fire truck arrived. Even the family dog and a raccoon his brother had raised from a baby.

There'd been an investigation afterward, and the fire marshal concludes that a candle left burning on a kitchen sill is the cause of this unthinkable thing. Even as she listens, Cat is amassing a fleet of silent prayers, thanking circumstance, divine intervention, or simple luck, whichever is responsible for keeping Gray safely removed on an overnight camping trip with a schoolmate on the night his family burns to death.

She is at once stunned and ashamed. As often as she has wrung hands over her own injuries and the efforts necessary to conceal them, she hasn't paused to consider that Gray might be carrying some of his own.

She drops her gaze, thoughts clenching tightly, imagining the impossible task of relaying such news to a young boy—to anyone—and how unfathomable it would've been for Gray to receive.

The pores of her face seem to swell with the friction of rushing emotions radiating up from a million points beneath the surface, her skin feeling too heavy to remain firm against her cheeks. She struggles to focus, trying to absorb the full actuality of this terrible thing he's told her. What does one say when handed such news? Where are the adequate words to fit the grievous scope of a thing so devastating?

His voice is a steady monotone, neither rising nor falling as he offers her the particulars. They are details she will recall often enough later, when she is alone and it is safer to think beyond this immediate moment and the necessary effort it requires to untangle all he is right now telling her.

Though the edge that will remain sharpest in her recollections, is the particular way he unreels the sequence of events—like someone repeating a tragic story they've run across in a newspaper. Touched, but not so deeply affected. And she knows if she is ever to tell her own story, it will require a similar distance—a span of safe detachment. The only conceivable place of endurance while in the throes of surrendering everything.

He talks and Cat listens, sensing she is not required to offer words as much as there is nothing for her to say. He is surrendering this piece of his history without expectation. Her role is simply to hear.

She slides her gaze toward Gray with undue caution; tenuous steps across a frozen lake—aware of the danger should she lose her footing, land with unnecessary force, crack the surface, and plummet through.

His face is unreadable, held within a faraway expression lending no suggestion as to how she might react or what she should say. Questions stream through her head in a deluge, yet she can see no gentle means for asking them now, or whether they can even be asked at all.

She might have told him then, that she, too, is alone. Alone even when her family was still here.

Their separate histories suggest little similarity other than vacancy—nothing about her losses that might ever conceivably align themselves to those distinguishing his.

So now, when Cat sees a window briefly cracked open along the edge of her vision, she nevertheless hears a steady internal mantra repeating over and over with the persistence of a returning tide, warning her to hold to her ancient oath. There is nothing from her past that belongs here hovering over-top the clean slate of her future.

She waits for him to continue, leaving his grave disclosure untouched where it lies in the air between them, neither shifting, rising, or swelling larger.

"You'd think it should be impossible to forget something like that—what it feels like to be part of a family. But I have. As if it's only something I heard about, but never actually had. It's been so long ... just a really long time."

He talks and she is grateful he leaves no open and obvious spaces for her to try and fill. Because isn't this the way it needs to be with experiences long extinct? The retelling of past horrors explained in statements of fact. Purposely devoid of the dramatics spawned by emotion, if only because they have already been well spent at the time the story first unfolded.

She listens to his quiet voice, anxious that she is not erroneous in interpreting his words for what they appear to be—a necessary recollection, and not an invitation. And yet, when he all at once turns his head to look at her, his expression is that of someone caught talking aloud in an empty room, distinctly embarrassed for having said any of it.

For the briefest instant she considers telling him, yes, she knows what it's like. She knows how it happens and how it feels. She so well understands the depths of aloneness. She might tell him, but won't. Because all too quickly she's lost the words. Possibly never even had them.

Three

It arrives with the sobering thud of a grim diagnosis. And even before she rips open the envelope, knowing to expect the folded pages will hold something wholly unwelcome simply in light of the hand that has scripted and sent them, Cat vows she will not care.

The envelope is devoid of a return address, but such particulars are unnecessary. Cat will recognize the aggressive points and angles of Maysel Carper's handwriting as long as she has eyes to see and thoughts to remember, and she is altogether certain Maysel knows this.

The postmark is badly aimed, running off the edge of the envelope, so Cat has no way of knowing how long it has been stuffed into the mail slot in the downstairs hall of the old hotel where she and Gray are currently renting a room. Impersonating an ordinary letter, when it is anything but. She instantly recognizes the missive for what it truly is—a venomous snake poised to strike—when she spies the letter nesting between a Piggly Wiggly store flyer and a catalog advertising ladies undergarments.

The chilling questions of how Maysel has found her, and why she would even want to, crash together with the force of a sobering slap as Cat slips her pinky finger inside the glued flap and slices it open. Her immediate impulse to toss away the poisonous thing unopened, holds firm even as she unfolds the sharply creased papers and her grim stare races over the sentences, jaw instinctively clenching against the injury of words striking in a volley of precisely aimed points.

She skims the pages—startled at first, then furious—disbelief rising in an uneven tide, slamming her hard with the stinging current of Maysel's tirade. Each deliberate blow a starkly familiar aggression culled from Maysel's personal arsenal of damaging remarks.

'Incredibly rude and insulting, thankless, selfish … unappreciative … never adequately repaid ... that I in any way deserve to be so humiliated … having to stand there smiling like the village idiot pretending that yes of course I know all about what you've done … running off and getting married to God knows who … it would be no surprise to hear that pregnancy is involved … and if you honestly think everyone doesn't know what this is about you're fooling yourself … no self respecting woman runs away with some man they just met unless they've gone and gotten themselves in trouble … and after everything we've done for you and your sister … everything we tried to teach you so you won't make the same disgraceful mistakes as your mother … that Curtis and I have been so humiliated is unconscionable … hear some of the things people are saying … though I seriously doubt you're embarrassed or ashamed whatsoever … so spiteful to the only people who ever lifted a finger to help … the only ones who did a cotton-picking thing to pull you girls out of that filthy mess …'

And even as her outrage swells—pulses madly with the injury of absorbing Maysel's hideous lies and accusations—Cat cannot force herself to drop the pages she holds in her hands.

How has Maysel found her? Cat has been so purposeful not to leave even a single breadcrumb along her trail. And yet this knot of paper filled with hateful words has effectively transported Maysel Carper into this very room with her—a flesh and blood apparition as real and threatening as she has ever been.

Cat assures herself that if she scans the pages quickly they will have no chance to settle, tripping over brief snatches of words and sentences for their familiarity, having heard the assessment of her character recited countless times before, even as she finds herself impossibly caught and held.

'Considering what you came from, maybe I expect too much in asking to be treated with some semblance of respect and dignity. Not that I care about my own feelings, but Curtis is inconsolable … when I think about everything we did for you girls … and this is how you repay us? This is how you show gratitude?

How conveniently you forget everything we did for you. You'd like to pretend you raised yourself, fed and clothed yourself … we saved you when no one else gave a damn what happened to you either way … if you put even a pinky's worth of effort into pretending to be thankful … appreciated even half of the sacrifices we made for you … managed to give a speck of thought toward anything or anyone other than yourself and your own selfish pleasures.'

They are accusations that might possibly matter if Cat allows them to settle, but she is steadfast in denying them weight. She refuses to care what Maysel has heard, embellished, or invented. There is no single detail, monumental or otherwise, Cat will allow to jar her interest. Regardless of what Maysel wishes or assumes, thinks or feels, it is no longer of consequence to Cat. In less than three days she and Gray will be gone from here. Far enough away to begin the process of believing this rotten spot on the world has never even existed.

It isn't Cat's intent to lie. She has no pre-scripted plan. She only knows she cannot tell him the truth. The beginning of the lie arrives without hesitation. Simply. Lands soft and painless. The lines so steady and clear they could just as easily be the truth were they not so false.

She understands that once she says these things there is no going back. Once the lie is spoken, it will become her truth.

"Oh … yes, that came the other day," she says. "Just a letter from my Aunt Maysel." She reaches for the empty envelope as though an afterthought, when the thing she most wants to do is snatch it away and mince it into fragments before his brain has the chance to record seeing it.

Somehow she's overlooked the offending sleeve of paper amidst the piles of confusion amassed on the kitchen counter where she'd been sorting and packing contents from the cabinets and drawers. Thankfully, the contents are long destroyed; the hideous pages burned in the kitchen sink, and the ash washed away while Gray is gone on a hunt to locate a fair-priced set of used tires for the truck.

Cat slides two fingers into the empty envelope, then, feigning surprise, "Hum… it's not in here, I wonder what I did with it," she glances over the surrounding accumulation as if genuinely expecting to spy the letter lying atop a stack of dishes or sprouting from the tangle of oddball tidbits upended from the kitchen junk drawer.

"Okay, so now I feel like a jerk because I don't remember you even mentioning you have an aunt."

"No? She's my mother's older sister. They're very close. Anyway, it was just a nice little note saying how sorry she is to miss meeting you," Cat says, hating how easy it is becoming to invent and embellish.

"Where does she live? We can stop on our way to—"

"No … well, that's the thing—she said she's getting ready to leave for China. She's going to visit the family. I'm pretty sure she's left by now."

China? What brand of madness compels her say China of all places? Her lies land decidedly heavy on her own ears, and yet they come with such ease, the compulsion to rein them in is all too readily dismissed.

"China? Really? For some reason I though you told me they were in the Sudan."

Cat stares at him, held stiff by the fear that he will see and easily comprehend the telltale marks of deceit crawling across her face.

And yet he altogether misreads her expression. "Um, uh oh … would I be correct in assuming what you said before wasn't exactly what I heard?" he smiles.

So simply he plants the necessary seeds to grow her recovery.

"No … actually, I probably didn't explain it so well. When I said they were missionaries I might not have mentioned how much they move around. Sometimes it's months before I find out exactly where they are. The only reason I even know they're in China now is because of Maysel's letter."

He reaches for her hand, his expression turning serious. "I know you like to pretend otherwise, but I understand how hard this is on you. When was the last time you saw each other?"

"It's been a couple years. Every time I see my sisters they look like they've grown a foot and they're only eight and nine."

"I can't pretend I'm not wildly happy you're here and not there. I never would've found you in China, or Africa … or wandering through some rain forest in Timbuktu," he says, enfolding her in his arms.

Cat presses her face against his chest, closing her eyes to keep from seeing the deepening fissures and ominous shadows swelling to accommodate her deceit.

They will leave for Maine in two more days, aiming for a town named Lost River, where Gray has a job waiting at a lumber mill. Cat doesn't quite know what she'll do with herself once they're tucked away in this place she's never seen, but her trust and purpose rest in the person and not the destination. Though, still, it is the greatest comfort knowing how blessedly distant that place will be from here.

Four

It's raining the morning they leave Columbus.

Cat insists on helping Gray load the meager collection of cardboard boxes packed with their clothes and a spare assortment of personal items, brushing past his determined attempts to steer her toward the dry shelter of the truck's cab. She stands beside him in the warm drizzle, watching as he arranges the cartons in the bed of his old Ford pick-up, ready to offer assistance when he lashes a heavy canvas tarp securely overtop their cargo.

And now they are truly leaving, pulling away from the curb. Cat takes a quick glance in the side view mirror, half expecting to see a wild-eyed Maysel running along the rain slick pavement, determined to extract yet one more payment against the balance of Cat's forever debt.

"Second thoughts?" Gray asks, downshifting, rolling the truck to an easy stop at the intersection as the traffic light winks from yellow to steady red. He turns his face, smiling at Cat in that particular way of his; an expression never failing to send her heartbeat into a crazy canter, reminding her just how far she's fled from the closed and emotionally void woman so long in residence beneath her skin. *Catherine Barnett, Catherine Barnett*—her voice repeats in silence, filling the space inside her head with the remarkable truth of who she has become. No more a victim held captive by the circumstances of her previous life. No longer gripped by the unforgiving tentacles of old, angry ghosts. She is someone else—is part of someone else—belongs to someone else.

She tips her head. Smiles. No second thoughts. Never. Only a giddy sense of gratitude which defies even the most carefully chosen or eloquent arrangement of words.

"There's just one thing …" Gray pretends a grimace.

"Uh oh, what did you forget?" she says, glancing up to see that the road map is there tucked above the visor, swinging her gaze to the narrow space behind his seat and spotting his jacket, his sunglasses on the dashboard …

She doesn't want to go back for anything. Not even for an instant. Never ever wants to go back.

He catches her gaze, "Just feeling a little guilty about uprooting a genuine Southern Belle. I'm pretty sure there must be a law or something."

She feels her limbs un-tense; the muscles in her face relax. "You, sir, are ridiculous. There's no such thing as a Southern Belle—such creatures only exist in old books and men's imaginations," she says, reaching for the lighthearted response necessary to camouflage the flare of angst stirred to the surface by his teasing proclamation. Of course he has no way of knowing how thoroughly she'd come to dislike all things Southern. That the only comfort she's ever received from this place of heavy old earth and sorrow is now, in leaving it.

"Cat? What's wrong? " Gray says, the teasing tone at once gone as he swerves his watchful stare from the slick blur of roadway to take in her face.

She nods away his question even as she invokes an immediate silent prayer—the same invariable plea she's repeated countless times over the past months—a fervent petition that Gray will never find out any of it. Will never know anything of the place or people she's come from—just how many starless galaxies span the distance between herself and any romanticized portrait of genteel fantasy.

"Nothing. I was just thinking how sad it is that yet another of your crazy Yankee misconceptions has crumbled to dust, and I hate being the one to give you the bad news," she smiles weakly, when her intent has been to produce a lighthearted grin. "If it's a Southern Belle you're looking for, you'll have to crawl between the pages of *Gone with the Wind* and hope you bump into one, because that's the only place they exist, my dear Rhett Butler—in fiction."

"If I really believed that, Cat, it'd break my heart."

She doesn't answer, opens her clenched fist to squeeze his fingers resting warmly on her knee.

They've been on the road for hours, yet the ongoing press of heavy grey skies and hard rain make it seem as though entire days have passed. They have stopped at a gas station in Maryland to fill-up and switch drivers, and Gray is already dozing. His head awkwardly slumps sideways, barely grazing the window glass.

Cat concentrates her stare through the rain streaked window, pinning her gaze to the painted line denoting the center of the road, anxious that slackening her attentions for even a second will send the trucks tires drifting from the blacktop and head-on into a tree, a ditch, whatever threat is there just beyond the moving wall of rain.

Her temples throb in rhythmic echo of the tapping fingers marching back and forth along a deepening groove inside her skull, and only when the truck swerves, tires unable to gain traction against the rain polished pavement, does she recognize she is going too fast. That at the same time she is pinching the bridge of her nose between thumb and forefinger in an effort to quiet the chaos scrambling inside her head, her foot is pressing down harder on the accelerator.

She lifts her foot, slows, grips the wheel like a lifebuoy and regains control. She shoots a fleeting glimpse toward Gray, thankful that the momentary crisis has merely caused his head to shift position, his sleep otherwise undisturbed.

Another hour gone.

The rain slackens into a momentary lull for several dozen miles, but now returns full force. Cat holds her attention steady on the roadway even as her thoughts drift … swirl and churn … not altogether aware when her focus shifts and she is all at once fighting the instinct to swerve and duck the reeling images of ancient things hurtling toward her. Broken segments of memory slam against the windshield, oncoming stones shattering on impact, releasing a pungent spray of unbreathable vapor. Unwanted remembrances twist her thoughts into a snapping crescendo inside her head, hissing like a volley of schoolyard taunts as they scratch sharp claws along the surface of her brain.

Why won't they leave her alone? Stop chasing her? She's remembered it enough … relived and relived it.

She considers waking Gray, anxious for the reassurance of his warm eyes and gentle strength reminding her that this is now—this is real and everything else is not. But she fights what feels to be a selfish urge. She has only been driving a few hours and it's clear he is all-out exhausted.

Her skin feels at once hot and cold as Henry's venomous growl rushes up from somewhere behind her, terrible sounds breaking loose as she tries to melt herself into the slender hollow separating the crippled old chiffarobe from the yellow stained wall—trying not to see, trying not to hear, trying not to take it in—willing her mind to slam shut. Safe and faraway. The grainy flesh of aged and flaking plaster strangely comforting where her fevered skin presses against the pocked surface. She hears Leafie crying. Terrified infant wails far off and yet so close it sounds as if they are coming from Cat herself …

Her hands wring the steering wheel, choking it hard; the white bones of her knuckles pressing up under her skin like a row of white porcelain knobs. She jerks her head, shooting a look toward Gray, holding her breath—releasing a soft, strangled sigh of grateful relief that his eyes remain closed. His own subconscious thoughts safely adrift and faraway.

The rain is endless. At times it slows and tapers off as if the skies have finally been wrung dry, but then the deluge returns, harsh and pounding, the wipers working harder to spank the curtain of water from the windshield.

Gray has reclaimed the wheel and he downshifts now, his foot easing off the gas pedal. The speedometer needle drops, barely touching 20. His hard stare, framed within a concentrated frown, holds intent focus on the blur of roadway undulating in watery sheets beyond the windshield.

Cat steals a glimpse at his profile, drops her lids for a moment before shifting her eyes back to study him. Her head is tipped sideways against the back of her seat as if on the verge of dozing, but instead her gaze travels his face. The familiar stir of liquid warmth leaks through her insides as she traces an invisible finger along the sharp line of his nose … the curve of one high-set cheekbone … passing over lips that smile easily, eyes as soft a shade as the color of his name. A face that sits nicely on the heart.

A surge of love and gratitude rushes up to the base of her throat, flooding out in a swell of impossible-to-contain adoration for this man who she is now tied to for eternity, unable yet to believe that they have somehow managed to find each other in spite of the mean-spirited defiance of the world.

She slides across the seat and clutches his elbow, hugs the firm crook of his arm tight against her chest, surprising them both. He turns his head, his gaze reaching out like a responding caress before turning his attentions back to the rain-washed roadway; a silent, fleeting exchange, pure in a way that reaches the very deepest depths inside.

"You know I love you madly, my Cat," he says, lifting her hand to his lips and gently kissing the palm, sealing the indelible imprint of these very same words laid out across her heart.

No one has ever been this happy. No one has ever been this close to true joy.

Five

Sharp needles of uncertain excitement prickle her armpits and dart along the perimeter of her scalp when he turns the wheel sharply and swings the truck onto the hard-packed dirt drive.

An unruly overgrowth of tangled blackberry bushes and thick knots of scrub pines have long ago rambled away from the dense population of mature ancestors hedging the deep edge of woods to crowd the rough suggestion of a driveway. Scraggly branches scratch along the hood and sides of the truck like witchy fingernails in those places where the disorderly growth has succeeded in reaching across the road to intertwine gangly arms.

The trail abruptly narrows, now little more than an uneven set of parallel tire tracks, and the truck pitches and rolls as they creep forward.

It is still early, but the sun is well on the way to turning the day blistering. Cat has tied her hair into a loose ponytail that lies damp and weighty against the back of her neck, the armpits of her white sleeveless blouse stained in widening crescents of perspiration. Even so, it is easy enough to ignore her discomforts as her anticipation climbs, eyes trained straight ahead, watching intently as the dusty hood of the truck rounds a tight half-moon curve.

Gray hasn't given any substantial details and Cat isn't sure what to expect other than something crumbling and ancient. What else can possibly be out here in the middle of nowhere-nothing acres? The past dozen or so miles have revealed little other than trees and briars. The lone suggestion of one-time human inhabitants—an abandoned trailer with a caved-in roof and shot-out windows.

The ongoing stretches of expansive emptiness strike Cat as well suited to the pocket-size settlement of Lost River, a place that appeals to her from first sight; blissful and excited that she is actually here, thousands of miles removed from all things unwanted and faraway. A yearned-for oasis even before she knows of its existence. Anonymous in the midst of quiet gentleness—shielded within the stark and tangled beauty of the ancient landscape.

It has been several weeks since their arrival, but Cat has seen little of the surrounding territory until today; content to navigate the small town where they have rented two tiny rooms.

Her initial and still-holding impression of the town is that it feels safe. Manageable. Neatly contained in the span of a few blocks. There are barely a dozen stores and businesses hemming the main street, but Cat has a sense that as long as the general store remains anchored at the corner of Eagle and Main, the town will succeed in holding itself together. After all, everything essential is contained within: wooden barrels full of fat sour pickles, fresh eggs and goat cheese from a local farmer, slabs of thick cut bacon and venison jerky from another, impossibly arranged pyramids of apples, oranges, and bananas, jars of penny sticks and nickel candy flanking the century-old cash register. Everything here feels oddly familiar—as if Cat has pushed through the whining screen door a million times previous and strode across the creaky wood floor to retrieve a cold bottle of pop from the cooler.

On the opposite side of the street is a diner, bookended on one side by the post office, a bank on the other. A trio conveniently linked by the bus stop designated at the curb fronting them. Further along the sidewalk, across from the Ford dealership, is what appears to be a souvenir/junk/craft store. Cat occasionally pauses on her way past, her attentions piqued by some intriguing object spotted amongst the cluttered disarray framed within the large front window, mildly curious, but not enough to go inside and find out precisely what's for sale.

It occurs to her that many of the people living in Lost River are not overtly friendly or solicitous, traits Cat especially appreciates, but which likewise doesn't inspire casual window shopping. From childhood she's found solace in holding to the safety and comfort of keeping inside herself, a preference that hasn't left her. Her only remarkable exception being the single crack she's opened just wide enough to allow Gray to slip inside and stay.

"Gray, what is—" she says now, angling forward, just short of pressing her face into the windshield, increasingly anxious to capture a better view of the large dark object all at once looming up beyond the dusty glass.

"Just hold on a minute," he flashes a grin, the glint in his eyes betraying his own barely contained excitement.

"But—"

"Hold on, Miss Antsy Pants."

And all at once it is there in full view, wide and rambling beneath a skin of weathered grey clapboards; a house rising up just beyond where the tire tracks end in a near improbable mirage abutting the tangled disorder of a feral front yard.

It is a brooding and ancient place. A wide deep porch runs the length of its face; a substantial portion of which is heavily curtained by an overgrowth of runaway vines twining into neighboring bushes. It seems to Cat there is an unusual abundance of windows for such a far northern place, particularly when she considers the loosely veiled references to the angry bite of Maine's harsh winters and punishing nor'easters that Gray has detailed on the drive up from Columbus.

"This is really … I just can't believe …" she starts and stops, pausing to take it in, words tangling with questions unable to catch up with her immediate thoughts. "Are you serious, Gray? This isn't a mistake?"

He grins with uncloaked pleasure as he springs down from the truck's cab, coming around to pull open her door. "I didn't want to tell you I was actually talking to a realtor all those times I said I was at the mill sorting out details of my future job incase nothing turned up worth considering. I couldn't see a point in both of us being frustrated and disgusted with endless weeks of show-and-tell. She just showed me this place a couple days ago—said it used to be somebody's summer place, but it's been empty for years. I did wonder for about three seconds if maybe it's too big for us." He reaches for Cat's hand as she hops down from the cab and tucks her narrow shoulders under the protective curve of his arm. She can feel the expectant press of his eyes watching her as she again scans the place, memorizing as much as she can for later recall.

Despite the clear evidences of long neglect, Cat senses the distinct edge of something else—something running deeper than the surface appearance of a house well aged and comfortably worn. Nevertheless, regardless of whatever it is tapping for attention at the back of her mind, Cat deliberately shoves it aside, deferring to Gray's as yet unvoiced inspiration in choosing this place. Because whatever his reasoning, she is wholly trusting it is something stronger and wiser than what anyone less crazy in love and abundantly happy might otherwise fail to see in this shabby, rundown, and potentially hazardous dwelling.

"Although—on the other hand—it won't always be too much house. I'm thinking we'll just grow into it," Gray says, the meaning in the shy curve of his lips speaking clearly of the things he needn't say outright: of growing children and large dogs, cats curled on sunny sills. And she easily envisions everything as he surely must, holding fast to every detail that comes shimmering along the surface of her thoughts in a trail of shooting stars.

And yet, all at once, even before the sweeping currents of elation have chanced to settle, a heavy load of reality lands with a sobering thud; loud and jarring in a way that instantly creases her brow with a press of discomforting weight.

"They must be asking a lot for a place like this, Gray. Have you somehow let it slip your mind that you not only married a starving artist, but you happen to be one yourself?" she says, making an effort to push a faltering smile past the harsh bite of disappointment pinching the corners of her mouth.

It's a perfect place. She is convinced of it. Knows even before she steps across the threshold to scan the rooms settled behind the walls. Not merely some impulsive reaction, it is something more—a distinct breath of certitude. Instantaneous love and affection without explanation or complication. If only for the fact that Gray has chosen it.

Not until much later will she venture to raise a tentative hand and part the gossamer curtains of blind love, noticing for the first time, the fragile, hollowed-out sigh quietly wafting through spaces too long abandoned. Just as she will note that despite the assortment of furnishings, dusty knickknacks, and unexceptional decorations already in residence, the rooms are wholly lacking in the genuine, durable touches reminiscent of a contented home.

"Not that I don't willingly offer to trade my entire collection of brushes and treasured whatnots should the owner of this place happen to be an eccentric loo-loo."

"I happily assure that no such sacrifice is necessary, Mrs. Barnett," Gray smiles. "This mighty castle is not as much as you might think. Apparently there isn't a stampede of buyers when one of these big old places lands on the market. Something about the insatiable appetite for repairs and the minor detail that they're just about impossible to heat beyond the point of barely tolerable. I got the distinct impression the realtor was waiting for me to give her the punch line when I said we might be interested. 'Dinosaurs past the age of extinction,' I think is the way she put it."

Cat's expression remains cautiously glum despite Gray's encouraging prognosis. What does it matter how minimal the asking price when they can just barely afford the pair of shoebox rooms they are now renting upstairs from the boarded-up movie theatre in town.

"And did I forget to mention this particular chunk of real estate is a bank foreclosure—unpaid taxes," he continues, his grin widening with the telling. "I did a little sleuthing on my own and no one I've talked to seems to know the whole story, but apparently what the realtor said is true. The owners abandoned it years ago—just packed up one summer and never came back."

"So what does—"

"If we pay the back taxes, we own it, Cat," he says before she can finish, pausing a moment to allow his words to settle.

"And before you ask, it just so happens the tax rate in this little corner of the world is relatively painless."

"Well, as nice as that sounds we still …" Cat starts, then hesitates, sensing from his expectant stare and ever-widening grin that there is something more. That of course he never would've brought her out here if he didn't already have an answer for all the questions she's likely to pose.

"There was some money … after I lost my family. Not a lot, but some. I told you that, didn't I?" He says, pulling Cat around to face him, folding her against his chest.

"Yes ..." Yes, of course, she remembers everything he's ever told her. Will always remember. Everything.

"What I might not have mentioned is that I didn't blow it all on women and wine as you likely assumed." He cups her chin with his fingers and gently tips her face up to meet his eyes. "All you have to do is say you want it, Cat. Say it and it's ours. Every drafty window and leaky faucet—all ours."

Summer bolts past at a gallop as they press to outfit the house for its first winter in a century of existence when it will be occupied, rather than closed up tight against the brutal Maine weather and left alone until the thaw in late spring.

It has always been a summer place, the assurance of which is readily apparent in walls lacking insulation and rooms that have never known the comfort of central heating. While the three rough-hewn stone fireplaces on the main floor and the trio in the upstairs rooms lend suitable warmth to late summer evenings leaning toward fall, Gray warns that navigating the winter months will require an abundant store of something other than romantic notions and steady armloads of split logs piled on the hearth.

"We'll need to take every ounce of pioneer stamina and willpower out of mothballs while we're hovering in front of the fireplace blaspheming the frigid north," he grins.

Cat merely laughs, shaking her head, never once entertaining the possibility that they may be in over their heads or in any way destined for failure. That they will accomplish everything they set out to do, regardless of anything nature or the world itself should care to unleash, is a confidence she holds without condition.

It is several weeks after moving into the house—once they have arranged their sparse collection of personal possessions amongst the shabby furnishings and eclectic assortment of knick-knacks left behind by the previous family, selected the room that will serve as their art studio and outfitted it with their treasured inventory—when Cat feels her suspicions stirring to the possibility Gray is withholding pertinent information as to the true dismal state of the antiquated plumbing. And she is in the midst of an early morning shower when confirmation of her skepticism unceremoniously arrives; the water pressure markedly diminishing as she soaps her torso and mentally scripts her plans for the day, ceasing to flow altogether before she's finished rinsing the lather of shampoo from her hair.

A slow moving finger of shampoo bubbles slide down her forehead toward one tightly clenched eye and she blindly reaches a cupped palm in panicked hope of collecting a last trickle of water. Yet when her fingers land just off center of the showerhead, she recovers nothing other than a moist hint of thoroughly vanished spray.

"Gray!" she shouts, squeezing her eyes tighter as suds cross the line of one eyebrow. "GRAY!" louder now. *Damn it. Where is he?*

She sweeps her arm in sightless search of a towel. "GR—"

"Hold on—I'm coming."

Cat hears his voice closing the distance as he ascends the stairs, a moment later appearing in the doorway clutching a sloshing basin of water.

"Bend down and I'll give you a rinse," he says.

"How did you—"

"Hold still. Here—just bend your head down."

"What happened to the water? What's going on?" she says once he's carefully emptied the basin of warm water over her head and hands her the elusive bath towel. "How did you know to bring up water?"

"Um, well, it was relatively easy to figure out. You up here screaming in the shower at about the same time it started raining from the kitchen ceiling," he says, his eyes laughing in obvious disregard of the thoroughly humorless nature of the situation. "I'm guessing a pipe must've burst somewhere between point A and point B."

"Oh, and this amuses you?" Cat stares in disbelief.

"What? The geyser shooting out of the ceiling? No, not in the least—that's definitely not funny. But the peeved expression on your face? Yes—enormously. It's oddly charming."

The beginning of a smile twitch at the corners of her lips, the furrows frowned between her eyebrows easing as her frustration drops from rapid boil to a simmer. Such is the magic of Gray.

"Okay, so, kindly remind me how many years it's supposed to take before we're sitting around here laughing about this big fat moldering mess we've gotten ourselves into?"

"Fair question. I'm guessing somewhere between eight and ten—assuming of course this colossal monster is still standing by then," he grins, reaching for her. "The way I figure, if we can somehow keep ourselves from mental collapse over the first dozen or so catastrophes, it'll be smooth sailing for the dozen or so after."

Cat lifts her damp arms to circle his shoulders, laughing against his neck, her anxieties so easily soothed by his simple assurance. Once again they have proven untouchable. Immune even, to the nocuous hands of all-out calamity.

Resolved and steady, they work through days that open early and close long and hard. Inspired mornings spill open with a current of enthusiasm that threads into late afternoons and wanes into deep-set evenings as they race against time and each other to accomplish as much as they can before the end of September, when Gray will start his job at the lumber mill. Just about the time, if estimates prove accurate, when the last of their money is gone.

There was a time not so long ago when the threat of parallel deadlines heading for collision would have chased Cat into an arc of nerve-splitting panic. But that was before, a condition of her previous life, when her accustomed habit was to hold steady, but paralyzed, braced for impact; unable to pull free from the grip of anxiety holding firmly at the roots. So much of her life has been driven by fear and uncertainty she's never understood before now that she isn't altogether powerless to close the door on guests she has no desire to receive, despite the insistence of their pounding.

As has happened with so many of her long indulged dreads, this one likewise has fallen away to be replaced by the genuine. Now, when emphatic demands of the immediate future lean in a little too close, Cat is prone to ignoring the discomforting burn of threats breathing at her neck. She understands there is nothing she need concern herself with other than focusing on the things Gray has promised, and the belief that the things they most need to do will get done. Everything else will be hit or miss, and that will be fine.

And it isn't the peculiar meals they share on evenings when they are both too worn out to cook or eat—cottage cheese heaped on saltines, tuna straight from the tin, bland soups that mostly taste like the cans they've been poured from—or the oftentimes dismal prognosis of returning life to a house too long neglected, which hold clearest in her thoughts over the span of passing weeks. But rather, it is the intensity of their shared passion producing the strongest, sharpest images. The great, leaping, loud, and boisterous life they spend wildly and freely within the walls and beyond to every other corner of their private world. Never thinking or otherwise conceiving that any of it can ever possibly change, other than to grow deeper, richer, and closer in distance to forever. Never believing for an instant that it could ever be gone.

Six

Cat wishes for memories that hold no detail. Paper scenes with neatly trimmed and changeable outfits she might alternate or discard on a whim. Something other than the dense palate rudely elbowing its way into her head, unexpected, uninvited, and immovable.

It is of little consequence that Maysel's poisonous missive was received and rejected months ago. The heft of its contents yet linger, crowded into her thoughts. The threat of its very existence working to resurrect long dead cadavers. She's certain this has been Maysel's intent all along. To routinely breathe life into what Cat has purposely wrung out and flung away.

It is a sure trick of remembrance—the near soundless approach from a distant nowhere. Softly falling steps slipping into her head with an artificial calm, unfolding from behind the gently undulating fringes of a faraway scene.

... *Leafie stops walking. Moves closer to the spilling cascade of wild roses trailing fragrant blooms along the length of split-rail fence at the edge of the long dirt driveway. Her small hands move deftly among the thorns, breaking off stems laden with pale pink blossoms, so intent on her illicit harvest she fails to see Cat watching from behind a nearby stand of trees, her brows pinched in disbelief over Leafie's continuing defiance in doing the very thing she's been punished for a dozen times already.*

There is little doubt Maysel is right now peering out from her accustomed sentry at the front window. Ever watchful. Lips drawn tight along the line of her teeth. One hand raised to part the drapes, her opposite arm crossing her chest—thumb and forefinger pinching the tender skin inside her bent elbow hard enough to make any other person wince.

And yet the certainty Leafie's been caught even before attempting a getaway has little effect, and she continues her crime. Assiduous fingers pruning blooms and adding them to the messy tumbling bouquet cradled in the crook of her arm.

Cat has all but given up efforts to warn her sister away from criminal actions already in progress, full-knowing Leafie will merely ignore her and continue with whatever it is she's doing. They are both aware Maysel's punishments carry a far greater weight than the deeds which earn them. An assurance which leaves Cat grudgingly fascinated by Leafie's stubborn refusal to be deterred from repeating her offenses; regardless of knowing Maysel will later force her to eat handfuls of the sweet smelling blooms. And Cat isn't so much envious of her sister's audacious feats of defiance as she is uncertain over Leafie's obstinate brand of courage.

To innocent eyes, it appeared a tranquil portrait reminiscent of a scene printed on the lid of a jigsaw puzzle: A neatly composed illusion dissimulating the truth. In fact, had she understood the meaning of the expression mixed blessing, Cat would have claimed it as a most apt summation of the Carper's out-of-the-blue appearance to whisk the orphaned sisters off to Memphis. The blessing coming when the sisters are rescued from their lost and hopeless existence within the orphanage walls to live with the Carpers in a brilliant, bustling town a million lifetimes times removed from the tumbling shacks dotting their previous life in the swamp settlement of Mudlick. The mixed being everything else that followed.

At first glance, the farmhouse settled at the head of the drive—a neat square box of white painted clapboards—appears a perfect fit for two lost girls arriving at Happily Ever After. But it is an assurance which endures only for the time it takes the slowly creeping car to reach the house—the filtered gaze of newness instantly falling away—blinders clearing to allow Cat a view of the obvious imperfections she's initially missed; the tired face of reality enabling her to see the knotted weeds clustered in the gardens edging the house, unwashed windows, splintered boards lining the porch floor, the rotten slats in the peeling picket fence.

Behind the neglected house, at the corner of the yard, is an ancient barn clothed in a molting red skin of sun-faded paint. And on either side, a wide field planted with shiny leafed tobacco plants aligned in unbroken isles.

A half dozen hens dart back and forth in the dooryard, scratching and pecking inside a circle of dust and gravel stirred up by scaly yellow feet. Two of the birds, then a third, momentarily disappear beneath a tangle of bushes hemming one side of the porch. The trio flapping back out into the sunlight an instant later, squawking excitedly as they dash and dart like contestants in the throes of some manic chicken sport.

"Come on then," Maysel snaps, breaking the silence crowded inside of the car. The two girls slide across the wide back seat of the Carper's station wagon, all but welded together as they stand staring at the bleak and looming house. "Your Uncle Curtis could use a hand carrying things inside."

Maysel instructs Cat how to prepare the cinnamon sugar toast she likes to set out for occasional visits with her lady friends—neat little triangles she is to arrange on Maysel's precious flower-patterned china plate and serve with tea; a simple brand of nicety Cat initially finds intriguing after a childhood thoroughly devoid of such particulars. But as it will become with all things ingrained during her years with the Carpers, even this small pleasantry will become one more thing to dislike.

By the time she is eight, Cat has learned to cook supper, bake Maysel's favorite red velvet cake, bone fish, dress a freshly killed chicken, polish silver, and clean house.

She also learns that when it comes to Maysel and Curtis Carper, no labor will ever be done right, anymore than it will ever be enough.

Cat shuts her eyes, swallows a sigh. Presses her temple against the receiver in an effort to quiet the throbbing in her head. She's been waiting for Gray to come home all day. Has in fact felt a yearning for his return even as she is waving him off to work that morning; an anxious sense of desolation rising with the clouds of dust churned up from the trucks tires as he rolls away down the driveway.

And now, Gray has called to tell her the foreman's asked some of the men to work a few hours overtime so they can finish sawing an order of lumber overdue for shipment to the west coast.

"This is a good thing, Cat," he says in way to suggest he hasn't missed the disappointment not so well concealed in her voice. "I think he likes my work. He only asked a few of us to stay over."

"I know, but—"

"And aside from the stroke to my ego," he says, and she can hear the smile in his voice, "you know we can use the extra money if we want to keep fixing up that ridiculous house you forced me to buy."

She knows he is right. Money is not a byproduct as much as it is a necessity, especially if they ever hope to reclaim their stalled artistic endeavors. But still, even the most reasonable logic crumbles against her impatience to have him home.

The strength of late afternoon light has lessened steadily over the past weeks, growing shallow as autumn days lean in closer toward oncoming winter. So now, as Cat heads to the kitchen, she snaps on a trail of lights along the way: an ugly ceramic lamp on an end table in the living room, the dim overhead globe in the hallway, twin fluorescent tubes centered over the Formica-topped kitchen table.

She retrieves the package of hot dogs she's taken from the freezer hours earlier and left to thaw on the counter, returning it to the refrigerator. With Gray not due for several more hours, she has plenty of time to reconstruct her original menu into something more elaborate.

She combs through cupboard, refrigerator, and freezer, analyzing the possibilities offered by the spare inventory of cans, cartons, and bags, before deciding on chicken. She selects a collection of ingredients not particularly extraordinary when offered solo, but which artfully combined will become something else altogether. She can do amazing things with poultry. Will in fact build a culinary arrangement of such magnificence, it will be impossible for Gray to detect even a shadow of the pitiable, emotional neediness poured into its brilliant creation.

Seven

She is happy in ways she's never imagined possible—as blessed and contented as any person can hope to be—and yet, there are moments—undeniable flashes—when Cat senses the lingering essence of distinctly sad and mournful things caught and held within these walls.

Her immediate fear is that she has done this herself, unwittingly transported some incurable strain of virus borne of ancient injury. And if this is true, what is the cure? If love and contentment aren't the antidote then what is? Does one even exist? Or will she forever be the potential threat walking around inside her own life?

She considers this as she stands in the yard surveying the forgotten landscape; sagging outbuildings, rusted hand pump no longer useful for drawing water from the underground well, teetering fence limping in a broken line beyond a garden of weeds. Maybe she's too quick in assuming responsibility for the fickle currents of melancholy waxing and waning like light and shadow on a shifting plane. Maybe what she senses is simply recognition of abandonment. Much like her childhood self, this house has likewise been forsaken by the family intended to care for it; leaving it to either survive or flounder on its own. A strange alliance, but only that. And just as Cat has reinvented her life to better fit the one she's designed inside her head, she is determined now to work a similar cure here in this faraway place.

One of the many things she hasn't given much thought to is the combed-over pate of earth reminiscent of a long-expired garden; a scraggly rectangle stitched together by a patchwork of weeds and grass barely distinct from the untidy edging of equally scraggly weeds and grass bordering the bed on four sides. With the barely shrinking roster of essentials listed on Cat's Of Immediate Concern page, considerations of tidying the yard or attempting to grow things have remained largely sidetracked.

But now, with the anxious arrival of a spring thaw too long in coming, Cat finds her thoughts piled high and spilling with battle plans for reclaiming the garden space from its runaway integration with the lawn. Armed with wheelbarrow and garden tools, she is confident this is a war she is equipped to win.

She aspires for abundance; fresh-cut flowers for the tables and sills in each dated and colorless room, orderly rows of robust and brightly hued summer vegetables thriving in place of runaway generations of vigorous weeds. Zinnias, delphiniums, carrots, cucumbers, tomatoes. Bounteous harvest. Permanence.

Uncertain of the essential starting point for setting her designs into motion, Cat makes her first ever visit to the town library. Until now, she's had little interest in combing the hive of tight-fitting rooms overtop the post office—an inadequate and clumsy space serving as temporary quarters since the original building burned to the ground fifteen years earlier.

It doesn't take long for Cat to sort through the brief selection of gardening and recipe books, dated volumes stilling hold the odors of smoke and ash. She leaves shortly after. Empty handed.

Even so, she isn't especially disappointed. As much as she would appreciate a helpful reference detailing methods for growing and eventually preserving her anticipated surplus of produce, she's confident she'll figure out the process when the time comes—even if it means having to resort to memory.

She's ever aware of their presence, which is precisely why she is so carefully determined to avoid glancing back and seeing them. Memories cannot, and should not, be trusted. Ever. Far better to assure herself she doesn't quite remember. That the vapory image occasionally glimpsed in a far corner of her mind is simply the recollection of a woman—any woman not her mother. A woman canning late summer vegetables to sustain her perpetually hungry family until the next harvest. Cat does not recall snapping the ends and pulling the strings from green beans, peeling peaches, tearing towhead silk and husks from corn, the sound of canning jars rattling gently as they boil in a pan of water on the stove. She doesn't recall any of it, is the assurance she holds to, even as the details bubble to the surface steady and clear. Only on the outside does she succeed in fooling herself with invented amnesia. Inside, the memories hold intact. Large and eternally real.

It is a much anticipated task undertaken at the end of every summer, when over the course of several days, her mother Reva spends long hours in the kitchen cooking and canning the generous offerings of kindhearted neighbors. Neighbors Cat has never actually met—since her parents share a certain disinterest in socializing and she has never seen either of them extend a friendly greeting or offer so much as a brief wave to neighbor or familiar face. And yet, every August, dependable as the setting sun, came an extravagant bounty gifted by phantom benefactors, allowing Cat a transitory sampling of kindness and fleeting solace that someone nearby was looking after her. Some sainted soul who miraculously cared how often she went to bed hungry only to wake even hungrier. She might've been crushingly disappointed when she came to learn no such entity existed. But instead, she merely felt foolish.

The truth, when it came, landed on a night typical of so many others; Cat hiding under the bed, attempting to quiet baby Leafie as Reva and Henry sparred in preparation of another long simmering battle. Accusations and aggressions, ugliness slamming across the room in vengeful blows carrying for hours. And somewhere in the mix, the gloating admission that the generous offerings of fruit and vegetables have not been freely given at all. There are in fact no caring and watchful friends, no concerned neighbors. It has been her father's doing all along; the spoils of Henry's late night raids from produce stands and roadside farm tables trustingly left unattended until morning, which appear piled on the kitchen counters under the guise of goodwill.

As is the routine duration of their brawls, the drinking, shouting, and breakage go on for days. And yet this time, along with the grudging cession of hostilities comes a significant turning point in their ongoing war. Because once the dust has settled and the heavy press of discontent is returned to a smoldering flame, Reva all but ceases to care about such necessary obligations as the care and feeding of her children. As if she's once and for all sobered to the conclusion such responsibilities are altogether insignificant once a person has surrendered the last of their reserves to a cause as all consuming as the maintenance of a hideous life.

But whatever became of the neat arrangement of provisions Reva had stored on the floor to ceiling shelf in the shack's dugout basement? The assortment of jars arranged on the shelf by color rather than variety; wax beans, yellow zucchini, green tomatoes, green beans, beets, raspberry jam, peaches, carrots …

Had her father actually shattered every one of those jars with the force of his poisonous rage—swung at the careful rows was a metal pronged rake until the shelves stood bare? Or was it something else that lays there splattered and ruined at his feet? Is it the remains of some terrible dream suddenly recalled? Or has she actually seen this?

Saturday morning Cat wakes with a chart of newly laid plans ready in her head. A ripe spring breeze lifts the curtains at the open windows, billowing the light cotton fabric into a chorus of full dancing skirts.

The steady drone of the mower drifts in over the sill. Cat parts the curtain with one hand and glances out to where Gray is pushing the machine back and forth across the patchy grass in neat parallel lanes. She is certain she will never tire of this amiable symphony; the sights and sounds composed against the backdrop of ordinary life. Blessedly uncomplicated doings which make their melodies all the more exceptional.

She reaches for yesterday's jeans where she's left them draped over a chair and pulls a clean T-shirt from the dresser drawer. She is humming as she skips down the stairs to the kitchen and grabs a brown freckled banana from the counter, peeling it as she heads out the back door and into the yard. She pauses by the truck and waves until she catches Gray's attention, blowing him a kiss as she pulls open the door and hops up into the cab.

She is not long standing before the revolving racks displaying seed packets in Peabody's Hardware Store. Cat has little interest in contemplating or otherwise studying the colorful images of perfectly shaped, unblemished fruits and vegetables. It is the names printed on the envelopes which will define her selections: Sugarsnax carrots, Deer Tongue lettuce, Sweet Gypsy peppers, Blue Lake pole beans, Purple King beans, Green Tiger zucchini, Moon and Stars watermelon. Hollyhocks, delphiniums, blue flax, and foxglove. Titles most befitting the sweeping landscape of her brilliantly blooming romantic notions.

The fruits of her labor prove no equal match to her ambitions, and weeks later Cat finds herself crouched in the garden, staring at the smattering of gently tilted heads on slender necks that have emerged in sparse, anemic colonies. All of which will vanish overnight, leaving the rows bald against the rumor of green sprouts.

The tomato plants appear the lone survivors of Cat's efforts, but they too fail to survive beyond their initial budding—fragile, pale green seedlings promptly drooping and withering back into the soil despite her concentrated frequency of watering and diligent attentions.

Still, she continues her hopeful watch, each day squatting between the planted rows to scrutinize the careful lines of upturned earth, even when the last of her plantings remain in absentia, declining to be birthed at all.

Aside from her initial sense of disappointment, Cat's failure to cultivate plant life doesn't matter as much as it might. Failure notwithstanding, there is no denial of the satisfaction that's come from the very effort of mapping a course, preparing the earth, planting the seeds she taps from the pretty paper envelopes into her dusty palm. After all, if there's any one thing she's come to understand, it's the assurance that only a very foolish person ever truly expects to reap what they've sown.

Far more meaningful and necessary is the pursuit of routines and duties composing ordinary life—the doings of regular, uncomplicated people. Mowing lawns, planting gardens. Growing, or simply attempting to grow things. Living quietly. Undisturbed. Steady and peaceful.

Each of Cat's ancient aspirations, once bulls-eye aimed and determined, sharp edged and solemn, have all but fallen away. And it isn't so much astonishment, or even surrender she feels, but the wonder of transformation; her hard corners gently rounded, rearranged in a way to make her former brittle and disjointed self nearly unrecognizable. A figure vaguely recalled when viewed from a distance, but up close, is altogether unfamiliar.

The unruly press of former ambitions have turned, resettled, comfortably arranged themselves into a place where she no longer feels a constant push of pained urgency. And when she glances back, she sees just how far she's drifted from the time not so long ago when nothing felt more important or necessary than chasing full throttle after a string of spectacular, multi-tiered accomplishments.

None of the things once driving her mean much of anything now that she is here with Gray. Living in a time and place where ill-formed pretensions have no bearing as much as they don't belong—no more necessary, as they no longer fit. Not when she has all of this. When she falls asleep every night with the weight of Gray's arm looped around her waist, and in the morning wakes curled with her back against his chest, the rhythm of his breathing steady between her shoulder blades.

She doesn't so much question where they're headed. What they'll be doing tomorrow or a week from now. Just as long as this beautiful quiet love entwined between them remains steady. As long as she always has this, the rest may simply unfold as it will.

There are two halves to any day; when Gray is gone to the mill, and when he is home.

Over the stretch of hours when he is away from her, Cat crawls through the list of repair projects they've started, but yet to finish; perched on a ladder with trowel, sand paper, or brush in hand, sweeping away accumulations of plaster dust and chips of ancient paint. Now and again she continues to devote an occasional morning to waging war against the unceasing regiments of weeds sprouted overnight in the otherwise barren garden, if only because her pride has not yet slipped low enough to concede surrender.

Even then, as she tackles each day's selected task, engrossed as outward appearances suggest, her thoughts shift away to rifle through the stores of ideas and mental sketches she has meticulously labeled and shelved. Not merely a jumbled collection of random thoughts and cloud-nine aspirations, her musing hold to a portfolio of designs in wait of the time when she and Gray will finally begin the murals they plan to create here; boundless stretches of vividly detailed landscapes spooled out across every bare wall throughout this house.

It is during the long drive from Columbus to Maine, in the midst of a storm update just outside Richmond, Virginia, when the radio in the truck makes a peculiar popping hiccup and immediately falls silent. Gray fiddles with the dial, swearing quietly under his breath when he is only able to retrieve the steady hiss of static. Cat holds a sigh of relief behind her lips, secretly glad for the quiet. Happy for the break from spotty songs and harpy chatter crowding the cab over the past several hours. Content to listen to the rhythmic conversation of tires slapping over the rain-washed highway for awhile.

She doesn't remember the first thing Gray says to break the silence, but she recalls everything else that follows. His gradual unveiling of deep-held aspirations gaining strength as they tumble loose and he breaks open the details of his determination to find the perfect place to settle into their sparkly new, forever-after life. And as his words continue to spill loose, she is gathering them to herself. Feels herself lifted heart and soul, swept up and carried along on the steady currents of his enthusiasm.

She is instantly in love with his description of this imagined house of ridiculous proportions, a rambling haven surrounded on all sides by a vast lawn, "On the chance we decide to get some goats, or chickens … a llama, maybe," he laughed. Their only neighbors will be each other, anyone else far enough away not to matter. And trees. An impenetrable forest dense as mountains.

"It'll be like living on an island. No one comes ashore unless we row out to meet them," he says in a voice full of smiles.

Cat nods her head, agreeing with everything.

And then he tells her about the walls. The walls they will fill with their own designs; together painting a flowing room-to-room masterpiece.

Over the course of the next several hundred miles, Gray laid open his thoughts piece by piece; aligning details for the murals he envisions climbing the walls from floor to ceiling, turning the pages inside his head until he's shown her everything.

Cat smiles her acquiescence with each description, effortlessly absorbing his vision as her own. She closes her head to the frowning voice of logic lifting now and again in a determined effort to talk over him with the insistence the very magnitude of his proposal is as improbable as it is bizarre.

It is in fact far too late for something as uninspired as logic. She is already lost to the boundless appeal of his imaginings.

The confidence of his passion so easily outweighs the burdensome heft of reality. And in the minute span of an instant, Cat feels her own certainty taking flight, sprinting forward into the promise of the absurd. The ridiculous. The altogether improbable.

Eight

His mind is seldom at rest. Charting, arranging, mapping. Some thoughts he will explain at length, others will appear as suggestions he then sets aside to either evolve later or quietly wither.

Sometimes, when Gray is explaining something particularly intricate, Cat allows her thoughts to drift beyond the boundaries of listening to wander through her own repository of collected designs and imaginings; incomplete compositions as yet devoid of absolute detail.

It isn't that she's lost the urge to paint or otherwise create; it's simply that she can't see how to go about pursuing her passion and yet still hold to her ideal of an ordinary, uncluttered life. The safety and promise of waking to mornings where fear is not the first face she sees or the first breath she breathes.

Cat is happier in ways she's never believed to exist until now. What other reason to explain why she doesn't know how to be away from Gray? An hour or two here or there isn't the question. It's his early morning departures for the mill—long before the slowly climbing sun crests the treetops—bringing her face to face with a disturbing sense of finality. Standing at the kitchen window, her coffee mug cradled in both palms, she watches him go. And even before his tires round the curve in the driveway and take him from sight, Cat finds herself staring into the truth that she hasn't yet learned how to be alone.

It makes sense and no sense at all. Considering how before Gray, alone is all she's ever been. And that's precisely how she wanted it. Solitary confinement. A state of being—but just barely.

In the years of living at the orphanage with Leafie, alone had been the flavor of the day. Day, into day, into day. It made little difference how many other hollow faces molded by loss, abuse, and abandonment were there—eating, sleeping, moving around her—Cat held to her isolated bubble and the safety it allowed her. Particularly once she came to understand how effectively her invisibility worked to further distance her from an unceasing flow of unanswerable questions.

"There's no one to come for you? No one?" She is asked time and again over the course of those first several weeks; less often as the months pile up, though still sporadically resurfacing on the chance some name had finally jarred loose from her memory. "Grandparents? Aunt, uncle … a cousin, maybe?" As if such dogged persistence might eventually prove successful in shaking out some elusive somebody from her family tree.

But always Cat would shake her head, stare at her feet, not sure how to make them understand there really truly positively is no one. And if there actually was, she didn't know who they were or where they might be, so please stop asking.

And once a year had passed, they did.

It was only the questions about Leafie which continued to come, and for good reason. If only because Cat carried much the same questions herself.

"Exactly when did she stop talking? Did she suffer an injury—an accident? Did someone hurt your sister? Did she cry as an infant? Has she ever spoken at all? A child doesn't simply go silent. It's very strange. Very, very peculiar. Of course a traumatic experience can short circuit the wiring and shut everything off for a time—particularly with children, but I don't think …"

And Cat would simply stop listening after awhile because she'd been asked these same things too often, and she didn't have any answers to offer anymore than she had a solution. She didn't tell them that, yes, there were times when Leafie did nothing but cry. For hours. Days even. It was only after that night when she shut up for good. But Cat doesn't offer this when they ask, because even a five year old knows such a reply will only bring more questions she doesn't have answers for.

And now is this life she so carefully protects—a future scrubbed clean from the past. A life where she never stops missing Gray; wishing him back even before he's gone. No matter how focused or absorbed she becomes with any momentary diversion, there is always some loud and anxious part of her conspicuously waiting for his return to this hard-earned place of consolation and safety.

Nine

The early weeks of spring fold into summer, slow and achy. Gray is putting in extra hours at the mill and when Cat impulsively pulls a face at his announcement of yet another late evening this week, he patiently reminds her how warming temperatures mean increased demands for lumber.

"It's spring fever, Cat. They want to build the stuff they've been thinking about all winter—an addition on the house, a shed, or barn … everybody has a plan."

Yes, but what about our plans? Cat shouts in her head, making an effort to hold her grievances unspoken when Gray's work days continue to commence earlier and finish later. She packs an extra bologna sandwich into his black metal lunchbox, ducking her face to avoid seeing the dull points of her own impending loneliness staring back at her.

She's being ridiculous. And needy—which is worse.

As tightly as she holds to the routine of her comfortable life with Gray, Cat cannot so easily avoid recognizing the beginning twinges of something which looks markedly similar to tedium.

The suggestion approaches quietly, tapping politely at the back of her mind in a bid for attention. And when she doesn't answer, it knocks louder, insistent to gain entry. Not quite boredom, but nearly. It seems in her determination to secure the comfort of the ordinary, she's taken a step a little too far in the wrong direction and tripped herself into something else.

There must be something here for her to do. Something uniquely hers and decidedly removed from running an ongoing marathon of home repairs. She needs to determine some necessary purpose. A uniquely fitted task or goal large enough to satisfy. Not so sizeable as to swallow her, but big enough to contain her.

For the better part of an hour, Cat rifles through the clutter squirreled away in the garden shed over the course of decades, feeling oddly invasive, and yet decidedly annoyed as she pokes through objects she and Gray haven't personally accumulated, but now own.

For lack of any other genius notion, Cat has decided to make a scarecrow to ornament her non-productive garden. Aside from the fact she hasn't been all that successful in growing plants, adding a whimsical figure to the sadly lacking plot will at least allow her the consolation of sprouting something indelible from the soil. A ridiculous notion that somehow makes sense.

She sets aside a dented watering can, a half dozen terracotta pots, several gardening tools resembling medieval weapons, a knot of bailing wire, and several badly contorted tomato cages, all of which she piles into the wheelbarrow and steers back toward the house.

In the two years they've lived here, Cat has yet to stumble across a single reason compelling enough for her to venture into the basement, more than satisfied to leave it wholly unexplored and deeded over as Gray's territory. Now, pulling open the twin slanted doors to expose the deep cavern beneath the house, she hesitates. Stares down the flight of bowed and splintered wood steps, unable to bring herself to descend to the dank and shadowy bowels.

What are the chances of even finding something useable down there? Something that isn't rusted, rotted, or covered with spider poop.

She bends down, but only to grasp the rusted door handles, slamming one, then the other, and closing the palpable ugliness back into itself.

Heading inside now, Cat climbs the stairs ascending to the attic.

Pale stripes of quivery light pass through a twin pair of narrow windows set high in the peaks at either end of the attic room, the dull fog of ancient dust lending a ghostly tint suggestive of things abandoned. She tugs the dandling cord of an overhead bulb, but apparently it is burnt out and there is no light forthcoming. She pauses, allows her eyes to adjust to the muted shadows draping the spacious cavern like unbounded yards of grey gossamer.

Dusty cartons line the walls in careless stacks. A lifetime accumulation apparently deemed unworthy of transport to wherever the owners have gone. It is truly startling how much has been left behind in this vanished family's flight. So unlike her own escape where there is nothing to leave behind other than memories—all of which have come with her anyway. Whether it proves to be an unexceptional assortment of ordinary things, or a startling trove of treasure, does little to answer the mystery of why it remains. Such all-out abandonment strikes her as unreasonable as it is jolting. Regardless of why it's here, it is, meaning one more problem she and Gray will have to eventually navigate. This weight of another's burden crowding into a space intended only for Gray and herself.

Cat shuffles boxes and splitting plastic wardrobe bags, overlooks wooden crates too heavy to move, and too dark to identify the contents of. She feels uneasy, even criminal poking though things which may very well belong to her legally, but not personally. She reminds herself it is accumulation without meaning. Left behind. Abandoned, non-descript, and apparently unimportant.

And yet there is something here … something uncertain but distinctly present. The air all at once cluttered with tangled memories—someone else's and not her own. Her initial desire to poke through the stacks and bundles in search for useful components for her scarecrow plummets sharply and she is on the verge of abandoning her plan altogether when she spies a forlorn tangle of furniture tucked beneath the eave in a deep-shadowed corner. At closer inspection, she finds that the snarl of wooden arms and legs includes a small table, three unmatched chairs, a narrow bench, and an oval footstool outfitted in faded upholstery fallen victim to feasting moths or nesting mice.

For several quietly drifting moments, Cat stands within the murky film of dim attic light accessing her discovery, crossing her arms as incoming thoughts pile into her head and take on weight. She can't quite determine her purpose for the forlorn collection—she is simply convinced there is one.

She hauls the assortment of misfits one by one down the narrow stairs and into the yard to join her earlier findings, trusting the crank and whirl of her imagination will have it thoroughly sorted out by the time Gray walks through the door.

He is late; once again held over with the rest of the crew to complete shipment of an important order of custom length boards. It's been nearly a week since Gray's last eaten—or at least that's how he feels. The hollow edge of hunger clenches his stomach in a hard reminder that lunch is too far past to register now, and as he races the dark roads home, his thoughts settled on the assurance Cat will have supper hot and waiting when he walks though the door, just as she always does.

And yet when he pulls open the door and steps into the kitchen, the anticipated aroma of a cooking meal doesn't swell out to greet him, and an immediate sweeping glance registers only a single pot settled on the stove over a burner that bears no flame.

He turns his gaze to the table. *No place settings.*

Cat takes little notice of his bewilderment as she rushes forth to greet him the moment he passes through the doorway, tossing all preliminaries aside as she launches into the details of her plans for the motley lineup of dusty furnishings she's arranged in the middle of the kitchen floor.

"Where did all this come from?" he says, making an effort to ignore the whining echo careening against the walls of his empty stomach.

"I went up to the attic thinking I might to find a few things for—"

"It's not a good idea to poke around up there," he interrupts. "It's probably not safe."

"Not safe? Aside from choking to death on dust, what could possibly be—"

The line of his jaw draws taut, then just as quickly softens. "Seriously? You really need me to remind you of the not-so-nice surprises this place tends to spring on us when our backs are turned? I'm concerned there may be loose or rotten floorboards up there where the roof was leaking last winter. One misstep and you'll be dangling from the ceiling. It's just not a good idea to be poking around until I've had a chance to take a good look."

"Okay, well, sure, I guess you're right. I forgot about the leak," she nods, even as she spins past his somber warning to recover her enthusiasm. "Alright, so anyway, what do you think? It's a great idea, right?"

"Well, yeah … sure you can paint them," he says, studying the pieces, a shadow markedly suggestive of doubt creeping into his eyes. "But stripping off the old finish could be a real—"

"I'm not saying I want to paint them just one color," she interrupts, pushing past the sigh of frustration gathering in her mouth. Clearly he isn't working very hard on his end to steer his thoughts in the direction she is driving him.

Cat pauses, turns to open the Frigidaire. She reaches for the last bottle of beer, pops the cap with an opener and hands it to Gray. "I'm going to paint them to look like people. Fun, quirky people. Very bold and bright. Lots of color and detail." She watches his expression as he palms the bottle for a moment, tilts his head back and takes a deep swallow.

"For instance," Cat says, sketching invisible details onto the chair with her finger. "The oval back would be the face—I'm thinking maybe an old man with a beard for this one—the seat will be his body, and the chair's arms and legs will be *his* arms and legs."

Gray cocks his head. The line of his lips slowly curves into the proportions of a full-on smile as she spills out her designs with animated fervor.

"Fine, go right ahead," she says, when she glances across her shoulder and spies his expression. "Why don't you just come out and say it—since you obviously think I've taken off on a lost marble chase."

"Lost marble what?" he laughs.

"I get it. You think it's ridiculous."

"Hey, I didn't say any—"

"Well you just wait and see. This might very well work out and when it does you'll feel like a big fat jerk for standing here making goofy faces," she reaches out and tweaks his ear, attempts a scowl, but a smile comes instead.

"It's hunger."

"What?"

"I like your idea, Cat. I think you're onto something, but honestly, another five minutes and I just might eat those chairs."

Ten

She's determined not to hear the mean-spirited taunts of discouragement creeping up to jar the quavering legs of her uncertain faith, but she does. Loud and clear. The same voice she's heard a million times before, scoffing with certain arrogance whenever she allows herself to believe she has something to offer—a talent uniquely hers.

Has she so soon forgotten who she is? Does she really think her name is on the roster? What makes her think she can steal away things never intended for her? Doesn't she remember how she got here? Aspirations like hers are designed and assembled for other people. Not her. Never for her.

It's an old familiar tune. A custom soundtrack composed just for her. She's heard it playing so long it's worn a groove inside her head. She knows the lyrics even in her sleep, regardless how resolved she is not to hear them.

She has no genius remedy or master plan for changing course. She will simply keep moving—taking one step and then another—persisting with a dogged steadiness to reach a place she isn't sure of, despite the fact she's always been headed there.

As much as she aspires to trust her talents and believe she possesses something, alive, breathing, and honest—a gift as true as she's always assumed it to be false—it is not something that comes easily. So when Judy Hines, owner of

The Birds Nest, calls to tell Cat one of the painted chairs Judy's agreed to put in her curiosity shop on consignment some weeks earlier has sold, she can't decide if she's gratified or incredulous.

"Who would've guessed, right?" Judy says when Cat drives into town to pick-up her first-ever earnings. "I figured your pieces would draw some attention, but I had no idea if any of it would move or not. People around here are professional lookers. They aren't all that adventurous when it comes to opening their wallets—particularly for anything costing more than a dollar ninety-nine," Judy laughs even as she shifts her gaze toward a lone browser paused outside the front window. Frowning when the figure beyond the glass moves on.

"Would it kill her to walk through the door and look around for a minute? Those front window snoops irritate the hell out of me. What's the point of shopping from the sidewalk? You'd think they're saving every dime for a trip to Fifth Avenue or something. What kind of woman doesn't adore a bar of scented soap?" Judy says, pointing to a careful arrangement of candy-colored cubes. "Every scent you can imagine, licorice, cucumber, chocolate bliss, lemon meringue—even one called Angel Kisses, for heaven's sake."

Cat smiles at the pun, wondering if Judy's even aware she's made one, hoping her effort of polite interest will coax the woman into remembering she has yet to pay Cat for the chair.

"All homemade. They smell so darned good I'm not even kidding when I say I'm tempted to try eating one.

"And these cute little clothespin refrigerator magnets—isn't this so clever how they're painted to look like kitchen utensils? You can use them to hold little notes or coupons." Judy squeezes one of the pins in assurance of their indispensible purpose before continuing with her narration of the store's inventory.

Cat nods, holding to her expression of polite interest as she silently questions both the taste and purpose of camouflaging extra rolls of toilet paper in wicker baskets topped by crocheted chickens in rainbow colors, or dressing a vacuum cleaner to resemble a cartoon cat dressed in calico.

She twists the hem of her hanging shirttail, at once aware that without a motion on her part to cease and desist, Judy is versed to continue straight through into tomorrow in her quest to entice Cat into spending her earnings in the store before the bills chance to cross her palm.

Cat glances at her wrist in an illusion of checking the time, hoping Judy doesn't notice she isn't wearing a watch.

A car horn bleats from the street outside and Cat snatches the opportunity to make her escape. "That must be Gray. I promised him I'd be waiting outside," Cat interjects before Judy has a chance to continue with her litany of crafts, collectables, junk, and treasure. "So, thank you again for—"

"Yes, well, like I said, I didn't expect many sales from my regulars—not to say they aren't intrigued," Judy says, counting out several bills from the open register drawer. "Having a close-up look at what you've been doing out there in the woods is the next best thing to having a peek in your windows," Judy grins. "Your furniture is certainly very clever, but one never knows what will eventually catch on around here."

If not someone from around town, who actually bought the chair? Cat wants to ask, but doesn't. Curiosity alone not enough reason to reopen the door to another of Judy's marathon explanations.

"Thank God and amen for tourists. They're not so practical—or cheap. This woman came in here with her sister and you'd think a chair painted to look like a person was the best thing invented since cornflakes. Let me tell you, those ladies were charmed to pieces. They positively adored it. They said they'd stopped in town for lunch and decided to have a quick look in here when something in the window caught their eye—and you know, I could just kick myself for forgetting to ask what it was. Just so I make sure to leave it there.

"When I mentioned how the chair people were done by a local artist they just ate it up with a spoon," Judy says. "Isn't that a hoot? A local southern artist!"

Again Cat smiles. She doesn't know what to say. No one can be more surprised than she is herself. Not that she hasn't been hoping … but nevertheless, such a surprise. She just might burst before she ever has the chance to tell Gray.

"When can you bring in some more pieces?"

More pieces? What pieces? It's a question Cat hasn't considered any more than she's expected it to be asked.

"I swear the tourist season gets shorter every year. Or maybe it just feels that way considering how dependent I've become on out-of-towners to keep this place in the black."

"Um, I don't actually—I, well, yes, I do have a couple things nearly finished," Cat says, reaching quickly for the lie, unwilling to admit in the delirious glow of the moment that the pieces she's already delivered comprise the entirety of her inventory. Or that the call she'd expected from Judy Hines is more along the lines of an impatient demand for Cat to come pick up her unsold junk.

How incredible that instead, on the strength of one sale, Judy now stands here grinning at her like she's the best thing to hit town since refrigeration. And as grateful as Cat is feeling at the moment, she knows not to pull the plug on this initial sampling of success by admitting the storeroom is bare. That there is in fact no storeroom and no inventory.

"Perfect. You be sure and get them in here as soon as the paint dries," Judy nods, the cool reserve she'd extended when Cat first approached with her untested wares altogether vanished in the warm glow of a single purchase.

But then, Cat has no way of knowing just how long it's been since Judy's store has carried something to inspire genuine interest. As it is, the occasional birdhouse or grapevine wreath carted away by vacationers passing through on their way to whale-watching boat tours and lobster festivals are the only things keeping the "Open" sign posted on her door. That, along with greeting card sales and the local kids who come in religiously with a fistful of coins robbed from their younger siblings' piggy banks to liquidate her inventory of homemade fudge.

Cat strides to where she's left Gray's truck parked at the curb and it is all she can do to keep from spinning across the pavement like a delirious baton twirler, trumpeting her bounteous joy with the explosive zeal of an unhinged cuckoo. She presses the carefully folded bills into the pocket of her jeans, thinking over the various ways she might surprise Gray with the news of her very first earnings as an artist; this glorious compliment heaped onto the spoils of her increasingly perfect life.

It's Gray's idea that they make the rounds of yard sales, flea markets, and auctions, in search of suitable furniture for Cat to paint. As much as she appreciates his enthusiasm, she isn't quite sure how a solo sale at Judy's store justifies excessive stockpiling, and yet Gray refuses to be deterred by Cat's initial arguments of caution and logic.

Mismatched chairs are the most common acquisition, but by summer's end they've succeeded in amassing a fair-sized collection of furniture cast-offs; tables, small dressers, benches, a desk, pie safe, and vanity.

It is late on a Saturday afternoon and Cat is helping Gray unload the truck of two chairs, a small trunk and shaky step ladder they've plucked from a trash pile heaped at the end of someone's driveway. They cart the trove across the grass and add it to the assortment of furniture stored within the dilapidated barn which until now has served little purpose other than to slowly rot away at the far corner of the back yard.

Over the past several months Judy has sold just three more chair people, but Cat nevertheless holds to Gray's unflagging optimism that given adequate time and persistent faith, her painted furniture creations will eventually catch on.

As determinedly as she aspires to succeed in her newfound passion, Cat doesn't fail to count her blessings for what she already has. That she is even here at all, blissfully tucked away in this safe and solacing place is only one of the impossible miracles that have soared in and landed on the face of her life—the first miracle being Gray himself. Never far from reach is the recurring sense of disbelief routinely drifting through her thoughts to remind her how implausible it all is. That despite everything, she has succeeded in finding this niche for herself which fits so well. Custom tailored to everything she's ever longed for or had the audacity to hope for. How incredible she has all of this. And it is very nearly enough. Nearly everything she needs to make her forget.

Eleven

Happy and full with contentment and purpose, Cat has no real concern the children she and Gray have dreamed into their future have yet to arrive. She has no reason to question or otherwise distrust her certainty they will one day grow their essential family—a big, boisterous, and colorful composition of love fulfilled. When the time is right it will happen, and this next portion of their lives will fall into place. It is a quiet and patient expectation gently hovering without urgency. After all, they are young and healthy and there is abundant time yet for claiming all the things they have blueprinted into their designs.

Unlike the pained sense of determination forever shadowing Leafie's measured efforts, Cat herself has never felt the urge to race after motherhood. Rather, she holds to the conviction it will come on its own. Simply arrive when it is time. When somewhere a clock tolls, a weight drops, a season changes.

Leafie had been three months pregnant when she disappeared. A silent matchstick of a girl, who despite being grown by then, was not altogether dissimilar from her dark-eyed toddler self, speaking by way of silent stares and hollow expressions. Her deliberate silence serving as a continuous reflection of the deepest horrors of a thick and bottomless night when her terrified screams shattered the dark like breaking glass.

In the locked space of Cat's memory, her sister has never matured beyond the girl she last saw all those years ago, and it is impossible to consider she has a child—is in fact someone's mother. And yet this is the thing Leafie has always yearned for—to the very depths of her silent heart—to mold herself into the loving, nurturing mother she's never actually experienced for herself.

She wonders if Leafie has finally been compelled to abandon her silence. Does she speak to her child? Read books? Tell stories?

For a time there were letters. Sporadic arrivals Cat is quick to pocket when she finds an envelope waiting in the mailbox at the end of the drive, ever aware of Maysel's watchful eye peeking out from the slice of a carefully parted curtain.

In her missives, Leafie promises she has not—even for a second—regretted leaving Memphis. Just as she assures her runaway flight is neither impulsive nor propelled by fear of whatever scheme the Carpers are plotting to cover the shame and embarrassment of a pregnant sixteen year old under their roof. She makes no mention of the unnamed father, but when the Carper's handyman, Tom, grew either weary or fearful of the accusing stares and innuendoes pointed in his direction in the wake of Leafie's vanishing, he'd simply stopped coming. Failing even to return and collect the tools he left scattered on the ground behind the garage where he'd been working to replace a rotted sill. And whether guilty or innocent of criminal fatherhood, his unceremonious leaving cemented his conviction in the eyes of the Carpers and anyone else paying attention, assuring all previous indictments and conclusions were nothing if not spot-on accurate.

For the most part, Cat wishes it is all true. Because stronger than the distasteful thoughts of Leafie with a thirty-five-year old drifter, is the fear her fragile and broken sister is in fact wandering the world alone.

It had been difficult if not near impossible, but Cat had somehow succeeded in holding steady and not surrendered to the grin tickling the inside of her mouth as Maysel blasted into a rant over Leafie's "selfish and humiliating abandonment" of the only people to step up to the "duties and sacrifice" of taking in the sisters after "that disgusting mess" with Reva and Henry.

"This is just the thing they warn in the Bible—'a child foolish enough to claim the sins of the father will likewise fall,'" Maysel said, pulling one of her ridiculous and altogether erroneous quotes from thin air. And while Cat was tempted to suggest the particular sinfulness of inventing scripture to suit ones tirades, the cost of such victories was too high. Far more beneficial to her best interests was to neither listen to, nor respond to, Maysel's blasphemous ravings, thereby avoiding the risk of being swept away into the heat of an argument and inadvertently spilling some detail of Leafie's whereabouts.

And then the letters stopped coming. Several weeks before the baby was due to be born—all at once, nothing.

Cat once again combed over each of the letters she kept hidden behind an upturned stack of flowerpots and piled fertilizer bags in the garden shed behind the house, but she hadn't discovered any telltale clues she might've overlooked in a previous panicked rush of clandestine reading. There was nothing. No secret code, hidden assurance, or pronounced cue. The meanings in the sparse paragraphs read much the same as they had at initial perusal—the main import of their existence allowing Cat to believe that Leafie didn't hate her.

That she held no anger or blame toward Cat for anything she may have done or otherwise failed to do.

Not that it much mattered by then. Either way, Leafie was still gone.

Cat awakens with a start, at once aware of the newly vacant, still warm space opened up beside her as Gray shifts his weight to the edge of the mattress and plants his feet on the floor. It is still full dark and Cat rolls her head to glance at the clock on Gray's night table. 5:00—another hour yet before he needs to get up for work.

"Gray? What are—"

"Shh … go back to sleep," he whispers, brushing away a strand of hair drifted onto her cheek. "It's a surprise. Stay right here until I come get you." Cat tucks her chin back under the quilt heaped overtop her, curious why he is up so early, but still groggy enough to willingly linger where she is.

This is nice, she says, maybe to herself, possibly out loud, as she drifts along the vacant trails coaxing her back to sleep.

Beyond the quavery edges of fragmented dreams, Cat recognizes the accustomed lyrics of a meal under construction. Cabinet doors opening, the chink of crockery shifted on a shelf, the dull clack of a pan settled on the stove, the rush of water coursing through silt-coated pipes—and then, the clear even pitch of Gray's familiar whistle trilling over a tune she doesn't recognize, as the tantalizing aromas of frying bacon and browning flapjacks curl up the stairs.

If she allows it, her life will be perfect. If she continues to battle and defeat the ugly burdens of memory—forces them to leave her for good—she will truly succeed in holding onto what has always felt impossible. She will keep all of this protected from the threat of ruin.

He has prepared a feast of delightfully ridiculous proportions. There is a pyramid of sausage links and bacon strips, a bowl of scrambled eggs, and a tower of flapjacks. Cat smiles past the logical question of whatever impulse it is that has inspired him to cook such outlandish proportions for two people at 5:30 on a Tuesday morning.

"This is amazing," she laughs, because really it is.

He grins sheepishly, as if nevertheless hearing the question she hasn't spoken. "I might've gone a little overboard."

"We can always have breakfast for dinner, too."

"And lunch—for the next two weeks," he grins, pulling out a chair for Cat.

She is surprised by her immediate hunger; the rich aromas of the steaming bounty stirring awake an appetite she normally wouldn't anticipate for several hours yet. Her customary ritual is to sit here at the kitchen table after Gray has gone off in the truck, absently sipping a second cup of coffee in the blue-shaded dark as she stares out the window into the yard, watching the morning leak through the lingering fringes of deep night.

It has become her favorite time of the day; when she allows her mind free reign to wind through the quiet echoes of the empty house, untethered thoughts spilling out into a maze of random corridors without purpose or destination.

She assumes this is precisely what every other living breathing creature must likewise do—quieting the outside world just enough to wade through the accumulated marshes of uncensored thought, planting and growing the seeds of colorful dreams. Sometimes not even thinking, but simply being.

And yet intermingled, are those thoughts she no longer wants to carry—moments when she inadvertently glances away for an instant, carelessly leaves the gate untended or forgets to relock the door—and the underlying threats of old things immediately press to the surface. Ugly things that draw deep and hold fast even as she wrestles to force them back beneath the lid they have leaked out from.

Sometimes it isn't until hours later, once her mind obediently settles into the slots and grooves of routines and tasks she purposely aligns in order to effectively stretch over the course of the day, when Cat reclaims the carefully cultivated sense that she is in fact ordinary. Perfectly, blessedly, ordinary.

"Gray … do you think there's something's wrong that we haven't had a baby yet?" She says now, and even as she hears herself speak it, Cat is horrified by her own question. She knows from the moment the words climb out past her lips that they are altogether wrong for the gentle intimacy of this quiet morning. She wishes she could pull them back. Swallow them before he has a chance to see.

And yet incredibly, miraculously, it appears Gray doesn't hear her.

She watches his expression from the corner of her eye as he piles a five-man buffet onto his plate, anxious for some sign of absolute validation that he is in fact so blissfully absorbed in the act of bathing his meal in maple syrup, his senses have been momentarily disabled.

What on God's green earth has possessed her to ask such a question?

She doesn't want to hear the answer, at once fearful of what he might say. Maybe he can see though her after all. Can see the damages her hideous omissions have caused. He knows about her. Of course he knows. How can he not? Her falsehoods are so transparent. It's a distinguishing mark of the guilty—poorly fitting lies.

He lifts his head and looks at her, his stare holding the heft of a loaded question—an assurance, that yes, he has very clearly heard her.

"It's just—I was—I mean, do you think maybe something's wrong?"

He takes a moment to finish chewing, swallowing, before answering. "What do you mean? Like what?"

"I don't know. Anything."

"There's nothing wrong, Cat."

And she knows of course this is why she's brought it up, because she expects he will say this very thing and the relief will be enormous.

"Why? Did something happen? Did someone say something?"

"No. But—"

"We've only been married two years, Cat. It's not so strange we haven't gotten that far yet."

"I know. You're right. It's not even that. I guess I've just been thinking a lot about Leafie and the baby lately," Cat says, hearing the mistake in the words leaving her mouth, but too late to draw them back.

"Leafie? Your sister? She has a child? I thought she was—"

"What … oh did I say Leafie?" Cat spears a forkful of something on her plate and quickly deposits it into her mouth, chewing slowly to allow her thoughts a moment to outfit her lie. "Oh, well no, not Leafie. Not with her crazy job—all that traveling she does. She's never even in a place long enough to change a diaper. Her career is her baby, that's for sure," she says, even as she wills herself to shut up. She can hear herself saying too much, trying too hard.

She reaches for her coffee cup, grateful it has grown tepid, allowing her to take a long deliberate swallow. "I meant to say, Lisa—I think that was her name—she was this nice girl I met at Judy's last week when I was dropping off that stool I just finished. Very sweet and completely over-the-moon baby obsessed," Cat smiles in feigned recollection.

Gray smiles without lifting his eyes, sectioning a flapjack, flooding it with syrup.

"I can't help but worry there's something wrong with me not to feel that way myself ... to not have that same passion to be a mother," her voice falls away, certain he is right now seeing the ugly glare of selfishness staring back from the too-bald confession she's spilled out between them.

"Look, Cat, stop doing this to yourself," he says and his voice is quiet. "There isn't anything wrong with you. We'll have babies when it's time. There's nothing wrong with waiting until we're ready." He reaches across the table and clasps her fingers in his hand, offering a reassuring squeeze before releasing them. "It's nice just being the two of us for a while. There's no rush. We have time. All the time in the world."

Cat once more lifts her cup to her lips, thankful for this diversion cloaked in the ordinary even as she returns it to the saucer without drinking. She bends as if to retrieve her dropped napkin from the floor, when in fact the folded cloth is still there neatly arranged across her lap. She is afraid to meet his eyes, terrified the comforting sincerity of his words have visibly shaken something loose, collapsing the blockade shielding him from seeing just how dishonest she is. As ashamed as she is horrified, her pattern of deceit has left no available vacancy for one day filling in the truth.

"It's only a guess, but it looks like you're over-watering," Gray says, bending to examine the toothpick line of shriveled plant stems for a moment before straightening.

He's much better at guessing than he thinks, considering Cat has been saturating the fledgling shoots with the garden hose every morning and again in late afternoon. She has a history of convincing herself she knows what she's doing, even when her suspicions strongly hint otherwise. *Jump in head first and hope the landing doesn't kill her.* Whether daredevil or simply foolish, the results of her experiments in artificial confidence remain as a string of casualties attached to her life like the tail on a kite.

Less offensive misdemeanors are the seedlings failing to thrive, an overcooked roast, unfortunate design or color choice when facing a blank canvas—near forgettable missteps easily overshadowed by capital crimes of serious consequence. Namely, her offenses of faltered faith, broken promises, lost hope, the destruction of her sister's trust, the lies she has told and continues to tell her husband.

Cat listens as Gray continues with his diagnosis, her attentions drifting, coming back when he asks a question, wandering off again when she all at once finds herself recollecting the long-ago baby bird she'd discovered in a patchy tuft of scraggly grass at the base of a dogwood tree in the Carper's backyard.

The fledgling not only survived its apparent freefall from a nest wedged in the tree's upper branches, but incredibly hadn't been detected by the Carper's wandering fleet of cats. A double dose of good fortune promptly rendered null and void when Cat set herself to lavishing it with a savage dose of over-attentive nurturing.

She'd wanted to impress Leafie by proving herself as remarkably skilled as her sister's hero, Dr. Doolittle. Instead, Cat had succeeded only in establishing her inexperience; force-feeding her tiny patient with steady intervals of food and water, pushing minced portions of dissected worms into the miniature beak with her pinky.

Leafie had refused to acknowledge Cat's existence for several days after the bird's tragically bloated demise. An interval likely to extend a good deal longer if not for another of Maysel's outbursts—this time off and running on a explosive tirade when she discovered a hardened pebble of egg yolk on a plate that had been washed, dried, and put away without detection by either of her indentured servants, Cat and Leafie.

"Do you see this? This is disgusting! Do I look like someone who would live with this kind of filth in my cupboards? You think you can do things any damn way you please and that's the end of it? You owe me and don't you forget it. You can bet nobody else wanted to take on the burden of you two and you damn well better learn to be appreciative. Life isn't some big handout—there are no freebies. You want to live here, you'd better earn it. You can get your lazy behinds into the kitchen and I want every damn dish in that cupboard rewashed," Maysel screeched, though she clearly wanted to shout. Taking a furious swat at each of the girls as they scooted past. Her rant promptly effective in reminding Leafie of the necessary importance of an ally in the midst of uncontrolled madness. Even should the only available consort happen to be a moronic bird killer.

Now, Cat sees how she has inadvertently assumed this same stifling role with the seedlings in her overzealous attempts at gardening; obsessively nurturing to the point of suffocation.

"Maybe you weeded out some of the seedlings by mistake when they came up?"

"For Pete's sakes, Gray, I'm not that much of an idiot," Cat snaps, lifting a hand to shield her eyes from the near blinding radiance of a high-sitting noonday sun.

"Don't be so touchy. I'm just trying to figure out why you haven't even been able to grow a carrot."

"I didn't plant carrots."

"Very funny. You know what I mean. This soil is really beautiful and dark—it's ideal for vegetables."

The sun hangs over the land like a physical weight. Cat feels the damp fringe of ringlets forming along her hairline and against her neck where several strands have escaped from the thick twist of hair scrambled on her head in a messy bun. She ducks her face, blotting the perspiration striping her forehead against the cotton sleeve of her T-shirt.

"It's blistering out here. Let's just forget it and go in and get a cold drink," she says, pulling up from her heels to stand, watching Gray as he chops at the earth with a hoe in an effort to dislodge a stubborn colony of weeds encroaching on the lone trio of surviving pepper plants.

It's not as if she really expects to achieve some blue-ribbon level of gardening success. When it comes to growing things, she has always been someone with ten hands and no fingers. It's a trait she's carried from early on, held intact from a time when her only success was in failing at so many of Maysel's demands. And she wonders now as she watches Gray, if this is what it's really been about. Has her true intent all along been simply to accomplish a task Maysel had been unable to wring from Cat, regardless of threat or punishment?

She is certain that Gray will understand, even commiserate, if she right now takes the opportunity to explain this miserable portion of her life. And yet again there is the tangled web. The truth she cannot say this one thing without possibly having to explain something of where it comes from.

She starts toward the house, pauses, glancing back when Gray fails to follow.

"Gray?"

He remains crouched in the middle of the garden as if he hasn't heard, leaning on the handle of the hoe as he bends forward, his fingers probing the soil to loosen something encased there in the earth.

He lifts his head, "I'll be there in a minute. There's a rock—" His voice halts, dropping away as he pries the object of his interest from the freshly churned soil, fixing a puzzled stare on what looks to be a rusted section of some ancient garden tool.

"What is that?"

"Just a rusty piece of pipe or something," he says, dropping it at his feet and turning away when Cat moves closer. "I'll throw it in the trash later—man, it's brutal out here. How about that cold drink?"

But there is something oddly familiar about the discarded object that effectively serves to draw her attention—a recognizable hint that lures her to bend and retrieve it. She turns it in her hands, her limbs instantly tensing, veins and arteries filling, rendering her insides solid and heavy.

"It's the barrel of a gun," she says.

"No, I don't think so. It's not—"

"Yes—a single barrel shotgun. Look, here's the sight," she rubs away the compacted earth from the raised metal spine with the pad of her thumb.

"Maybe … yeah, I guess it could be," he says, a cloud flitting across his brow, then gone.

But she knows for certain she is not mistaken; knows indisputable details about the shape, feel, and workings of guns without wanting such knowledge.

"It's not the first peculiar piece of junk we've found lying around here, and I'm sure it's not the last," Gray says as he turns toward the house and strides away without looking back.

And it is only once she hears the screen door slap shut, breaking her from the forceful pull of memory, that Cat rises to follow him.

Twelve

Gray has thrown away the rusted relic, but it is already too late to quiet her mind.

Guns were a far from uncommon thing in her years growing up in Mudlick. Possessing one gun, or several, was no more exceptional than owning a refrigerator or stove. Whether stowed in the back of a closet for hunting, tucked behind the seat in a pick-up truck, within reach on the nightstand, or snugged into a waistband, common knowledge assured guns were only as threatening as the hand holding them. Which is precisely why Cat had been afraid of Henry Baldwin her entire life. Even now, when the only way her father might possibly reach her is if he should stretch up a tortured hand from hell and somehow succeed in grabbing hold.

She has every reason to forget—has been impossibly blessed with the perfect someone to fill the void from seam to seam—and yet something as unexpected as a rusted steel barrel encased in dirt has been the thing to send her reeling backward.

And on this morning when Gray picks up his lunchbox and heads off to the mill, Cat holds to him a moment longer. Kisses him harder. Misses him with a pulsing ache even before the truck's tires have stirred the dust and taken him from sight.

We are not them. We are nothing like them. They are so far away and long ago they have ceased to exist.

She refills her coffee cup and carries it out to the front porch where she sits on the porch swing despite the chill. She feels safer here outdoors where there are no walls to hold her captive should she need to make a desperate or immediate escape. The world here is so expansive as to feel endless—spacious in a way that keeps ancient threats safely distant. So bright and clear and blue, it is impossible to consider anything broken or ruined might ever dwell here.

They never had anything like this. They never experienced a life like this. Would they have even wanted it? Didn't they choose the life they had?

As it is, Cat can't recall a time when Reva and Henry hadn't fought. In the storehouse holding her remembrances, the rough-hewn and damaged images denoting the span of her parents' marriage glare back from portraits lining her memories in one long evil stretch. The sharp edges of anger are always there. At times spitting and clawing like opponents in a ring, at others, unmistakably obvious in the deceptively quiet and mutual hatred hovering along the surface of poisonous actions turned upon each other.

Even now, some twenty years later, Cat holds to the certainty had that night not ended as it did, she may never have fully come to understand just how many degrees their union was removed from normalcy. May never have wholly understood not all husbands and wives came to finalize their vows with an embrace of deepening aversion. She only knows on the night they at last succeeded in putting an end to their terrible life together, it felt more an inevitability than an accident of circumstance.

It was shortly after Cat's fifth birthday when they finally came undone—broke apart and loosed the awful craziness long twining out between them. She'd seen everything—rigid within the grasp of paralyzing fear—struggling to breathe past the ponderous weight of horror pressing into the back of her throat in a suffocating surge of silent screams as the terrible sequence unfolded frame by frame.

Even now Cat instinctively squeezes her eyes shut against the burn of his wicked words and the shameful sight of Reva's near naked body when the images reappear behind her lids.

It is this dull ache of memory that continues to survive intact, deeply rooted in hostile soil. Regardless of how far she's traveled or the distant track she's taken, it holds steady, barely withered, deviously waiting to spring back, full, thick, and immortal. She can see the darkly swirling poisons, some days more visible than others, reminding her the shadows of the past are right here looming where they've always been—just on the other side of the glass—threatening to spill a river of pernicious toxin all over the freshly papered rooms of her pretty new life.

Thirteen

There isn't an exact instant of recognition or notable metamorphosis; rather it comes as a subtle comprehension. The moment when Cat recognizes her life with Gray is no longer racing with a stride of starved intensity, but slowing now, shifting to rest like a hand cocooned within a comfortable pocket.

The days hold to something of an affable pace, closely reflective of the deepening cords of love and devotion twined between them in an intricate, life-sustaining network of arteries and veins.

There has been so much work to tackle on the house—is still so much to do—but Gray is pulling longer hours at the mill and not arriving home until early evening. He makes a valiant effort to shake himself loose from the pull of what has become his routine state of nightly lassitude, but the span of his flagging energies reach only as far as eating supper, and afterward, propping himself in a chair in the living room where he attempts to read the newspaper. Dozing intermittently as he makes slow progress beyond the first page, seldom reaching the last.

Dreams have been set aside to accumulate a fine powder of gathering dust. The art studio lies quiet and unused behind the closed door at the end of the hall, and designs for the murals they planned to one day decorate the walls are no longer mentioned. They have lived in the Maine house nearly five years, and Gray's grandiose blueprints have long since waned from immediate to someday; set aside to allow necessary space for those things comprising ordinary life.

For Cat, there is a quiet taste of accomplishment with the occasional sale of a chair, bench, or bedside table—once a special order for a chest of drawers—a novelty that never feels anything other than extraordinary.

But there is a certain cost.

Even as her spirit thrives in the light of renewed creativity, there is a true sense of remorse nettling her conscious as to Gray's own sacrifice, having selflessly taken on the obligatory position of supporting their life at the expense of himself.

It is a Saturday morning late in September when Cat heads downstairs, tracking the tantalizing promise of brewing coffee enticing her from under the covers. Her senses fogged from too-long sleep, she cinches the belt of her robe as she pauses on the landing, lifting her head when she all at once detects the familiar odor of something other than the waiting pot.

Paint?

She hurries the final few steps, eyes instantly widening at the sight of Gray perched on a ladder in the front hall, outlining a network of broad strokes across one wall with a stump of charcoal.

"Hey, Van Winkle, finally decided to join the living, have you?" he says without turning, and there is no mistaking the grin in his voice.

She silently watches the wide and extravagant strokes of his arm slicing heavy charcoal lines across the bare-skinned wall like a scalpel drawing black blood.

"So … what do you think?"

"I think I'm stunned and amazed is what," she smiles when he turns his head to throw a questioning glance back over his shoulder. "Stunned and amazed in a good way. Assuming of course, I've happened upon a surge of inspired creativity and not my adored husband's decent into madness."

"The latter. But I promise it'll be a nice quiet madness. Civilized even."

"I was afraid you'd given up the idea of doing this."

"Nope, just temporarily sidetracked," he says, turning back and adding several contrasting contours to the skeletonized lines of the life-sized tree trunk he's planted in one corner.

That finished, he steps down from the ladder and moves it several feet, thoughtfully positioning it to accommodate his reach for the next section ready to be sketched.

Leaning her hip against the newel post, Cat stands quietly watching for several long moments, then sinks to sit on the stair, her eyes following Gray as he continues the lines of limbs and branches stretching out onto the adjoining wall.

How passionately she's needed this. Quite possibly, even more than Gray himself. His life has been too long postponed from accomplishing the things he's set out to do. And although he never complains, it's a hard thing for Cat to swallow. That one of them should shelve their aspirations as sacrifice for the other has never been part of the plan. And although he has only just started on a project that will require a significant investment of time in order to see completion, Cat can right now feel the earth shifting under her feet as she watches him work; a profound sense of excitement rushing in to assure their shared aspirations are no longer derailed, but picked up, dusted off, realigned. At last running on parallel tracks. The load equally distributed as originally intended, and not the lopsided cargo where Gray brings home a paycheck and Cat follows her heart's desire on a solo path.

Her original pursuit of waiting coffee all but forgotten, Cat folds her legs up and tucks her cotton nightgown around her bare feet, rests her elbows on the ledge of her bent knees. She is curious to hear details of the scope of his plan, but she doesn't ask now, unwilling to disturb his thoughts or interrupt his movements; the soft scratch of charcoal drafting curves and lines across hard plaster, twining a melody through her head that melts down over her shoulders in an intimate embrace.

It feels as impossible as it is startling when she considers how long it's been since she's last witnessed the passionate explosion of his creative madness—seen him unwind into the ecstasy and fury of creation—so thoroughly absorbed into the near mystical act of transferring the things of imagination into tangible existence.

The sleeves of his softly faded denim shirt are rolled to just below his elbows, corded muscles visibly moving under his skin with each stroke of the charcoal; firm flesh and sinew signifying the strength existent there, even while engaged in this decidedly careful and precise endeavor.

He pauses and turns without speaking, his gaze holding her face with a smile not yet arrived on his lips—staying with her for a smoldering instant before returning to his task. And she knows that he, too, is remembering; is right now recalling those improbable, once-upon-a-time days when they'd first found each other. The savior prince stepping from the pages of a fairytale, patiently gathering the pieces of her hideously bruised and misshapen heart, and returning it to her whole.

And she hadn't seen it coming. So thoroughly absorbed as she hung on a ladder painting birds in flight onto the mural she was helping illustrate on the brick wall of an abandoned textile mill in Columbus, Georgia, she hadn't immediately noticed Gray's arrival that morning—simply another face planted amongst the curious audience paused to watch the misfit assemblage of artists at work.

They hadn't been long working on this newest mural, Cat and the ragtag band she'd claimed as a replacement for her missing family, all of whom unofficially deemed it their collective charter to beautify the city's vacant buildings one inspired tableau at a time. Or at least until someone inevitably came along reciting a litany of legalities, chasing them off to stubbornly pursue their next project in another forgotten section of town.

Over the course of a year and a half, they'd composed nearly a half dozen murals on the City's abandoned buildings, but only recently had the misfit company of brush-wielding vagrants begun to garner the first sputtering sparks of public interest. And it was no longer an unexpected phenomena to find themselves in attendance of inquisitive stares when they set-up shaky ladders and makeshift scaffolding to begin the work of transforming another wall of brick and chinked mortar into a freshly laid canvas of vivid life and color.

Despite the fanfare of onset wonderment, Cat and her compatriots knew to expect the majority of initial onlookers to soon lose interest and disburse; occasionally slowing to offer a questioning stare as they strode past, but no longer halting to a full stop in order to scrutinize progress.

But then there was Gray. Unlike the usual transient passerby, he continued to reappear every morning, nursing a bottle of cola as he sat watching from his seat on the poorly patched curb across the street; unwrapping a bologna sandwich from a paper bag as the hours wore past.

Cat had been aware of his appearance from the very first day of his solitary vigil—assuring herself it was only because she found it impossible to ignore the press of his stare against the line of her back—and she'd been purposeful to avoid meeting his eyes or otherwise acknowledging his presence. There was too great a risk in an action as simple as turning her head. Too much of a chance she would one day pivot and find, not a stranger, but Maysel Carper's nodding glare, smugly satisfied at having finally found where Cat had gotten off to.

She believed herself very effective at pretending to ignore him, when in fact she was making rapid assessments of his features at fleeting intervals, whenever she deemed it possible to do so unobserved; evaluating the components of his face in the quick thorough manner of the artist perpetually at work in her mind's eye. *Neatly put together—honest good looks. Warm eyes—approachable. Nose—long thin, nice line. Lips—well shaped, pleasingly formed.* A visage immediately inspiring Cat to caution—for no reason other than its unquestionable appeal.

Then rain. For two weeks the sky wept without restraint. Tired from excess sleep, of pacing through tightly stitched hours of endless boredom, Cat waited out the days, trapped inside the deeply echoing warehouse currently serving as home. She watched the lengthening gloom from behind broken window panes. Stared out to the street below though there was nothing there to see—everything colorless, slick, and empty—waiting impatiently for the weather to turn. The passage of each carbon copy day lending to the growing sensation that it never would. That this was all there would ever be—long stretches of unfillable emptiness.

Until finally dawn broke with a quavering shimmer in a distant corner of the sky—a weak band of tangerine light leaking across the low mantle of surly clouds and melting them across the horizon like a string of dirty snow.

She assured herself she didn't care. She didn't care and she wasn't watching for him when he failed to return to his sidewalk station. Just as it wasn't a cold lump of disappointment felled to the floor of her stomach like a splintered oak when he didn't.

Idiotic foolishness. After all, he was no one. A stranger. Mildly curious, but otherwise ordinary. No one of consequence. Forget it. Forget him. Clearly he'd picked up and returned to his steady and comfortable place in the world. He wasn't a drifting cloud of vapor like Cat. Wherever it was he came from and wherever it was he'd returned, he obviously belonged somewhere inside a real life.

But then one morning he was back. Returned to his place across the street, bottle of cola settled on the curb beside his bent knee, paper sack resting on the pavement between his feet. And he was there nearly every day afterward, far enough removed to be unobtrusive, yet close enough to eventually meld his way into the overflow of their loose and easy camaraderie.

Considering how little thought or interest went into whether someone might be joining or leaving them, it wasn't until the mural was nearly completed that someone finally thought to hand him a brush.

From the first, Grayson Barnett had proved himself an easy man to know and even now Cat recalls how surprised and uncertain she'd felt because of it. Her life, after all, had forever revolved around an essential need for caution; doors locked and shades drawn, ensconced within the dark and shameful family circumstances marking her inheritance like a still smoking brand. The ache of years trailing away from her childhood had left her thoughts too fragile, too unsteady, too injured to exist anywhere other than propped inside her own head like a chronically broken limb.

It was several weeks after making his acquaintance when Gray approached Cat to ask if she would consider helping him with an expansive seascape he'd sketched out across one entire wall in his rented flat.

"Let's just say I had a moment of supreme overconfidence," he said earnestly, though there was no missing the smile in his voice.

His simple but thoroughly complicated invitation had immediately sent her insides soaring, landing her in a place somewhere poised between anxiety and elation even as she nodded her acceptance.

"I'm a little surprised your landlord's letting you do this," Cat said, shading a bayside cottage she'd painted in the foreground of the shoreline unfurled across the entire length of the wall.

She took a step back, pleased with the effect of silvery wash stroked across the clapboards of the diminutive cottage, satisfied she'd rather effectively captured the effects of sun, salt, and sea.

"I'm pretty sure he'll be surprised, too," he grinned, dabbing a lather of frothy surf along the edge of sand.

"Honestly?" She threw him a startled glance across her shoulder. "You didn't ask if it was okay to do this?"

He didn't answer, the devilish curve of his lips saying everything. And when he turned his gaze on her— a rush of bottomless light landing with a force that sent her insides catapulting—she'd had to look away quickly, contracting her stomach muscles in a concentrated effort to calm her wildly slamming heartbeat.

How many emotions was it possible to feel in any one instant? Pleasure, elation, desire, fear, incertitude … all there together, blindly, wildly, whirling like an incoming cyclone.

In the brief time they'd been acquainted, they'd already shared dozens of conversations. Ordinary and unexceptional dialogues which in fact had spoken volumes. It didn't so much matter what he said, because regardless of content or immediate import, she remained purposely alert; gathering his words, cataloguing and meticulously storing them away for later analysis, searching for hints of meaning that inadvertently passed her ears unrecognized when first retrieved.

"I promise not to be insulted if you tell me you want to call it quits on this," Gray said several days after they'd started.

Even with the safe barrier of her back turned to him, Cat could feel the press of his eyes along the knobs of her spine as he waited for her answer.

"What makes you think I'd want to quit now and miss out on the grand jubilee of finishing when we're so close to being done—unless you forgot to mention you've decided to add a fleet of ships—the Nina, Pinta, and Santa Maria maybe?"

Just that morning he'd come to the conclusion that the scene looked sparse and unfinished and so had added a section of grassy dunes and a line of broken fence—weather-torn, salt battered planks tipped toward the sand.

"Hum, that might be a good idea, now that you mention it," he grins, then, "I just don't want you thinking you're stuck here doing this if you have other things to—"

"No, we—I don't." Cat paused, watching him as he neatly stroked in the lines of the fence. "Kimberly's pregnant. She just told us yesterday," she said, grasping the first subject to fall into thin air because she didn't want to think about finishing or leaving or any project other than this one here with him.

Kimberly was the only other female aside from Cat living in the warehouse and Gray had met her the day he'd finally crossed the street and they'd all exchanged introductions.

"Does she want to be?" he asked, his careful tone suggesting he'd misinterpreted the concern in Cat's tone.

"Yes, desperately. But it's not an easy situation," she says, declining to mention the obvious complication that an abandoned warehouse is not an ideal place to raise a baby.

He took a moment to respond. "I know women who've had kids and never stopped being angry about it."

"Oh … that's kind of—"

"Sad. I know. It doesn't make a lot of sense."

"Especially when you consider someone like Kimberly who'd have a dozen babies if she could."

"I hope it works out for her."

A restless quiet fell back into place and Cat bent forward, slipping off her shoes, carelessly tossing them on the floor beside the chair where she'd draped her jacket hours earlier.

Her knees and the backs of her legs felt stiff and unyielding from long-term crouching and she stood for a moment, sharp pinpricks of discomfort swimming down the backs of her legs like electrified minnows.

Cat massaged the fingers of her right hand with her left, kneading the line of her knuckles. Her eyes slid sideways to study the back of Gray's head as he stroked paint onto the mural; her gaze gently combing the thick auburn hair waving along the creased edge of his shirt collar.

She built his face in front of her, replicating the details of features already etched deeply in her mind. She watched the smooth rolling movements of his shoulders beneath the faded cotton fabric of his comfortably worn shirt—the head-to-toe length of him, neatly cut and well formed.

He'd mentioned he was a recent graduate of the Art Institute in Savannah, and this place where he lived was precisely the sort of dwelling she would've designed for him in her head if he hadn't already occupied it.

The former warehouse of a long extinct shoe manufacturer, the enormous brick building had been converted into apartments by Clifford Nast, a well-known developer in Columbus. Gray's apartment, comprised of three average sized rooms and a small bathroom, was open and airy, sparely decorated with a distinctly masculine collection of bare wood furnishings—sharp lined and unfussy—all of which added to the sense of ongoing spaciousness.

This stark, uncluttered environment struck her as a perfect fit for Gray, in part because it was so thoroughly removed from any resemblance to the eclectic décor outfitting the vast echoing space of the abandoned warehouse where she herself lived.

The place she called home was a nucleus of self-claimed territories appointed with the prized accumulations of street life; oddly shaped scraps of wood; repurposed bicycle parts refitted into a Frankenstein sculpture bedecked with cracked Christmas balls; vintage ties and accessories draping a moth-ravaged dress designer's dummy; three legged chairs; twisted bits of metal transformed into sculpture; an ever-growing assortment of peculiar decorations carried in from the streets outside.

Even without knowing all that much about Gray or his life, it struck Cat that his neat, spare place was a perfect fit. And for reasons she hadn't yet paused to analyze, the fact he apparently preferred his private world unadorned and clutter-free, merely served to illuminate his appeal. By all appearances, his life held none of the messy complexities tied to family, and so harbored no baggage or hidden complications. His life as beautifully stark and clean as a blank sheet of paper.

"There's cola and ginger ale in the fridge if you'd like something to drink. Maybe even a beer if you care to poke around," Gray said, his voice opening up a hole in the quiet.

"Thanks. I was just taking a minute to un-kink. You want me to get you anything?"

"A glass of water if you don't mind—with a lot of ice please."

"I'll put your drink here," Cat said, returning a moment later, setting the glass on the shiny surface of the end table nearest him.

"Thanks."

Cat stood sipping from her glass of ginger ale, surveying the mural and mentally chronicling all that was left to finish before their masterpiece would be deemed complete. With a sinking heart, she realized it was altogether likely they'd be done that afternoon—the following morning at the latest. She was nearly through with the slope of sand dunes she'd been painting all morning; complete now other than for the grassy areas which wouldn't take long no matter how she procrastinates. And once they finish—then what?

"Am I in your way?" Gray said, interrupting the dismal plummet of her mood.

"Only if you mind me hovering over you. If I bring in a chair from the kitchen I can work on the section above you. It shouldn't take long."

He nodded. "It doesn't bother me unless you start dripping paint in my hair," he smiled, returning his attentions to the corner of fence he'd added on the whim of a second thought.

While she'd later strived to reclaim details of how that afternoon had unfolded often enough to render them uncountable, Cat could never quite paste the collected components together in a way that formed one solid sequence. There were only ever pieces—still-life fragments gathered and aligned side by side, but otherwise unconnected within the protective embrace of remembrance.

He bent to dip his brush in a can of paint adjacent his knee, his shoulder grazing her stocking foot where she stood on a chair positioned beside him. An accidental contact. Brief enough even to seem an illusion.

The upper dunes finished, Cat stepped down from her perch and nudged the chair aside with her hip. Gray glanced over and they exchanged a wordless look. It was nearly done. She started in on the lower section of dunes.

His elbow bumped her knee. "Sorry," he said, without looking up.

Cat nodded, saying nothing.

Her mind resisted all attempts to focus, instead dashing back and forth between destinations like a burning thing skittering across hot coals.

Gray reached behind her to replace the lid on an open can of paint and his forearm brushed along her thigh, his fleeting touch sending a surge of heat rushing up the backs of her legs and along the track of her spine—splintering out in fiery sparks at the base of her skull. She tilted her head sideways, stealing a quick glance at him, but his face remained turned away, eluding her gaze.

Did he notice how her hand quavered when she dipped her brush into the paint?

The mural was nearly done. Almost finished. Any other time, in any other circumstance, this would've brought satisfaction, but now yanked on her senses with a sharp snap. Reeling hard, she worked to dislodge the smoldering knot clenching her insides—wrestled against the massive pulsing contradiction that lay in the project's finality.

Cat leaned forward, blending a hint of color into the swell of sandy mounds. It was the last area yet to be sprouted with the pale green wisps of seaside grasses, leaving little more to do other than offer to help Gray with the cleanup of paint and brushes—and then leave.

They held to an easy routine of amiable conversation interspersed with long stretches of companionable silence through the deceptively placid stretch of afternoon; occasionally returning from their separate silences to break the quiet with a simple comment or observation.

Yet even in the span of stillness, some indescribable something remained entwined between them, something warm and calming and safe; silently coiled, and yet fully awake. And it wasn't something born from anything said or otherwise conveyed by eye or touch, but simply there, alive within the luminous expectancy of unvoiced possibility. A nearness. Something Cat might've reached out and touched as effortlessly as she stroked the blades of grass along the cape of sand with her brush; absorbed within the intimate aroma of paint and turpentine, a familiar perfume on warm skin. Intoxicating in a way that fluttered in balmy ripples behind her ribs, so that she'd had to lower her eyelids, dizzy with the spiraling effort to reclaim her spilling senses.

Everything had fallen out of place, shifted—the room, this man, the painted scene spanning the wall. Herself. All of it far off and unrecognizable. Displaced even in time. As if she'd tumbled headlong into the imaginings of a newly drafted story and was now attempting to form pictures from the unfamiliar words she found there.

Had she reached out to him? Or did Gray's hand touch her first?

Unlike each earlier contact—self-conscious and apparently accidental—when Gray's fingers grazed her arm this time, they didn't brush past, but remained. Cat lifted her head. She could taste the heavy pulsing of her heart in the back of her mouth as their gaze locked and held. His eyes stared steady and deep—somber and full like a voice calling to her from a long time ago. She thought she heard him say her name, but she couldn't absolutely recall seeing his lips move.

He leaned forward, pressing his face into her hair where it curtained her neck. Her skin warmed like wax touched by flame, and when he moved his face to kiss her, she felt the touch of his lips everywhere, on her face, her eyelids, along the rise of her cheekbone, hearing the litany of his words mumbled low against her neck, "I'm sorry … I'm sorry, Cat …" over and over between kisses.

She lifted her arms to grasp his shoulders and his fingers moved in her hair, touching along the back of her neck, traveling the length of her spine. His kisses turned harder, demanding, as something like love and desire sent them crashing together, and she'd pressed herself against his chest to keep from falling away. And she knew without question—maybe had known even before then—that she was thoroughly lost to him.

From the very beginning it had felt almost too perfect. Like a gift too pretty, too expensive, too preciously fragile to risk opening with her clumsy fingers. In the weeks that followed, Cat found herself all but obsessed with studying her treasure, gently turning it in her hands, touching it, inhaling it, tasting it like a delectable sweet dropped onto her tongue—her impossible-to-believe romance with Grayson Barnett.

She doesn't immediately notice when Gray stops sketching and turns his stare on her. But now, feeling the imprint of his eyes, she tilts her face to catch his gaze, both of them smiling, saying nothing.

It is all still here, those original sensations and emotions, though somewhat changed over their years together, now grown quieter even as they become stronger and increasingly durable. A life as hopelessly beautiful, she is certain, as all those scenes they have yet to paint.

Fourteen

For a long while Cat lies quiet and still, listening for the disconnected sounds of Gray moving about in the rooms below. But she hears little beyond the loud and persistent throb of night.

She rolls onto her side, shifting clumsily beneath a press of anxious concern. She lifts her head and steals a glimpse at the clock perched on the nightstand flanking Gray's side of the bed; glow-in-the-dark numbers a soft and steady proclamation in the dark. 2:27. She squeezes her eyes shut against the charcoal-shaded murk in a determined effort to reclaim sleep, even while knowing she will not. Not so soon. Not for a while yet.

The pattern of Gray's middle-of-the-night wanderings over the past several weeks have become familiar in such a way she knows it will be hours yet before he creeps back upstairs and carefully returns his weight to the mattress. And while his restlessness is by now a condition Cat has come to expect, she has yet to arrive at a possible explanation or understanding of it.

And each time she rolls over in a groggy state balanced somewhere between wakefulness and sleep, turns her face in expectation of feeling the warm security of Gray's shoulder touching against her cheek, she is more bewildered than distraught to discover the vacant expanse of mattress stretching out beside her like a hollow field.

"Insomnia," he tells her. "I just have too many ideas running around in my head at once."

It's an easy enough explanation to accept. Although it's been a while, Cat has owned such restless fervor herself.

And yet, once several days of Gray's sporadic sleeplessness have stretched into four … six … eight weeks, Cat feels a ripening sense of unease, threads of uncertainty stringing lines of questions across her thoughts.

The tide carrying her concerns rolls in harder and stronger, rubbing emphatically along the fragile edges of her apprehensions. Nevertheless, Cat accepts his vague and simplistic responses to her carefully placed inquiries, readily sympathizing with his assurance he is simply frustrated by a recent stretch of over-long days at the mill which have kept him from working on his masterpiece.

As the hours composing his restless wanderings pile together like weighted slabs, filling the nights with a bludgeoning press of unease, Cat forces herself to swallow the simmering brew of her insecurities, waiting for the disquietude to pass. She leaves Gray on his own as he distinctly prefers, until the moment inevitably arrives when the space left by his vacancies spreads too wide and deep for her to continue ignoring it much longer.

Again Cat wakes to find Gray's side of the bed empty, the forlorn tangle of sheets working to press his vacancy somewhere deeper than an ache. A white stripe of moonlight melts through a narrow slice in the filmy lace curtains stirring loosely at the window, laying a ghostly ribbon along the sill and onto the pillow where Gray's head should right now be.

She squeezes her eyes shut against the hard knot of white-knuckle fear clenching tight fists behind her lids. She has made every effort to avoid staring face to face into the truth there is no such pattern without cause. There is always some underlying reason or specific agenda attached to erratic behaviors. And as much as Gray insists otherwise, Cat is unable to fully convince herself to believe his sleepless wanderings are in fact nothing of importance.

What has she done? What has gone wrong? What does this mean—what is it about? How can she fix it? Can she?

Somewhere far off an owl hoots, forewarning of its presence in the dark. Cat tosses onto her back like a parcel tumbled by invisible hands; throws an arm across her face in a shield against the moon's watching eyes.

The night moves restless and deep around her, closing in like a threat as the minutes crawl past. She rolls onto her side and wraps her arms around Gray's headless pillow, embracing it like the single buoy in an enormous sea, listens hard to the silence even as she strives to pretend it away. Assuring herself it is no darker than any other night. Just as hollow and echoing. Just as loud and screaming.

How is it that every evil thing in her life has ultimately managed to find its way inside by creeping in with the absence of light? The dark of night, an endlessly diligent herald of unwelcome things. More than just a shifting of hours, Cat has long been alert to the infinite boundaries separating night from day. An awareness exemplified by Reva and Henry's routine of drinking through the daylight hours, biding time until nightfall when they would unleash their mutual crazy.

"Two boozed-up vampires," Cat would sometimes say in an effort to make Leafie laugh; another weak attempt on her part to minimize past horrors to something of a manageable size. An endeavor which felt increasingly necessary as their life with the Carpers accelerated downhill; piling up bricks of heartache to add to a teetering wall, in a sad assurance that the only thing the sisters had accomplished thus far in life was to leave behind one brand of crazy for another.

Maysel Carper made no secret of her obsession to *fix* Leafie. That Leafie was a child who didn't speak simply made no sense to Maysel, particularly when there was no medical diagnosis forthcoming as to why she couldn't. Or wouldn't. Even at those times when Leafie was stirred to crying silent tears, such emotive displays were of little consequence to Maysel in her determination to cure Leafie's affliction.

"If they can't prove she's really deaf then she's just stubborn. And if there's one thing I can cure, it's a stubborn child," was Maysel's ready diagnosis and subsequent vow.

As might've been expected, Curtis took his wife's vow as a personal challenge to be won and celebrated himself. Over the course of several nights, he alternated tactics with a barely concealed sense of gleeful cruelty, resolute in his determination to trick Leafie into speaking.

He initiated his plan as the house lay sleeping, slipping into the room shared by the sisters and creeping up alongside Leafie's narrow twin bed—leaning in close and blowing a whistle next to her sleeping face. His success in waking her was immediate—her eyes springing open in wide-eyed terror—yet her unhinged mouth remained soundless, even as everything living and dead for a thousand miles rolled in their graves, tumbled off cliffs, splintered into microscopic shards.

"What the hell? Curtis? Curtis! What the hell is going on?" Maysel's voice barreled out from her bedroom down the hall. Her shout accompanied by a neighborhood dog howling a complaint somewhere in the dark.

He was the perpetual childish bully who never tired of cruel and foolish antics; sneaking up behind Leafie where she sat cross-legged on the floor turning the pages of a picture book and slapping his hands together next to her ear; kicking her slender calf with the hard toe of his shoe as she climbed into the back seat of the car. Each stunt earning a startled jump, disbelieving stare—occasionally fear—but otherwise, not a single syllable spilled loose from his victim.

In the end it wouldn't be Leafie who eventually broke the silence, shrieking in horror for him to stop, but Cat herself, on the night she'd inexplicably blinked awake—rocketing upright with the realization someone was there bending over Leafie's bed—her sister's pillow no longer cradling her small blonde head, but pressed over her face.

And Cat had screamed. Had screamed for days without shutting up. Without ever shutting up again.

It feels as if hours have passed though the moon has not drifted and the sky is not yet beginning to lighten. Cat pulls herself upright, twisting to free herself from the tangle of sheets shrouding her legs. She swings her feet over the edge of the mattress, the cool touch of wood against her bare soles at once sobering. She pauses. Listens past the loud silence of nighttime things as she moves to the door.

She finds him in the downstairs hallway, dappling green paint onto the dark branches of a second spreading tree he's sketched onto the wall over the course of some previous night.

"I just felt like working on this," he finally says, but only after an aching stretch of silence has suffered past.

"I know, it's just that …" Cat begins, but doesn't finish, all at once uncertain as to what it is she intends to say.

The piling questions and carefully worded declarations she's lined along the shelves inside her head over the past months, glare back with a note of bristling hostility and not as the litany of concern she intends. Because now, as she faces the closed barrier of his back, her suspicions leap forward into the conviction that he is deliberately withholding something of consequence—the true reasoning behind his nocturnal wanderings.

"It's so late," she says at length, feeling foolish, because what she hears in her voice is everything she doesn't say. And she has no doubt he hears it, too.

He doesn't answer as he continues to dab and stroke green leaves amongst the knobby branches filling the wall. She waits for him to say something, anything, but it seems he's already pretended her away—one quiet minute climbing onto the next until she feels as if she will suffocate under the heft of piling silence.

"Is something wrong, Gray? Did something happen?"

He leaves the question to grow large in the silence. And when at last he shifts his gaze to stare at her, his expression holds something of agitated confusion; the look of someone elbowed roughly, only to turn and find a face he's never before set eyes upon. "What are you talking about? Why would you even ask that?"

Her insides immediately tense, jolted as much by the unfamiliar insolence in his tone, as she is by his harsh reaction to her guiltless question. And for the first time since she's known him, Cat feels disturbingly, frighteningly, unlinked to him—train cars dangerously uncoupled on a blind curve.

It is a sensation so thoroughly startling that months later she will still vividly recall how truly awful this moment feels.

As if he is gone. His very essence swept away and recklessly replaced with this stranger staring back at her.

"Gray, I—"

"Please, Cat," he interrupts before she can finish, his eyes large, and deep, and unreadable. "There's nothing wrong. I just feel like working on this, alright?"

"Yes, but why in the middle of the night? It's been weeks now. How can I not think something's wrong?" Cat implores, hating that she sounds so needy, so grasping, so unreasonably insistent and yet unable to temper her plea or readjust her tone.

He turns away. An obvious dismissal. "I just need some time to myself. That's all, Cat. It shouldn't be such a big deal."

And his words are no less painful than if he slammed her in the chest with a two-by-four and left her mortally wounded.

When Cat awakens, it is with the caustic taste of his rebuff still clinging to the inside of her mouth, a chalky paste impossible to swallow. The sick sense of disillusionment peppering his emotional desertion is still here knotting her insides—squeezing with the tension of a closing spring. She shuts her eyes against the lifting dawn, unable to motivate herself to take the initial step required to maneuver herself into the day.

They are changing. Their lives no longer parallel, but subtly shifting course, drifting toward a destination just off center from the place they've always been. Cat sees the oncoming lights of an undefined something steadily closing the distance, but cannot grasp a ready solution for realigning the tracks and avoiding imminent impact.

She hears a creak on the stairs outside the bedroom door and shifts onto her side, opening her eyes to the pearly tint of rising light. She watches Gray cross the room to sit on the edge of the mattress beside her. He sets a steaming cup on her night table and bends to press his face against her neck.

"I love you more than anything, Cat. You know that, right? You believe it?" he says quietly.

"Yes," she whispers when her full voice doesn't come, at once understanding the morning has returned him to her whole and undiluted.

"I never want to hurt you, I just—"

She touches her fingertips to his lips, closing the words in his mouth. "I know," she says, sensing his struggle for an explanation and all at once feeling like she doesn't require precise words. His familiar self is here again and he loves her.

And mostly it is enough; though sometimes she still needs to remind herself of this when Gray's episodes of nighttime wandering stretch into weeks and she can't so readily press down the sense of mourning over her exclusion from this secretive place he occupies. She simply tries to understand. Not that she begrudges his quest for privacy, but because she somehow senses the import of whatever it is that stirs him to wakefulness and carries him away into the realms of necessary solitude. This unspoken something that drives him from reach—shuts the door and leaves her standing alone on the other side without a key.

And always is the question of, why now? What is it that's transpired, erupted, or shaken loose—taking on flesh as it grows larger? Jolted the foundation and splintered the sill of his comfortably settled self.

More often as the days and nights slowly drift, one easily blending into the next, it feels not so much a sporadic pattern of restlessness as it is a habit increasingly established. It is now less of an effort for Cat to return to sleep when she wakes and finds herself alone; pressing her face into Gray's vacant pillow and losing herself to the comforting scent of him; gradually tumbling back into a place of uncertain dreams as the night continues to tick past.

Even then, there are still nights when she finds herself staring wide eyed into the shadowy dark, straining to see what she has missed as her mind reels back in search of the precise moment when Gray flipped the page and turned the corner. But if there is a hint or clue alluding to the telling point when everything shifted, tilting their lives off kilter ever so subtly, she has yet to find it.

Fifteen

Cat is on her knees combing through the deeply shadowed recess of the narrow closet in the upstairs hall. She pushes aside a stack of magazines crumbly with age, flakes of brittle paper breaking off with the brief pressure of her fingertips, and retrieves a straw hat crushed flat by a pair of cracked rubber fishing waders. Next she pulls out a dented shoebox stuffed with a collection of curling receipts, a wicker sewing basket holding a jumbled confusion of thread wound on wooden spools, loose buttons, a pincushion impaled with rusted straight pins …

Her outstretched palm lands on something cool and flat tucked against the back wall where the space narrows to accommodate the attic stairs angled above it, and she drags it forth with her fingertips. She glances briefly at the tin box then adds it to the uninspired assortment of items amassed in a haphazard pile behind her, increasingly agitated over the question as to what she and Gray are supposed to do with this worthless inheritance willed upon them with purchase of the house. She only knows that her resentment over having to cohabitate with somebody else's pack-rat clutter is scaling the heights of maximum capacity.

The pile shifts and a cardboard box tumbles open on the floor, spilling out a collection of box tops and paper labels neatly cut from cans of soup and vegetables. Cat blows an exasperated sigh past her lips. It will be a far better thing for all concerned if she trains herself to adopt Gray's mindset that anything concealed in a closet or otherwise tucked out of sight, in essence, doesn't exist at all. "Ignore it and it's not there." Maybe he's right. It would certainly eliminate what she's doing now—sorting through and throwing away infinite miles of worthless junk.

She stuffs the scraps of paper back into the box and edges it toward the 'convicted and condemned' garbage pile, then shifts sideways, reaching behind to retrieve the recently added tin.

As it is with everything else here, the box clearly wears its age. And, as it is with everything else here, it is altogether unexceptional—a rusting cookie tin from some bygone era.

She almost doesn't open it, easily assuming the contents are yet another uninteresting archive of yellowed clippings, paper labels, or grocery store savings stamps, any of which will assure it a place on the swelling mountain bound for discard.

Cat pauses to study the muted outlines of the picture painted on the lid. Animals—cows, she thinks—grazing in a meadow sprinkled with pale yellow flowers. It is a difficult scene to decipher, the image muddied beneath a dull coating of dust lacquered by time and spots of brown rust, and she tilts the container in an effort to catch a hint of the late afternoon light fading beyond the window at the end of the hall.

Something shifts inside the box, a subtle movement, but enough to lift her curiosity. She rocks back onto her heels and works the edges of the lid with her fingers, prying it loose.

How thrilling it will be if she actually finds something of value or serious interest hidden away within this otherwise unexceptional hoard. A stack of bills thoughtfully tied with faded ribbon that Cat will set alongside Gray's place setting at the kitchen table. Saying nothing when they sit down to supper, pretending ignorance as she innocently piles her plate and waits for him to notice the windfall.

Farfetched and unrealistic, yes, but the remote possibility nevertheless spurs her heartbeat as she loosens the lid and lifts it away—

Photographs.

She stares at the uninspired collection of old snapshots, disappointed, though she knows she shouldn't be. She picks up several from the top of the pile, leafing through the images with abstract attention if only because they are here in her hand.

As would be expected, it is a collection of unfamiliar and equally uninspired scenes; horses standing along a fence, their dark eyes turned on the camera; several shots of a waterfall tumbling over a narrow rock face in a setting of tightly edging woods; a stand of trees paced at a distance; an automobile parked near the dark stretch of a lake in the background … Cat pauses her shuffling, her curiosity at once sparked and shifting to the forefront. She stares at the familiar wide rambling porch on the equally recognizable house planted squarely behind a grouping of people posed in the foreground.

She flips over the print in her hand and moves it closer to her face in order to decipher the faded scribble recorded in one corner—1953. How incredible that this house should appear virtually unchanged over all this time, as unmistakably forlorn and untended when captured in black and white then, as it is now in color.

The pubescent lilac tree in the photo, planted at the far corner of the porch, is easily recognizable as the mature version currently aging in its same place. Although it has multiplied in thickness and height over the passage of years—now several feet taller than recorded in the snapshot—the familiar bent elbow of a far-leaning branch is easily identifiable. And when she draws the black and white portrait closer to her eyes, tipping the image to catch the light, she can just make out the outline of what appears to be a swing hanging from the rafters supporting the porch roof; although if such an object ever actually dangled there it is long gone. An assimilation that leaves Cat sharply disappointed.

What does remain is the discernible sag in the center of the third step rising up to the porch. And Cat can't help but grin out loud at the remarkable familiarity of it; the previous occupants as disinterested then, as Gray is now, to consider the need for repair.

She studies the next photograph with interest: a slender dark-haired girl in a modest bathing suit sitting on a blanket neatly arranged on a sunny patch of lawn, the meadow rolling out behind her. The girl's expression strikes Cat as eager and yet somehow shy—the uncertain look of a near-teenage girl hovering within the threshold of puberty. How well Cat recognizes this look and the accompanying sense of disarray. It isn't a time so long past in her own life that she can't recall the stubborn nuances of this particular age—the sense of floundering—and how much she'd hated being on the other side of it herself. The way she'd just wanted to be done with it, through it, past it all.

Cat sets the photo aside and lifts out several more—a boy of seven or eight perched on the edge of a lawn chair as if anxious to take flight at any moment. He faces the camera, but there is a sense of distraction, the solemn cast of his eyes lending to the perception that he is in fact staring out at something beyond the lens, some distant focal point holding his gaze.

She continues leafing through the glossy images until another catches her interest—this one also a young boy. The inferior quality of the print makes it difficult for Cat to clearly decipher whether or not it is the same child posed in the lawn chair. She combs the narrow face intently, her stare held by the subtle but undeniable essence of something recognizable in the invisible shadows layering the child's grave expression. She feels the sharp prod of unspoken fraternity, the brittle sting of ugly things deliberately tucked away but nevertheless detectable. She knows. She understands all too well—can right now feel it moving through her insides like a resurrected curse.

The photograph has been taken at a poor angle, the glare of an improperly posed sun leaving a distortion of pale light stippled across the boy's face. Standing beside him is a tall slender man, the pair decidedly ill at ease in their Sunday suits, their mutual stiffness suggesting fabrics stitched from burlap and reinforced with cardboard. The salient span of palpable discomfort connected by the man's large-boned hand laid awkwardly atop the boy's shoulder.

Cat fans her fingers through the remaining photos, occasionally pausing to examine her home in a distant time; familiar settings separated by years, yet brought close enough in these images that this unknown family's portraits might just as easily meld into her and Gray's own.

She stares into the closed expressions of strangers that speak wordless volumes—images that tug in silent determination to pique her interest. She feels an eerie sense of foreboding drawing her in, senses the load of unseen things amassing on the horizon, edging in like a bank of storm clouds. But even then Cat is unable to look away.

She selects several more photographs, pausing to study each one thoroughly; a small boy hanging upside down on a tire swing; a young girl sitting on the porch steps, bare feet neatly crossed at the ankles, the seam of her lips just slightly lifted at the edges to suggest the possibility of a shy smile had the camera lens remained long enough to capture it; an older boy holding up a line with the dangling prize of a good-sized fish, his pride over the catch mirrored in his mile-wide grin, an expression particularly memorable since it is the first suggestion of genuine happiness she's come across in the entire sober collection.

The light is rapidly fading beyond the window, a reminder of how thoroughly Cat has lost track of the time. She hasn't considered what she'll prepare for supper or even what she has time to cook at this late hour if she hopes to have a meal ready and waiting (or at the very least, simmering) when Gray walks through the door.

She flips through the remaining photos, gazing absently as she mentally maps the contents of downstairs cupboards, refrigerator, and freezer for supper options. Until suddenly, her wandering thoughts cease whirring in mid-motion, cogs and gears stiffening to an immediate grinding halt as she stares at the horrifically mutilated photograph in her hand. *Is this the same tall man from the earlier photos?*

His face has been exactingly exorcised from the paper's glossy surface, scratched away to leave a deliberate void yawning atop his neck. Arms, legs, and chest, likewise crisscrossed with disfiguring slashes inflicted with the killing force of a ballpoint pen. She holds her stare to the image as if nailed in place, searching for some clue or suggestion of the murderous intent behind the attack, even while knowing the unlikelihood of finding such a motive on paper.

Several long moments tick past before she finally sets the photo aside, eerily discomforted by the pained sense of intimacy stirred awake as she peers too closely into the crux of another person's rage.

But there are others, each defaced portrait precisely mutilated as if to excise a demon. And impossible as it would seem some twenty years past the date printed on the back of the photos, Cat is certain she can feel something of it now—a coiled knot of deep-sunk hatred still here roiling along the surface of each ruined image.

Why some and not all? Why has the man's portrait been so exactingly purged in some images and left untouched in others?

She once more shuffles through the stack of prints she's set aside on the floor beside her, locating the only two pictures of the man that remain unspoiled. As with the others, the quality of the images is poor, the subjects distant and faded. Cat scrutinizes the lines of what she decides is a handsome face, though maybe it is the 'almost grin' teasing along the line of his mouth that draws her in. Even so, charming visage notwithstanding, there must be something she is overlooking—an essential clue alluding to traits markedly sinister.

And yet there is nothing readily discernible in the stranger staring back at her across the decades, nothing to justify the immediate hoisting of a red flag.

Her mind races with steadily piling questions as she once more returns her attentions to the images, scouring for details which might've slipped past in her initial scrutiny—girl on the blanket, boy on the swing, boy on a chair...

She presses past the steady rhythm tapping at the back of her skull in a Morse code of persistent warning, urging her to consider whether she really wants to see anything beyond the safety of her initial assessments. But she's read too far into the book to consider closing the cover now. Certainly not before she takes a shot at determining the ending.

She starts from the beginning, training her lens to refocus past deductions made at first impression. Again she stares at the girl in the photograph and is at once startled by the immediate recognition of the error of her earlier assessment. How was she so ready to assume that it is a cast of uncertain timidity overlaying the young girl's expression, when now, under the sharpened beam of newly birthed suspicions, what initially appeared as more or less ordinary, is clearly something else? The girl staring out from her black and grey existence looks not so much timid as she does wary. Not so much shy as melancholy.

And the boy in the lawn chair—is he simply a distracted child temporarily held in a fleeting pose? Or has Cat too easily overlooked the anxious cast in an expression alluding to secrets unwillingly held.

But of all the images here, most jarring in a way that slaps and bumps along the surface of her increasingly startled senses, are several prints of the tall man and a woman Cat assumes to be his wife. Although the woman stands only a single step away from him, her quietly simmering visage easily suggests a distance of oceans, detached and unsmiling, as if mentally preparing to remove herself from some future insult.

Instinct urges Cat to shift her stare, cease her scrutiny and return these people to the quiet isolation of their closet coffin. But she cannot force herself to look away from the woman's face—a pointed sense of delayed repulsion slowly yawning wide behind her eyes. Because she knows what this is. She knows what it means. She recognizes the closed expression of a woman who has already given up the fight.

This woman's face might just as easily belong to Reva Baldwin for all its resemblance to Cat's own lost mother. Just as whomever it is that has engraved their pained rage across the handful of colorless photographs could just as readily been Cat herself.

The dusky boarders of afternoon tighten around the house, closing in with silent stealth; the outline of full evening no longer subtle tracings, but thickly edged and deepening.

She gathers up the tragic assortment of images cataloging this vanished family's life, hesitant to return them to their forgotten metal tomb. She briefly glances over each print with newfound consideration as she replaces them in the box, unable to shake loose from the tangle of uncertain emotions stirred and heavily settled on the floor of her stomach.

This house, so unchanged—and yet so much so. And what of this mysterious family who once called it home? Where are they now? Why did they leave? What's become of them? Did they too feel the undercurrents of undefined melancholy wandering through these rooms as Cat sometimes does? The children will be grown now. The parents quite old. Maybe as dead and gone as her own...

She is layering the collection back in the container as closely resembling of the way she originally found them—as if this is somehow essential—when she is struck by a lightning bolt arriving from nowhere. The brilliant illumination of an otherwise obvious detail she's somehow overlooked despite long scrutiny, possibly because she's simply been looking too hard.

Is she mistaken? Is the discrepancy merely the result of a differing pose or varying camera angle—the presence or absence of high heels?

She aligns two comparable photos alongside each other, edges touching to access the man's countenance in both, the unmarked visage in contrast to the mutilated one.

How has she missed this thing that screams so loudly now? How did she manage to overlook the telltale indications that the two men are not actually one and the same? The ink-slashed form is bulkier, thicker through the torso than the other man, an inch or two shorter in stature when compared against the height of the dark-haired woman accompanying each man in their separate photographs.

Somewhere a clock stops, allowing the minutes to fall away uncounted as Cat again studies the conflicting images. Two men, one apparently loved, the other despised— at least for a time. The woman herself offers no clues of explanation. No readable hints as to the possible nature of his crime. Who is it then that he's wounded so deeply? So critically injured.

Cat stands in the kitchen staring at the stove, her mind suspended in a place of spontaneous amnesia. Her thoughts are running too fast to pause and process the accustomed and ordinary. On the counter is the package of limp beige pork chops she's plucked from the freezer hours earlier and left out to thaw, but any interest in preparing a meal is altogether evaporated.

There are too many memories racing circles inside her head— all the more convoluted because they are not hers. They belong to these other people. The ones she's lifted from a dented tin box and unwittingly resurrected. And try as she does to set it aside, she can't quite shake her mind free from the stinging disappointment that this house—her and Gray's house—has not always been a fortress protecting ironclad assurances of love and security. Because now there is this—the ponderous weight of another family's unmistakable discontent.

"You found these where? In a closet?" Gray asks, taking the photograph Cat proffers; studying the image for a long instant before handing it back.

"Uh huh, the one in the upstairs hall. Now take a look at this one," she says, holding out the portrait of the pen-slashed man.

"Whoa …" his eyes widen, as clearly startled as Cat has been at first sight. "Somebody must've been pretty worked up over something. Maybe one of those kids wanted a pony for Christmas but didn't get one."

"Seriously, Gray, do you think this might be them—the people who abandoned this house?"

"Maybe. I mean, I suppose it's possible, but I don't see how we'd ever know for sure. There's probably been some renters in and out of here over the years," he says, turning away, his fleeting spark of interest already snuffed out and swept away in lieu of more pressing matters. "Is supper ready? I'm starved."

"Just about," Cat answers, disappointed that he clearly isn't seeing the photographs in the same burning light of fascination as she is, even while understanding why he wouldn't.

Her comprehension of damaged people is hers alone. Gray will forget these unknown persons even before they drift back around the corner into oblivion, but Cat will hold on. Because as unreasonable or improbable as it may very well be, she senses an undeniable connection to this unknown family—linked by the palpable strands entwining things unnamed, yet assuredly similar.

Now, rather than spreading out the prints as she's intended, eagerly outlining the intriguing clues and revelations she's decrypted over the course of the afternoon, Cat replaces the lid on this other family's past and relegates the tin to the table in the seldom used dining room. She returns to the kitchen just as the chops she's left frying on the stove are beginning to burn.

A litany of questions and accompanying suspicions continue to tickle at her thoughts; deliberations over the unearthed photographs rising and falling in her mind like a changing tide. Even so, Cat holds to her determination to rebuff the temptation to re-open the cache of faded prints. She easily recognizes it doesn't so much matter whether her observations are real or invented, because regardless of what she's interpreted in the images, there is no point and even less purpose in revisiting what is past and gone.

She reminds herself to ignore the strangers in the box and forget their disquieting expressions, telling postures, and suggested injuries. Every hour through every day, she pretends them away even as she listens for the distinct sound and constant pull of old injuries rekindled beneath the innocuous lid of the cookie tin. Threats dangerously discomforting for their similarity to the ones she's long raged against herself; these dull and tarnished strangers aligned shoulder to shoulder with her own fractured portraits. And if she doesn't step away from the edge—move back and steady her footing—she knows she might easily tumble over the side, landing in the very place where she's so methodically buried her own ugly corpses.

The silently taunting box and its menacing contents remain untouched over the next several weeks, not so much forgotten as they are deliberately ignored. It is clearly Gray's simple assessment that holds closest to the truth. His logic that the mutilated pictures are merely the result of a child's impulsive flux of anger toward a parent makes sense; the inevitable arrival of shame over a ruinous misdeed, inducing the offender to hide away the evidence of naughtiness in a bid to avoid certain punishment. Perfectly logical sense. A far more reasonable assessment than the rapid evaluation of tumultuous discord and mental suffering Cat has been so prompt to feed her imagination.

The best thing, the wisest, safest thing, is to return the troublesome collection to the very place she's pried it from; remanded to the back of the closet amid the dust balls and darkness where it has peacefully nested all this time.

She knows that to further mention it to Gray is to assure his suggestion that she toss it away with the assorted troves of bric-a-brac and worthless clutter they occasionally collect and haul away to the town dump. Unlike Cat, he is neither sentimental nor protective of things which hold no inherent connection to either of them, and these abstract souvenirs from another's distant past are without exception. His opinion, whenever the topic arises, is unchanging, "If we're going to live in a house crammed with worthless junk, at the very least it should be our own worthless junk. Eventually we need to get serious about cleaning it out of here—crumbs and all. Anything that came through the door without our original fingerprints on it goes."

Only now, when she returns to claim the troublesome object from the dining room table, knowing for certain that this is where she's left it, she finds it's gone. The ensuing search proving only to clarify what she's already determined—that the tin isn't anywhere else either.

It isn't so much a mystery as a surprise, that despite Gray's lack of interest in the photographs when first presented, his curiosity has apparently been stirred after all. Cat assumes he's found himself leafing through the collection during one of his late night forays; stirred awake, but minus the required motivation to sketch or paint.

And yet, if she's assumed correctly, and all he's done is transfer the snapshots from one spot to another, then how is it they're still nowhere at all?

"Where did you leave that tin of photos, Gray?" she remembers to ask hours later, all at once recalling the morning's fruitless search, as she scrapes dregs of meatloaf and mashed potatoes from the supper dishes.

He doesn't answer, continuing to leaf through the stack of junk mail accumulated on the kitchen counter.

"Gray?"

"Hmm?" he murmurs without glancing up, his attentions caught and held by a catalog advertising camping equipment.

"That old cookie tin—the one with the pictures in it—have you seen it?"

"Cookie tin?"

"Yes. The one I showed you a few weeks ago," Cat says, feeling the mild stirrings of annoyance at his blatant inattention. It isn't as if she's unearthed so many crummy old cookie tins he can't guess which particular one she's referring to.

"No, I don't—"

"I left it on the table in the dining room and now it's gone," she interrupts, no longer making an effort to mask her impatience. "You must've done something with it."

"I don't remember seeing it," he says, lifting an eyebrow in brief recognition of the perturbed shift in her tone before returning his attentions to the catalog and turning the page.

"You are aware that there are only two people living in this house, right? It's a simple process of elimination. If I didn't move it—and I didn't—that leaves you."

"Well, you obviously must've misplaced it, Cat. I haven't seen it since the night you showed it to me," he says, at last lifting his head and affording her full attention. "What's so important about a bunch of old pictures of people we don't know?"

Important? What's so important? She's seen things in that box she understands. Felt things. Recognizes the certain possibility that they've been to the same places—her and that family. They have a connection. It's her responsibility to return them to the place she's taken them from on the chance someone comes back to collect them one day. Because they very well could. They are important for a dozen different reasons—none of which she can right now explain to Gray.

Waves of irrational frustration slam up against the walls of her skull in a seasick tide, yet when she speaks her tone is wholly dispassionate, steady and quiet, "I just really liked the tin. The scene on the lid gave me an idea for a table I want to do for Judy's shop."

"Unless it accidentally got tossed away, you must've put it somewhere and just forgotten. It'll turn up," he smiles. "Right there alongside all the other crap we've lost track of around here."

Despite her annoyance, Cat knows he's right. Not that the pictures will eventually turn up, but about the thing he hasn't said with words—the understanding she reads in his expression. The assurance this missing item is of no real consequence because whatever truth is there in those black and white images has no place here with her and Gray. They belong back where she found them, closeted in the dark. Unseen, forgotten, and entirely left alone.

Sixteen

Cat dreams that Leafie has lost her baby. Not lost, as in unborn, but lost as in all-at-once gone—there and then not. She sees Leafie running from place to place, frantically searching, all the while screaming, lips pulled so tight they seem to vanish inside her mouth, unhinged in an unmistakable definition of terror. And just as it is in life, there is no sound. The urgings of her face, a moving portrait drawn to express all the words she does not speak.

It is an image so real, so vibrantly authentic, it remains even once Cat jars herself into the safety of waking consciousness. The icy edges of deep-set fear still here framing the unsealed edges of her thoughts as she plods downstairs and throws herself into the task of preparing breakfast; purposely focused as if it's the most essential task she's ever undertaken. *Everything is normal. Her life if normal. She is here and this is now.*

And yet hours later, the bitter remnants of the dream remain firmly in place, stubborn grounds pasted to the walls of her mouth, resisting her efforts to dilute and swallow. She feels the forceful pull of a deep-seated regret that appears distinctly like guilt; the two emotions squeezing close enough to feel like one and the same. Guilty regret? Is there even such a thing?

If only she can make herself believe she is reading it all wrong. That her reoccurring dreams are the runaway ramblings of a vivid imagination and not full-to-breaking reminders of unresolved sorrows.

Where would she even begin to look for her lost sister? Is it as uncomplicated as picking up the telephone and dialing? Dialing who? Where is the list of rules detailing the task of finding a carelessly misplaced person?

She can't explain her cowardice in doing nothing any more than she can stomach the infinite stores of pitiful excuses and quavering resolutions she's allowed herself to accumulate. They are difficult sins to confess, and so she doesn't.

The perfect conclusion would be to find Leafie safe, happy, and cared for. But what if her sister is none of these things? What happens should Cat stumble into a tangle of answers she doesn't know what to do with? When ignorance is no longer an option large enough for her to hide behind?

She has too easily allowed herself to become a shallow observer of her own invention. Deliberately taking a step backward without pausing to reassess her motives whenever persistent curiosity threatens to collide with desperate concern. Because she is afraid. Even of those things she doesn't know and cannot see. Especially those.

Finding Leafie doesn't require a goal so much as a destination. To discover where her sister has gone and what she's become is only one bite-size portion of an eternally roiling stew; a culmination of unhealed injuries; broken hearts, twisted insides, abandonment, fear; painful things stacked against a poorly constructed wall, forever teetering, threatening to fall.

They are scenes that snap open without prelude, slam shut without warning, waft through her mind in a ghostly vapor even as they grow increasingly brittle.

They hold no purpose, are no longer of consequence, yet they continue to come; returning Cat to the slow bake of Memphis in August. The long lonesome seasons in the Carper's house where Maysel lorded over every minute detail between waking and sleeping. Governing her kingdom by an unholy list of commandments set in stone—chores, duties, obedience.

The sisters arrived at a quick understanding as to the costly consequences of disobedience and so mostly did as they were told. Most disheartening was Maysel's rule forbidding them to associate with the boisterous cast of children running wild and free across neighboring yards, assuring that Cat and Leafie's only connection to life beyond the separate shore of their lonely island were brief glimpses of their carefree peers playing red light-green light, or enviable shrieks of laughter carried across the yards from a high-spirited contest of Duck-Duck-Goose.

"Oh I'm sure those ragtag ruffians would get quite a charge playing games with a mute—or playing games on a mute," Maysel smirked when Cat summons the courage to ask why they must remain isolated.

"I'll talk for Leafie."

"Oh really? And when you're crawling with ringworm and scabies like those filthy hooligans, are you gonna talk your way out of that too?"

"I suppose I could."

"You'd do well to watch that fresh mouth. Your mother might've let you run wild, but that's not how I raise children."

Desperate loneliness, bitter sadness—these were the unchanging edicts held intact over the span of years lived with Maysel and Curtis. An accustomed state of being that made the unexpected spill of Maysel's close-held secret all the more remarkable when Leafie disappeared.

"It's not fair. It's shit. It's just shit!" Maysel railed at Curtis with the discovery of Leafie's vacant closet and empty dresser drawers. "All these years I've tried to have a baby—all these years hoping and praying and wishing and bawling my eyeballs dry and that little whore gets pregnant with one poke. It's not fair. It just bullshit."

Maysel has wanted a baby? Cat would laugh herself silly if it wasn't so ridiculous. It simply couldn't be true that this hateful, brittle woman has pined for a child. Hoped, and prayed? Never. Not when she so passionately disliked the two living right there under her roof.

Stark determination, denial, and invention—these are Cat's collected antidotes against her injurious past—only now she questions if they are somehow losing potency. She knows how to wait out the burdens posed by memory; how to hold fast through oncoming strings of sore and tender days. She knows to tighten her grip when unwanted things return with disturbing clarity—mindful that her apparitions will diminish as long as she continues to deny them.

Or confesses them.

And what if she does stop pretending? If she simply surrenders and offers up her burden of stagnant secrets? Exchanges the fairytale history she's invented for a corrected version of the truth.

But even as she considers it, she knows she won't. Not when her imagination is so ready to fill in the blanks with shifting images of Gray's gentle countenance melting into a cool bottomless stare—surprised, maybe angry, possibly disappointed, certainly confused. *Why?* Is the question that will slam to the surface. Why such distrust?

Distrust. It's a motive she will vehemently deny even though he will be right. Because isn't that what this ruse of deliberate omission is about? Distrust in the foundations of Gray's love for her; uncertainty as to its strength or durability once he sees the uncloaked face of her mistruths, and the person he believes her to be crumbles to dust.

Seventeen

"I'm thinking about quitting my job at the mill."

Cat lifts her head, uncertain if she's heard correctly over the tangled sounds of a chilling rain riding hard on the back of a blustery wind outside and the rapturous chords of classic symphony swelling out from the old console radio planted in a shadowy corner of the living room.

They've been painting since early morning, and the arrival of afternoon finds them progressing at the same comfortable pace. Gray has been up since before dawn, propelled by a fixed determination to finally make something of real progress on this newest mural—a project started weeks ago, but which they have been too tired, too occupied, too absorbed with other things to pursue.

"Quit?" Cat repeats, far more surprised than she is disturbed.

"I've been thinking about it for a while, but I figured maybe I was just being crazy."

Cat crosses the room and switches off the radio, the magnificent energy of the dramatic music all at once an annoying distraction. "Did something happen?"

No, he indicates with a shake of his head, laying his paint brush across the mouth of an open can.

"Then what's wrong?" Cat moves to sit on the floor across from him. More to the point, she hasn't seen this coming. Has not caught so much as a hint or reason to suspect such a notion is even stirring in his head. So now, on the tail end of a decidedly quiet and easy afternoon, the arrival of his statement feels akin to a tornado spinning in through a crack in the wall.

A distinct sense of confusion pushes up hard against everything he's said and everything she doesn't—a surge of questions pooling in her immediate thoughts and spilling over her face in obvious shades of concern, even as she strives for an expression which pretends otherwise. And she knows from the laugh tickling at the corner of his eyes and the grin creeping across his lips, that her thoughts are far from invisible.

"Hey, hold on there, kitty Cat, your shock and horror are showing," he laughs softly. "I'm not saying I never intend to work again, I'm just saying I want to do something that's more about us—about me. The mill was fine for a while—while we were getting settled and putting our life in order—but sawing and stacking lumber isn't exactly the grand scheme I had planned for my life. It's getting harder to pretend I don't feel like I'm driving ten miles in the wrong direction when I leave for work in the morning."

He cups her stocking foot in his hands, pressing his thumbs against her instep in rhythmic strokes as he talks. "Okay, your turn—and don't skimp on the honesty—I can take it. Go ahead and tell me how selfish I sound."

"Straight up and between the eyes?" she says, her initial surprise quickly settling to be replaced by something else. "For starters, it never really made much sense why you'd want to come up here just to slice up trees. You're an artist, for Pete's sake. An amazing, knock-your-socks-off master of the brush," she smiles, but his expression has already turned serious. All signs of lighthearted amusement gone.

"But I thought this was what you wanted," he says, tipping his chin to indicate the house and all things in residence, his eyebrows pinched in a suggestion of just how difficult it is for him to admit his restless discontent. "I thought all of this was important to you."

"This is what I want," she says, squeezing his fingers still holding her foot. "You are what's important to me."

She waits through a long moment before he finally returns his gaze to meet her eyes. There is something going on here that Cat doesn't altogether recognize. She senses the thing Gray most wants to reveal isn't necessarily contained in what he's already said. There is something more. Something hovering along the surface that causes her instincts to pique—step closer, stand straighter, listen harder.

His voice is low. Her foot remains cradled in his hand. "Sometimes it feels like I've spent my whole life wandering around looking for something—trying to find the one place that feels like the right fit. For a long time this felt like it. Like this was the place. But that's only because you're here, Cat—because you are the place."

It isn't so much his words, as it is the press of his gaze holding to her face that pilots her to the understanding he is neither explaining nor announcing. He is asking.

"If I leave the mill, we might end up starving for a while—maybe risk losing the house. I need you to be sure you understand all of that before you say anything. I know how much you love this place."

"Gray, I love this place because you brought me here. I promise to love anyplace you take me." She could tell him that she sometimes wonders if she likes this house at all. She pretends not to notice the drifting motes of discontent—the undefined sense of sadness that sometimes wafts through on a passing current of melancholy.

He smiles, but his expression is uneasy. His words are a cautious confession. "I guess what I'm saying is I think I want to jump in the deep end, but I'm not all that positive I know how to swim."

"I know you can swim, Gray. I've seen you."

His fingers tighten on her ankle, tugging gently for a moment before releasing her. She shifts her legs, bends her knees and slides closer. "It's not about having my name on something or any of that," he says, and she leans into him, touching her forehead against his chest; the steady cadence of his heartbeat riding over her flesh like a gently stroking hand.

"Not like that would be a terrible thing—but this is something else. I want to create things that come from all the stuff I'm carrying around … an assurance to myself that I'm really here. That I passed through once. Am I making sense, Cat? I promise I won't hold it against you if you tell me I sound like a whiney burnout looking for a way out of getting up every morning and going to a real job. Honestly, I won't."

She nods her head. "There's not one thing you've said that doesn't make perfect sense," she clasps his hand between both of hers, squeezing an assurance to match the sincerity in her words. "What makes me sad is thinking maybe you've felt like this for awhile but were afraid to say anything."

She would be telling the truth if she told him how passionately she understands. That she's felt all of this herself. Years ago; her ambitions flamed by the determination to prove to everyone, herself especially, that regardless of any ugly thing Maysel or Curtis Carper have ever said, Catherine Baldwin exists in this world for a purpose. She is more than a body occupying space. Despite all those things she's been told over the course of her life, she is in fact someone of worth. She is not a mistake, an injury, or unfortunate predicament.

Only, she's put away the pressing urge to prove herself a forever ago, slowly but steadily changing direction from the moment Gray came falling from the sky to land on her heart. The White Knight, valiantly determined to sidestep the tight barricade strategically placed around the tumbleweed-strewn core of her life. He'd succeeded in the impossible—trundled through the dark shadings of nothing years Cat had piled up around her in a protective fortress, striking against the walls with patient fists until they fell away like crumbling ash.

Not that she's lost the taste for accomplishment. It's simply that her ambitions have changed course and she's willingly traded complicated aspirations for the more durable treasure of full-blown contentment.

There is an immediate sense of relief washing in, trailing his words as Cat realizes he has in fact given her the very thing she's been searching for—an answer to the question of sleepless nights, solitary wanderings, and uncharacteristic moodiness accompanying him over the past several months. Even as she wonders how she hasn't recognized it before now—the sharpened point precisely aimed at the beating heart of his unfulfilled need to compose something of significance.

Cat leans forward, tips her face into his neck, her lips holding to an immediate prayer of gratitude.

Finally, finally, finally it all makes sense.

Eighteen

Cat opens one eye in a tight squint against the stark white light. She swipes the air with a briefly lifted hand to discourage a fly darting in schizophrenic flight above her face, sitting upright only when the insect remains maddeningly elusive and unaffected by her midair strikes.

Judging from the position of the sun, it isn't quite noon. She'd come out into the yard hours earlier, dragging the lawn chaise away from the deep stripe of morning shade clinging to the back of the house, intending to stretch out for just a moment. Only now this handful of minutes has all too easily distended to eclipse the entire morning—along with any potential glint of motivation which may have originally come out here with her.

It's become her habit of late to hurry through necessary tasks early in the day while her patience for the mundane is still pliable; leaving her afternoons free to dabble with ideas and evolving projects for Judy's store.

But today she is tired. The previous night has been a difficult one; hours sharply punctuated by restless bouts of wakefulness and shallow sleep, her tangled dreams a crazy-laid patchwork of old injuries and lingering torments. *Why do these things refuse to leave her alone? Hasn't she carried them long enough?*

Cat drops her legs over the side of the chaise. She touches the soles of her bare feet to the cool grass and leans forward with the intent to rise, hesitating just long enough to decide she prefers to remain where she is; lifting her legs back onto the chaise, reclining back and closing her eyes when the motivation necessary for drawing herself upright fails to take hold.

Summer has come early, dropping a premature shroud of uncommon heat over the hours spanning dawn to dusk. Even then, it isn't the discomfort of unseasonal warmth working so effectively to keep Cat distracted and anxious, but rather the amassing crowd darting and whirling through her thoughts in wild abandon. The twittering, gibbering audience that never quiets—knocks and bumps and pushes hard to throw her off balance with the constant static of empty words.

She makes a determined effort to align her thoughts with other things, and for several days she is wholly immersed in painting the small chest she hopes will wow Judy well enough to afford Cat a place for it alongside her two unsold chairs. But just as swiftly as the inspiration appears, it is gone. Her zeal for the project veering off without warning, leaving the chest half finished and abandoned in the barn.

And then there is everything else; sheets on the bed in need of laundering, a bathtub long overdue of a proper scrubbing, floors to be swept … She considers over the waiting list of things in need of doing with reluctant guilt, fully intending to tackle what most requires attention at least a dozen times a day and yet unable to summon the necessary push to follow through.

Mostly she thinks about Gray. Gray and the now-stagnant plans Cat cannot bring herself to leave alone even though he has. The memory of that afternoon is still too vibrant in her thoughts, and her gratitude that he has at last shared the desires of his heart feels no less significant.

But it has been weeks and Cat is still waiting for something to happen, increasingly frustrated as the days tick past unused for any purpose other than the ordinary. Despite everything he's said, Gray continues to rise with the dawn and drive off to work—sawing and stacking lumber five days a week and the occasional Saturday.

Whether unrealistic or not, Cat has anticipated an immediate change to arrive shoulder to shoulder with his pronouncement. Instead, the very next morning, with the giddy excitement of the previous afternoon still piled up like a row of shiny gifts waiting to be opened, Cat is stirred awake in the dim morning light by the sound of Gray rummaging through his dresser drawers.

"What are you doing?" She rolls onto her back.

Cat watches him button his flannel shirt then tuck the hem into the waistband of his jeans, waiting for his answer.

He lifts a quizzical brow. "Going to work," he says, threading his belt through the pant loops.

"Can't you just call and tell them you quit? Do you really have to go in person?" she says, fully awake now, sliding up against the headboard.

"When I said I wanted to quit, I meant once I have something lined up. I can't just take off and leave those guys hanging. They've got enough problems going on down there. I have to do it the right way. I can't be a jerk about it, kitty Cat."

She understands the logic of what he is saying, that the right way to do things involves considerations of fairness and responsibly, but even so, she isn't quick enough to dodge the incoming rush of disappointment. Whether insensible or not, she has unequivocally fallen in love with the notion of being together every day; once again working side by side, dreaming, painting, creating beautiful and fantastical things.

The prospect of immediate change has left her head-over-heels intoxicated. So thoroughly enamored that accustomed obligations and future concerns such as property taxes, utility bills, maintenance and repairs, have easily lost their footing in her thoughts. When he'd warned they might starve for a while, she not only accepted it, but just as readily anticipated it. Now. Not later. And certainly not someday.

She wants to remind him it isn't so much about planning, as it is about putting dreams—life—in motion. No less complicated than taking a grand leap over the edge of uncertainty and only then seeing what lies below.

Everything else—the ordinary ingredients of life, the uninspired details—will simply need to take care of themselves. And should that eventually mean having to leave here, walking away as the previous inhabitants have done and landing somewhere else, then they will. It makes little difference to the grand scheme. Her life is with Gray. Their home is anywhere they settle. The greater tragedy is to do nothing. To stand still and do nothing at all.

In the short span since Gray's revelation, Cat's visions have grown so large and all-encompassing it is impossible to distract herself from hearing the whine of her own disappointment when the promise of change fails to take so much as a single step forward. The mundane is still here large and screaming—so loud it is becoming harder for Cat to detect the quieting heartbeat of all those things as yet unlaunched.

The idea of opening the house to the population of Lost River for a summer party arrives like the majority of Cat's ideas; a gently drifting mote moving through her thoughts, steadily gaining weight, landing with a deafening thud once it becomes too heavy to stay aloft.

It comes in the middle of an ordinary morning as she works a lather of cleaning foam along the bottom and sides of the bathtub with a sponge. A spark of an idea that rapidly swells from simmer to boil by the time she is swabbing the kitchen floor with a mop an hour or so later.

The longer she rolls it back and forth in her head, the more brilliant it becomes, and she spends the remainder of the afternoon outlining her scheme on paper. By the time she hears Gray's tires crunching over gravel in the dooryard, she has composed her plan down to the minutest detail.

Her brain is generating thoughts too fast to fit words, and it takes all her concentration to slow the details jockeying to rush from her mouth in an incomprehensible avalanche.

"We can put up some posters around town and I can ask Judy to mention it to people who come in the store. You can give personal invitations to your friends at the mill," Cat pours forth, barely pausing for breath, unwilling to see or otherwise acknowledge the immediate sobering cast sweeping across Gray's expression like a lethal spill.

"Nobody around here even knows you're an artist, Gray. Can't you just imagine what they'll say when they see the murals? I think we'll be able to finish the one going up the stairs before the party. As long as—"

"No," Gray interrupts. "I don't think so," he pauses, continuing before Cat has a chance to register disappointment or interject argument. "I really don't like the idea of a horde of strangers wandering through our house." His tone is quiet, yet holds a certain air of finality that sends

Cat scrambling to grasp hold of her confidence before it plummets headlong into the chasm instantly opened up between them.

"Strangers? This is a pretty small town, Gray, I'm sure most people around here know who we are by now," she says, feeling the metallic taste of injured pride pushing up into her throat. "Okay, so maybe it sounds like a little too much at first glance, but just think about it for a minute. It'll knock their socks off when they see—"

"I appreciate what you're trying to do," he says, glancing down at the pages Cat has laid out across the kitchen counter.

Cat stands watching him, her arms crossed tightly against her chest. She digs her fingertips into the skin of her upper arms, stubbornly holding herself stiff when he lays his hands on her shoulders.

"This house is our sanctuary, Cat. We've always believed that, haven't we? I'd be a liar if I said I wouldn't hate having carloads of amateur art critics stomping across our lawn scrutinizing our life here."

"But you don't understand, Gray—" If he will just listen. Allow her to lay it out for him as perfectly as she's designed it. A shimmering summer evening. The gentle lift of conversation rising and falling in admiration of the talents and vision of a man they've never suspected to possess such gifts. They will mingle here for hours, no longer simply mill workers, farmers, merchants, and housewives, but art lovers mesmerized by what has been right here under their noses all this time.

She struggles to produce the necessary words to effectively replicate the picture so carefully nurtured in her mind's eye, even as she sees its eminent death crossing his features.

"No. Okay. Just no. Our life here is not for sale. You just ..." he pauses and Cat can see him searching for words she will not want to hear no matter how careful or gentle he is in presenting them. "You try too hard, Cat. Sometimes you just try too hard."

And she thinks maybe he doesn't try hard enough.

If not for her prideful insistence in holding to the armor of indignation, Cat might be quicker to admit Gray's rejection of her grandiose plan has been the right one. But instead, for a time at least, she allows herself the comfort of believing she is both disappointed and hurt by his disinterest in the proposal, rather than horrified by her own ill-conceived enthusiasm for what now stands clearly as a ridiculous suggestion.

Everything she has proposed is in fact unthinkable. After all, from the start, haven't they shared a mutual vow to protect their private world from both the prying and the curious? Why would she ever believe any of this has changed?

And maybe Gray isn't as correct in his thinking, as Cat is so terribly wrong.

She stands at the kitchen window gazing out across the yard at the accustomed things of autumn—the slow waltz of red and orange leaves drifting down from nearly bare limbs—when the screen door snaps open and just as quickly slams shut. She swings around, momentarily startled since she hasn't heard Gray's truck come up the driveway.

Her heartbeat lifts as she hurries to pull open the heavy storm door, then instantly plummets when she finds he isn't there on the other side of the door anxious to greet her. She re-latches the screen, ceasing its lonely thumping in the wind before moving back to resume her sentry at the window.

She's been waiting for Gray to come home all day, her mind tuned to catch the familiar sounds of his arrival even when she knows the unlikelihood of such an early return.

"A dream assignment," is Gray's enthusiastic assessment when he first spies the advertisement in the back pages of the *Down East Gazette*: Seeking knowledgeable artist to restore nose art on vintage airplanes and create designs for reproduction models.

Cat agrees it sounds intriguing, even as she prepares for the inherent frustration of Gray's accustomed standard of procrastination, anxious the position will be long gone and well filled by the time he gets around to inquiring after it. All of which makes it that much more surprising when Gray telephones the number listed in the ad the very evening he reads it and arranges for an interview the following week.

"I wish it wasn't such a long drive, but you know how much I want you to get this," Cat says, watching Gray dress in the grainy light of early morning.

"And I wish I wasn't so damned nervous," he replies, tucking the tail of the shirt Cat has meticulously pressed the night before into the waist of his trousers. "I'll need the long drive to figure out how I'm supposed to keep from sounding desperate at the same time I'm groveling for this guy to hire me."

Gray moves to where Cat sits cross-legged on the bed, her own nerves darting in skittish trails under her skin. She rises onto her knees and places a hand on either side of his face—kisses him firmly on the mouth as though to transfuse him with an essential portion of her boundless confidence in his abilities.

He pulls her tightly against his chest, holding her there for several long moments, saying nothing, his breathing warm and steady against her hair. "I don't know how long it'll take to get there. I've never been to Madison, but I figure it won't be more than a couple hours or so. I'll call you after the interview and let you know how it turned out, okay?"

She nods, silently questioning how she'll ever be able to manage the next several hours of expectant waiting. "I'll fix a thermos of coffee to take with you."

It's an impossible undertaking—waiting when there is no other option—and Cat attempts to quiet her mind as she moves through the hours, supercharged with giddy energy. Little of what she plans to accomplish in his absence is remembered, her thoughts continuing to stray off course as she obsesses over the minute details of Gray's immediate whereabouts.

She is certain her nerves will explode from her skin if she glances at the clock one more time only to see the hands have barely moved. And so she makes her best effort to pretend it away; washing the meager collection of breakfast dishes stacked in the kitchen sink before heading outside to rake the newly laid carpet of red and gold leaves dropped by the wide-spreading maple in the side yard.

Over the next couple of hours she works vigorously, random thoughts hop-scotching across the minutes until it feels as if enough time has passed that she can at last go inside and wait for the telephone to ring. She drops the rake where she stands and hurries across the yard to resume her station inside the house, leaving the accumulated mound of her labors to re-scatter on the October wind.

She is sitting on the bathroom floor, arms hugging her bent knees as she studies her freshly painted toenails, when the telephone in the hall at last rings. It is just after two o'clock in the afternoon. Gray's voice on the other side of somewhere sounds as distant as it is impossible to read.

"He said he liked my portfolio, but he still has a couple more interviews before he makes a decision."

Say the right thing. Something to fortify him on the long drive home. "Is he seeing anyone else today?" she says when the perfect words, the ones evenly balanced between hopeful and promising, fail to arrive.

"I don't know. He didn't say."

"Oh … well, did he spend a lot of time with you?"

"Yes. He seemed to like my designs. He went through them a few times—asked if I'd leave a couple with him," Gray says, and still Cat in unable to decipher his mood or potential level of discouragement. "But I don't know. He was hard to figure. He said he'd be in touch."

Again there is a brief pause. Wide open space for Cat to fill. "Gray, I just—"

"Look, I better get going. I'll be home in a couple hours."

"Okay. I'll have supper ready. Drive safely," she says, about to hang up when she hears something that brings the receiver back to her ear.

"Cat?"

"I'm still here."

"Maybe it's not so bad. He seemed like he might really be interested."

"He is. I've had this unshakable feeling all day—like the planets are aligned, the birds are singing, there's peace in the world—I know it went well. Better than well, perfect in fact," she lies, because the truth she's been anxious and jumpy from the very moment of his leaving is a confession best unshared. Just as she will never tell him how the very thought of him never fully achieving his dreams is something she can't bear to think of, let alone believe, even as it breaks her heart into a million little pieces.

And now the waiting. The days move like cement heels dragging through the piled debris of withered expectation. Endless hours flavored by the caustic taste of quiet agonies accumulated in anticipation of a phone call too long in coming. Cat struggles to pretend away the clashing swells of hope and dread in an effort to shield Gray from what feels more and more like eminent disappointment, knowing he must in fact be doing the same. Both silently suspended in a limbo of uncertainty, if only because there is nowhere else to go while they wait. And wait.

Nineteen

It's still early afternoon, but the storm clouds rolling in heavy and low across the streaky orange and charcoal sky lend to an illusion of encroaching evening.

Cat has felt oddly disjointed and uncentered all day—the murky shift in the weather maybe—though in truth it feels like something else. Something hard edged and threatening that she can't quite define other than to recognize its unmistakable presence.

She purposely turns her thoughts away from incoming waves of anxious yearning, deliberately avoiding the grasping embrace of stormy day heebie-jeebies and the ripening seeds of unreasonable fear threatening to fall. She knows that the moment she hears Gray's truck rolling along the driveway this weight will lift. Once he is here this weird sense of angst will settle.

Too often of late, whenever Gray is gone for any length and she is alone in the house, Cat finds herself wrestling against the fallacious pull of uncertain apprehensions; a sense of foreboding settling in and rapidly multiplying to eclipse all but the furthest glimmers of light.

If she wasn't so weary of striving to understand herself—of trying to put words to what she has no explanation for—she might share her unreasonable fears with him. But she lacks the necessary courage to admit just how needy she's become.

How can he possibly respond should she admit how essential it's become for her to look up and see him—to pause in the midst of doing some ordinary thing in order to remind herself he is here—just around the corner in the next room? Simple yet necessary assurances to remind herself she is not alone.

Cat glances at the clock above the stove for the third time in less than twenty minutes. It is not even 1:30 in the afternoon. Too late to begin anything of consequence. Too early to start supper. She runs through a list of ingredients in her head, wondering if she has all those necessary to bake a pan of Gray's favorite cornbread. It will be a nice accompaniment to the roast chicken and vegetables she's planning for later, just as it affords a welcome dent in the wide open stretch of time dragging past now.

She finds herself smiling at the thought of Gray dashing across the yard in the rain-drenched darkness, pushing through the kitchen door into the waiting warmth within, where the first thing to hit his senses will be the fragrance of a hot and ready meal.

Even as she orchestrates the scene and sets the stage with her perfectly selected props, Cat recognizes her true purpose in composing this model portrait is not as earnest and pure as it would otherwise seem. Maybe the larger part of her motivation is driven by efforts to veil what she doesn't want to see.

Increasingly, the thing Cat most fears is that she and Gray have been too careful to conceal certain close-held anxieties in a misguided effort to shield one another from disappointing and painful blows. They have in fact become so efficient at hiding away their worries they have no way of knowing how often they are actually secreting away the very same things.

Most silent, even as it screams loudest, is the phone call that doesn't come, and now seems unlikely to come, considering how much time has passed. She senses the enormous glacier of their mutual disappointment dense and piling, and though it remains unspoken, Cat believes it impossible Gray can feel any more devastated than she does herself. She so desperately, passionately wants this for him. For all the gifts he has given her, visible and not, she longs for him to have this particular something in return.

It is enough to make her laugh out loud with the confidence of a fool—the thoroughly perverse truth that she has never liked or believed in fairytales—yet with childlike faith clings to this one now. The one where the prince and princess live content in their castle, perfectly ensconced within the assurance of happy-ever-after.

The sky and woods beyond the kitchen window rapidly fall to a cast of thickening gloom as if somewhere a switch has flicked off—a shade drawn, a door slammed shut. Bulging, low-hanging clouds spread thick and full to eclipse the last glimmering streaks of afternoon light. Evening shadows at midday.

The first spits of rain ping against the glass.

Twice last spring, power at the mill has been knocked out by heavy winds and rain and the men sent home early. Gray's unexpected arrivals in the middle of the afternoon have since encouraged Cat to adopt the habit of launching an immediate prayer for an early homecoming at the onset of every storm passing through Lost River. A simple request for downed wires or a random lightning strike to some distant power box; a minor act of nature without threat of physical harm or serious destruction, just enough to deliver Gray promptly home. The very thing she prays for now.

The house feels damper, colder, as the rain falls harder. The outside chill easily seeps through the drafty old windows regardless how tightly they are shut. Ordinarily she is quick to light the woodstove, assured it will bake a comforting pocket of warmth into the shivery air within a half hour. But although the past several weekends have been spent chopping and stacking wood in preparation of rapidly encroaching winter, Gray has forgotten to fill the wood box in the living room as he's assured her he will. Just one more "will do" he intends to get around to as soon as he isn't sidetracked by something else. She only wishes now she'd taken the initiative to do it herself.

She moves away from her sentry over the roasting chicken, passing through the long hallway into the front room where she will most clearly see the sweep of headlights when Gray pulls into the driveway.

Even after six settling years of marriage, Cat seldom strays from the ritual of Gray's daily homecoming—eagerly rushing to the door, melding into him as he crosses the threshold of their comfortably worn-out house—ever grateful of the deep sense of love and reassurance that comes with receipt of his greeting kiss. Soft and warm and true. Promised solace without the unnecessary clutter of words.

Only now, there is this other thing pushing hard to crowd the accustomed assurances from her mind. A shadowy weight arriving without notable purpose or distinction—spilling over her with a presence invisible as it is indelible—tightening with the heavy cadence of heartbeats thumping in her chest.

She hears the deepening echo of a strange and uneasy plea creeping along her spine in a mimicking threat of the darkening sky, working its way upstream into her thoughts. Quietly nagging at first, tugging harder as she works to thrust it away.

A sharp wind blows the rain hard against the house, peppering the glass like buckshot and rattling the wooden frames. From somewhere upstairs comes the sound of an injured shutter slapping back and forth in a ghostly knock. The dull rhythm working to dislodge the dust of faraway things; jagged sections of long-ago memories splintering loose in an aching trail curving along the back of her skull. Sharp fingernails scratching deep, etching bone.

That night had been so similar. Except there'd been no rain. It's the suffocating press of yawning emptiness that is the same. The dark, oily fear that spills out to encase everything, swallowing every last glimmer of light like an insatiable mouth. The settling of dread—the final grains of sand sifting through a narrow tube of glass …

Cat pulls away from the swelling current of unease crowding closer in an attempt to settle. It's a recurring war she's waged a thousand times, but failed to win. An assault that grinds the workings of her insides to a halt. Presses hard against the back of her eyes. Squeezes her heart with hands determined to wring loose the final vestige of breath.

The playing out of their deranged drama is enough of a habitude she might just as easily have missed the evil turn this time, and yet she hadn't. She'd sensed the presence of something uglier—markedly threatening. Something so utterly devastating she can still recall the bitter taste—the sickening odor of ruination—a noxious poison eternally steeped into her mind by the determined force of memory.

In the silence of empty rooms distinctly taking on substance, Cat chastises herself out loud, admonishes her mind for allowing unwelcome thoughts to climb inside so freely. And yet it stubbornly remains, too long carried to so easily discard. She feels the hot breath of reawakened terror sweep against her cheek and she quickly turns her head—looks away and slams the door. But still she hears it breathing.

Accustomed as she is to their frequent drunken battles, the subtle shift that night is perspicuously evident even as it is impossible to describe. Cat only knows it feels too sharp, too clear. Surreal as it is painfully acute.

There is a sudden and immediate urge to disappear but nowhere to go. Cat folds herself into the narrow concavity between wall and chiffarobe, watching without wanting to see when Henry grabs her mother.

She squeezes her eyes shut against the burn of his wicked words and the sight of Reva's thin shoulders convulsing with her noiseless weeping, and yet the terrible scene remains intact behind her lids. The caustic bite of her mother's degradation too bitter a taste to hold or swallow.

"Stop it. Stop it—stop this." Cat shakes her head, fighting hard to dislodge the grainy images quavering in the space behind her eyes. They are ancient taunts that haven't lost their sting—forever remembrances working to shake her loose and wretch her away from this place of safety she has found with Gray. This life she needs as much as cherishes.

They are the shattering sounds of killing. The dull thud of a closed fist striking flesh. Reva's cries of agony never having a chance to accumulate in her throat or spill outward as Henry hammers the fullness of his rage into her face and chest—slamming into her again and again—one hand twisted into her long, dark hair, keeping her there to assure receipt of each killing blow.

And his assault ceases only when she folds into a lifeless parcel of pooling blood and broken tissue—clutching his leg as she sinks to the floor at his feet.

Of course it's the climbing intensity of the storm which proves so forceful in throwing her imagination into full-blown overdrive. The ominous veneer of early dark so effectively working to blend the threat of distant shadows into the here and now.

And yet, just as likely, it is none of these things. Maybe she's become so effective at spooking herself when she is alone because it's that much more difficult to pretend this house feels like a perfect home when Gray is not here to distract her traitorous thoughts from settling. *This is their home. This is the place where everything important resides, safely removed from false starts and imperfect history.*

Has she carried something here with her? Or is she merely imagining the sharply defined echo of unseen things? The whispers of … something … an unrecognizable plea she cannot describe other than to know she can feel it.

Back in the kitchen, Cat again peers into the oven to check the roasting chicken. Perfectly golden brown now, she lowers the temperature to warm and covers the bird with foil to keep it from burning.

She busies herself putting away the breakfast dishes washed hours ago and left in the rack to dry. Next she dampens a sponge and meticulously wipes the countertops of non-existent crumbs. Wiping, rinsing—once again swabbing the length of Formica she has only just passed over—purposely engaging head and hands with unnecessary tasks as she endeavors to keep from thinking over, or otherwise acknowledging, the aching press of too long waiting for Gray to pass through the door.

But whatever is here, hovering just out of reach, will not leave. She feels it stealthily creeping—back and forth along a sharp edge of recognition—and all at once—the distinct sensation of something rolling away just off center. The caustic burn of immediate and absolute dread rises into her throat, coating the walls of her mouth as it floods upward with her breathing.

She reaches for the phone, no longer capable of subduing the incoming tide of irrational fear—knowing even before she assembles the words or considers the sequence of numbers necessary to make a connection—she will call the mill and ask for Gray. And she'll do the very thing she's often considered but never followed through—just this one time—she will allow herself the consolation of surrender. Just this once, she will ask him to come home.

But when she lifts the receiver there is nothing there beyond the faraway echo of dead air. No indication of a dial tone. Only a deep-running void of silence pressing back against her ear. The lines have gone down somewhere after all.

Twenty

Cat pulls her bulky wool coat from the front hall closet. The ghostly echoes winding through the rooms of the cavernous house have swelled from discomforting to persistently loud—all at once suffocating. The shadows draw closer, casting deep into empty corners wholly unqualified to hold the rapidly amplifying proportions of trepidation funneling a steady drip of poison into her thinking. She pulls open the heavy front door and steps out onto the porch, filling her mouth with hungry gulps of air.

Rain-drenched wind whips tendrils of hair spilled out from beneath the hood of her coat and slaps them against her cheeks. The air feels painful and raw in her lungs, yet there is an odd sense of comfort in its sobering sharpness. She continues swallowing large, greedy breaths as if she might somehow drown the oncoming waves of panicked anxiety rolling in from the heavy sea of gloom pressing up against the house; a persistent force swelling with each unfolding hour.

In the painful slow tick of passing minutes there is a silence so complete for a frozen instant Cat believes Henry has somehow succeeded in killing her too. And if her lungs continue to intake and expel air, she doesn't feel it. Only her eyes remain alive, watching, waiting for him to react in some way to the horror of what he's done.

He doesn't move. Continues to stand there. His back turned to Cat. And while her eyes never leave him, her thoughts run ahead to whatever it is he will do next.

In her mind's eye she sees him reaching for the dark bottle of sour potion he's started drinking hours earlier. He will drain the last of it. Stumble out into the dank heaviness of a too moist night. And once his drunken mind un-fogs and he grasps the full import of his murderous act, he will run. Will never stop running until he is vanished forever.

But she's surmised wrongly. Because what he does next is the one thing Cat least expects. He cries. And it is this image of his weeping that remains as the single-most disturbing lie in that final fatal interlude between her parents—the way he'd wept after working so hard to silence her. The stunning hypocrisy of those parallel lies coursing over the cadaverous hollows scooped out below the sharp line of his cheekbones—crocodile tears wholly ineffective at washing away the murderous black rage still there shadowing his eyes.

She is being ridiculous. Thinking crazy thoughts. Not working hard enough to deny what serves no purpose. The rust and sorrow of her vanished family has no place here. And whether negligent or merely foolish, Cat is disgusted she has allowed this long-banished ugliness to settle back inside her head; knowing even the most minute hairline crack left unsealed will require excessive labors to repair.

Stop it. Stop it. STOP IT.

She recognizes this demon as the one she's warred against her entire life. It is always this same monster riding in on a tide of irrational panic—recognizable symptoms invariably commenced by a flaming sensation ignited behind her eyes, heat fanning out across her brain to leave her nauseated and weak.

But why now? Why when she is here long settled with Gray and so far removed from ancient shadows. She wants nothing from these memories and yet they continue to arrive without invitation—an avalanche of unharnessed fear and dread slamming in from nowhere with a steely determination to knock her from her moorings.

The rain doesn't slacken and the wind blows harder, great wet gusts sweeping the pounding torrent up under the porch roof. Before long Cat will be soaked all the way through, and yet she stays where she is, feeling safer here in the madness of the storm, than she does inside the empty house.

She reminds herself, not for the first time, that there is nothing living in the past which holds the power to touch her. Just as the inexplicitly rekindled sense of panic and dread are not so much akin to psychic revelations as they are irrational fears. They hold no potency anywhere other than the space she's allowed them to settle in her head. She repeats this logical mantra over and over in an effort to make it stick; as often as it proves necessary for her to hear.

And she stays where she is, rooted to the rain-washed floorboards. Staring out at the rain hammering the earth with intent to harm.

A numbing chill settles into her toes, inches up the backs of her legs, and wicks deep into the center of her bones. She understands how foolish she is to stand here taking on water—*doesn't she know well enough to get out of the rain?*—but it takes less effort to hold to the fragility of optimism out here where there are no walls to capture and hold her terror.

She prays with a fervor to rival the storm thrashing wildly around her; a passionate litany running on a constant loop inside her head—"*Please, bring him home soon … Please, bring him home … now … please, God … please, please, please … Please, God, bring him home …*"

She leaves her coat hanging in the front hall, dripping rainwater onto the floor.

She has ceased watching the clock hours ago. The turbulent afternoon long since collapsed into evening when she at last sees the headlights of Gray's truck swing into the lower stretch of driveway. And just like that, in the blink of an instant, incoming waves of precious relief sweep in, washing away the ponderous wall of dread piled up astride the long, empty hours of waiting.

She stands watching from the front window, her hard stare holding to the twin headlights reflecting a silvery path through the driving rain. And it is as the vehicle creeps toward the house with the slow caution of the unfamiliar, that Cat's initial sense of relief takes a downward dip, quavers with the recognition that, no, this won't be Gray after all. Not unless he is a passenger. The shimmering orbs are set too low in the approaching vehicle to belong to his truck.

She continues to peer out beyond the pane, her vision determined to force a part in the curtain of rain, following the moving globes of light as she anxiously waits for the car to roll to a stop alongside the porch. She rushes to pull open the door even before it receives a knock, eager to gather him in.

"Gray—" she manages to exclaim in the wink of a second that whooshes past even as her voice dissolves like melting granules in her mouth. She stares at the rain-soaked visage of a uniformed police officer framed in the open doorway. Her immediate question—not whatever reason it is that brings him here—but why he isn't Gray.

She throws a confused stare past his shoulder, suddenly aware of the presence of another figure. And it takes her a moment to recognize Charlie's face—Gray's friend from the mill.

The officer's features swirl together beneath her rapidly fragmenting stare. The details of his face torturously blurred within the space of her vision—his eyes shifting to collide with the side of his nose, mouth slipping to his chin, eyebrows melting down his face—a disjointed Picasso madly tilting, breaking apart in the surge of bludgeoning fear racing upward with a roaring crescendo.

Cat presses her palm flat against the doorframe, forcing her eyes to find focus on the shield winking from the uniform jacket filling her vision—a shiny surface glistening with quivering drops of rain. His name is evenly stitched onto the fabric above it. *Rhodes. His name is Rhodes … Rhodes … Rhodes …*

And she knows in the deafening horror of an instant, what it is he's come to say. Knows even before his lips move to form the words. It is all there on his face. In the tight set of his jaw. The nervous tick of a muscle just below his cheekbone. The bottomless stare mirrored on Charlie's face suspended in the darkness just beyond the officer's broad shoulder. Though more than any other thing, she knows it from their very presence here. Because they are here and Gray is not.

She waits for the words to come, frozen in a horrible conscious state of a nightmare crashing down. Watches the officer named Rhodes as he speaks—her eyes following the moving line of his lips as they form the impossible phrase. Her lungs collapse inside her chest with receipt of his words. Her heartbeat throbbing out through her skin. She struggles to grasp a mouthful of air only to find it has all been sucked away the moment she opened the door. And she feels herself dying with every syllable.

Twenty One

It is the heavy pounding sort of rain that comes after a long absence.

The water lashes against the glass and washes onto the sill where Cat has neglected to close the window. And even as the drowning deluge pours from the heavens in powerful sheets—rapidly puddling on the bedroom floor and trailing off into a handful of spreading tributaries—she doesn't move to shut it now.

She doesn't care. She will never care. Never again.

She rolls onto her side, presses her face into Gray's pillow, wishes herself away.

His scent has dissipated months ago, yet if she concentrates with every cell and fiber of heart and mind—floods her head with the atoms and molecules forming her memories of him—she can very nearly smell him here. The delicious warm scent of pitch and spruce gum on his skin and in his hair. Wet bark and sawdust. The essence of Gray.

And sometimes—if she succeeds in reaching deep inside, stretches her mind taut and sentient—she can very nearly trick herself into pretending him back inside this house. Can create entire moments and conversations they might have should he still exist here under this roof and continue to lie beside her in this bed.

She feels the familiar sensation of wetness on her face. Again the tears. Forever and always the tears. They melt over her face with such regularity they have become an accustomed occurrence—her eyes crying rivers while her body turns weaker, scarcely able to function much of the time, but still painfully alive.

Even after so many months have passed, she cannot fully fathom that Gray is truly gone. Thoroughly impossible. Just like that—gone. To one moment be happy, and then not. To have everything, and then nothing.

So often, in the middle of some meaningless task or nondescript moment, Cat will all at once hear a voice shouting madly in her head, admonishing her for thinking any thought beyond the only one that will ever matter. *Don't you realize Gray is dead? He's gone. He's gone and you're alone. You'll never feel the warmth of brushing against him in sleep—his arm draped across the curve of your waist. Never glance up and find his eyes watching you. Never speak to him or share another thought. Nothing. Gone. But you don't believe it, do you? Because it's impossible.*

I-M-P-O-S-S-I-B-L-E.

It is a blow that never softens—every instance of sudden awareness as sharp and crippling as the first. She senses time moving past without her actual presence. The painfully torn edges of absence, the one thing holding steady.

The days are identical, opening wide into a bottomless echo, drawing her through the halls of memory. Long empty stretches when she does nothing other than sit and stare at Gray's possessions, all still here, alive and breathing around her. His favorite wool cap hangs from a hook on the back of the kitchen door; the book he'd been reading left on an end table in the living room, a playing card with a torn corner marking his place—the ten of clubs she knows from the countless times she's opened the pages and dusted her finger over the card's glossy surface; his boots where he left them at the foot of the stairs, patiently waiting to receive his feet; a flannel shirt hanging over the back of a chair; a pen he particularly liked left on the kitchen counter; an assortment of coins collected in a jar on his dresser—saving for something she believes was intended to surprise her. All things she is hesitant to touch for fear of erasing the prints made by his living hands.

She struggles to call him back, to reverse in her mind the wicked unfairness of fate. But always she is unable to move beyond the act of bleeding tears, helplessly listening to the sound of one minute piling onto the next; the loudness of it thudding hard against the acute edges of her constant screaming pain.

She finds herself talking out loud to a God whose existence she's never actually doubted, but whom she hasn't known how to approach until now, when propriety no longer seems to matter. Or at least not as much as does the minimal comfort offered by her own voice coming back in the quiet.

They tell her it was a tumbling stack of hardwood sawlogs that killed him. A prematurely released cable sending forth an unstoppable avalanche as a truck is being unloaded onto the log deck. A freak accident, they say, as if it is explanation enough. They are careful to omit details, but Cat's imagination is not so sparing or kind. In wakefulness and sleep she sees the full horror of what no one will tell her—the impossible blow of an instant that robs Gray's life and recklessly spits their dreams into oblivion. Her perfect, beautiful Gray, crushed and broken. The men shouting as they frantically work to haul the logs away, hoping for a miracle. A miracle … even as his precious blood steadily leaks into the mud splattering their boots and the legs of their denim pants, and the pounding rain washes it all away.

There is nothing left to think about or plan over. The days unroll vacantly, passing as if they've never been. Piling up into an infinite heap of vacuity, each one duller and emptier than the one before, and worsening with the next.

It is weeks before Cat will allow herself to cry, aware that once the tears break loose there exists no means for making them cease. But she understands now they don't matter—the tears. Not really. Of far more consequence is the sound of nothingness screaming a trail through her brain, slamming against the fragile curvature of her skull like a fist—day into night into day. The awful silence that signals her unstoppable decent into the realms of a solitary madness.

There is only one expression Cat is capable of offering in reply to the thoughtful condolences and kind sympathies extended to her over the loss of her husband, and it is held in the silence of her wordless dull stare.

She is aware of the misunderstanding generated by her discomforting failure to say something when really anything will do, and yet not one of those persons who drive out to the house or approach her in town seem to comprehend her deadened response as the only one possible. That nowhere in the whole of existence is there a single word or phrase to fit. No appreciative look she might tender that won't result in an immediate breakdown of irretrievable proportions. There is no one who senses or feels the dangerous edge she is teetering on. Just as there will be no one to reach out and grasp her back when she inevitably begins to fall.

Cat knows it is Charlie Alder's visit more than any other episode since Gray's death that will best serve to cement what everyone in Lost River is already thinking.

She'd first met Charlie years earlier; one afternoon when she'd had a list of overdue errands to tackle and had borrowed Gray's truck. Her final stop had been Judy's store, with the intention of dropping off a finished step stool, and she'd been wholly surprised when Judy handed her an envelope containing the commission for an end table sold earlier in the week. Even as Cat left the store—heading to the truck with a buoyant stride bordering on a skip—she'd arrived at the decision to stop at the mill and share her news with Gray before whisking him off to lunch at the diner on Main Street.

She was standing outside the mill waiting for the noon whistle to blow, when at last the two men passed through the side door carrying their identical black domed lunchboxes, Charlie laughing over something Gray had said. Spotting Cat leaning against the fender of his truck and clearly pleased to see her there, Gray tipped his chin, smiling that particular smile of his which never failed to toss her heart.

He brought Charlie over for a introduction, and afterward Cat had seen him often enough to remain familiar; bumping into him now and again when she and Gray were in town on a Saturday morning—exchanging a few words or the wave of a hand at a distance.

Several of Gray's friends and co-workers have come out to the house to offer condolences in the early weeks following Gray's death, but it is months before Charlie arrives on her doorstep. Cat is on the front porch painting a chair when she hears his truck round the curve in the hard-packed earth driveway. She doesn't lift her head until his tires roll to a stop.

"I tried to come out here a dozen times before now—I wanted to—but … I don't know … I guess I was waiting for the right time. But there's no such thing as a right time, is there, Cat?" Charlie says, pausing to clear his throat of an unknown obstruction.

"I realize you don't know me very well, but Gray was a good friend and I know he'd want me to try and help you out as much as I can. Make things a little easier, if it's at all possible."

Cat nods, immediately wondering how it is he's managed to miss what she suspects is the community consensus—that she is clearly someone who cannot be helped. But then maybe his coming here is about something altogether different. He'd been Gray's closest friend. He'd talked with Gray every day. Laughed with him. Had possibly been standing with him when he died.

"Would it be okay if I come in for a minute?" Charlie asks, and only then does Cat realize she hasn't thought to offer.

"Yes ... of course. Sure," she says, instantly flustered in the manner of someone who has fallen out of touch with society. With conversation. Visitors.

"Can I get you something to drink? Coffee, pop … a beer?" *Gray's beer. Four cans neatly aligned on the bottom shelf in the refrigerator.*

"No, thanks," he says, without quite looking at her. "I figured we might just talk, if that's alright."

"Sure. Do you mind coming back to the kitchen? I was just about to wash up," she says, and for the first time his eyes drop to register her paint-splotched hands.

"Hey, this is incredible," Charlie says as he follows Cat through the hall into the kitchen. "Gray told me you two were painting the walls, but I couldn't really picture what it might look like. I definitely never imagined anything like this."

"This was the first one—Gray did it by himself," she says, turning to watch Charlie's gaze sweep across the wall, feeling something of pride and pain come crashing together.

"My God, I had no idea … it's beautiful," he says, an expression of honest admiration mirroring his tone.

"Thank you, Charlie," she says quietly, an immediate flux of liquid pressure building behind her eyes. "I'll show you the others before you leave if you want."

Charlie pulls out a chair from the table as Cat stands at the sink soaping her hands; methodically working the frothy lather halfway up her arms, rubbing at the splotches of paint coloring her skin.

"I don't really know where to start, Cat, so I guess I'll just get to it," he says, but then hesitates as if hoping she'll lead him toward some particular juncture clearly indicating what direction and at what speed he may proceed safely.

She waits silently through the discomforting pause, her fingers kneading the soap along her forearm, leaving him to decipher pace and progression for himself.

"Are you doing okay, Cat? Are you managing alright?"

"Yes … I'm okay." *Doing okay? What is okay? Does he realize how foolish a question that is? How can she be okay? How can she ever possibly be okay again?*

"The guys down at the mill still aren't able to talk about what happened."

I don't talk about it either, Charlie. I will never ever be able to talk about it.

"My wife Rachel wanted to come out and see if she could do anything for you. She thought maybe if you wanted to talk or something … but she's a little shy about just showing up, what with neither of you really knowing each other and everything. She wanted me to be sure and tell you how sorry she is though."

"I appreciate that."

"Yeah, she felt real bad about it. We all do."

Cat doesn't answer, waits for him to get to whatever it is he's really come to say. Some other time—a time before all of this, when good manners still felt like a necessary effort—Cat would have said or done something to ease his obvious discomfort in broaching whatever it is he struggles with now.

"I'm guessing you've probably gotten the check from the company by now? I've heard they're pretty good about that."

"Yes, they are," she says, continuing to massage the lather over her skin. "I wasn't really thinking about it. At least not so soon after—" her voice falls away without finishing. *After Gray died. So soon after Gray died.* Although she's heard these words a thousand times a day inside her head, she still hadn't learned how to say them out loud. Is in fact certain she never will.

There is another long stretch of discomforting silence. Cat rinses her hands in the warm flow of water surging from the faucet, washing away all traces of soap. Continuing to hold her hands in the cleansing stream even after there is no longer purpose in the action other than to distract herself from an immediate sensation of near crippling pain—a sharp point embedded in the base of her skull like an ax splitting skin and bone.

Stop this. Stop this right now. Stop this.

A flush of heat rushes up, fans out behind her eyes, presses hard against her temples.

"It might seem that money is enough for you to take care of yourself, the house and everything, but it isn't, Cat, it really isn't. I know this is the most impossible thing to think about right—"

She swings around sharply, all at once recognizing where he is heading, slicing his sentence off at the joint before he can finish. "Just what is it you're trying to say, Charlie? Whatever it is please just say it."

He is clearly startled by the unexpected bite in her tone, the sudden flash from nowhere, but he recovers quickly. "I'm trying to say I think you should go after them. They figure they just send out a check and that's the end of it. It's over for them and back to business as usual. They're counting on you being too grief stricken to do anything but deposit the check and move on."

"Go after them? For what? Go after them for what?"

"For what you deserve. There's a very strong chance they'll offer to settle the minute they get wind you're taking legal action."

The room shifts, walls slanting like falling timbers, the floor tilting in a threat to spill her to her knees. Cat grips the edge of the counter, presses the base of her spine hard against the edge in an effort to keep herself upright, his words spinning in her head like a crumbled page caught on the wind.

"Settle? Settle what, Charlie? Is there some question whether or not he's dead? That maybe he really isn't in that box in the ground?"

She hears Charlie's voice carefully pacing toward her across the miles, steadily patient in the face of the rekindled tide of grief and anger rising up and folding in on her, as if he's somehow known to expect such a reaction and has so prepared himself to receive it.

"I've been going over this whole thing in my mind ever since it happened, Cat. It's impossible not to think about it. It's right there every day waiting for me. From the minute I open the door and walk into that place.

"I'm sure Gray told you about everything going on down there—all the changes over the past couple years. Some we knew about, others we only suspected. But once they brought in the new foreman—well, it all pretty much exploded. We didn't miss what was going on for a second—all the talk about layoffs was just a threat to keep us in line. But you can't pull that kind of crap on grown men and not expect things to turn ugly sooner or later," Charlie says, meeting her gaze, but obviously misreading her expression; assuming grief, when what she's feeling is stunned confusion.

"I'm sorry to rehash all this. I know you've already heard it from Gray a hundred times."

Cat nods, assuring that, yes, Gray has shared all of this. Explained all of it in anticipation of her thoughts, opinions, assured comfort. And yet he hasn't. Had never said a word.

"But knowing Gray, I'm guessing he wouldn't have mentioned the worst of it. How it was becoming more and more obvious that someone somewhere was making a lot of very wrong decisions in order to save money. Cutting corners on things like legitimate repairs to broken equipment and the quality of materials being ordered for the machines. They seemed to think we wouldn't know the difference—a bunch of half-educated local boys sawing and stacking lumber. Figured no one would ever complain as long as they handed us a paycheck every Friday.

"Gray never should've been out there unloading those logs, and sure as hell not in the middle of a storm like that. That's the loggers' job, shorthanded or not, it's their problem. Except that's not the boss's way of thinking. He didn't give a damn how those logs got unloaded just as long as they ended up on the log deck. To throw a sawyer like Gray out there to unload was bullshit. And to partner him with a greenhorn kid who didn't have a clue what he was doing—Gray never should've been out there, plain and simple. He died because some guy behind a desk wanted to save a few bucks—that's the truth. It never should've happened.

"I know what you're thinking, and you're right—money won't heal your heart, but it'll help you live. It will help you, Cat. Maybe not now, but later when you need—"

She shakes her head in a determined effort to throw off his words. "What I need is for him not to be gone. That's what I need. To still have him here."

Charlie pulls up from the chair and steps toward her. "I know how bad this feels. I was there when it happened—it's all I think about. I can't get away from it, just like you can't. But you need to do this. Later, when you're thinking clearly you'll know this was the right thing to do. You have to think of the future before it gets here, because by then it will be too late."

She lifts her head, held steady by the unbearable heaviness of his hand reaching out to touch her arm. The sharp features set into his broad face swirl together in an indistinguishable blur as her heartache congeals into a thick mass behind her eyes.

"I don't want the future. I don't believe in it. If I could, I'd give it away. Just hand the damned future over to anyone who wants it."

"Gray would want—"

"To still be here. That's what he would want. To still be here."

Charlie drops his gaze, looks away from the pain he sees in every part of her, the raw ache of it leaking into his hand even once he releases his hold on her arm. Several long moments pile into minutes before he finally succeeds in forcing his eyes back. "Just think about it, okay? I can help you do this. You won't have to go through it alone. When you're ready I will—"

"How do you stay there? If you really believe everything you're saying, then how can you stay?"

"Because I have to," he says quietly. "I have a wife. Kids . . ."

"I appreciate your coming out here, Charlie. I do. It means so much that you were Gray's friend. But I've given you the only answer I'll ever have. It won't change. I'll never be ready to accept a check in trade of Gray's life," she says, the steely resolution in her words braced in an indisputable barrier firmly set to intercept any possible argument he might think to offer. "I don't want to talk about any of this again. And I won't. Not ever."

She has every intention of holding to her vow that the circumstances of Gray's accident are a subject forever dead to her, but still, Cat knows to expect talk of Charlie's visit will make the journey from mouth to ear to mouth with the remarkable efficiency afforded such topics in small towns.

It's easy enough for Cat to gather from the sprinklings of conversation carelessly drifting within range of her hearing in the following weeks, that aside from her condition as an understandably grief-stricken widow, most believe she has clearly taken leave of her senses—an unfortunate condition which only time, prayer, and distance may potentially hope to heal.

It is a thoroughly erroneous sentiment which only proves to confirm what Cat already knows, the truth she is wholly alone in her comprehension of the impossibility of any such recovery. Nowhere within the deep recesses filled to overflowing with the heft of her deadened thoughts does a place exist for things of the future. No corner or crevice capable of holding the cumulation of time, vacancy, or sorrow which might otherwise enlist some potential for lessening her grief.

For several months Charlie respects her issuance, making no further advances or attempts to contact her.

Even so, Cat suspects this is only a temporary truce extended with the expectation the encompassing fog of her grieving will effectively clear, allowing her to recognize the import of what he is trying to tell her.

When Charlie once again drives out to the house, he finds Cat sitting on the porch steps. She listens without comment as Charlie repeats what he's already said on his previous visit, declining to utter a word in response until he is finished.

"Cat?"

"I can't," she says with an unmistakable firmness that is impossible to misinterpret for anything other than the final verdict it is intended to convey. "I won't."

She feels the press of Charlie's eyes staring down at her, easily sensing his purposely careful manner has taken a slight shift into something else. Frustration? Impatience? Annoyance? She doesn't quite know for certain, but it makes little difference either way.

"I realize this probably sounds confusing and overly involved, but it won't be all that complicated. Like I said before, once they've been notified Gray's widow intends to hit them with a lawsuit, it's pretty certain they'll—"

"No one's ever really told me about the accident, Charlie—I mean the details. You said you were there, but you haven't told me what I need to know," Cat speaks past him, neither hearing nor listening to anything he is saying.

"Telling me he was crushed by a tumbling stack of logs because of someone else's mistake isn't enough—in fact it doesn't mean anything. It's the same as telling me nothing at all. I want you to tell me everything, Charlie. I want to know how he really died. I want to know what he felt," she says, turning now to look at him, meeting his eyes for the first time, watching his expression dip and wane—whether in confusion or stunned disbelief, it doesn't matter.

"You're saying you'll describe it in a courtroom, so that means you can tell me the truth now. I want to know. I want you to tell me what you saw—everything the way it really happened. Did he die instantly? Did he feel anything? Did he say—anything? Did he say my name, Charlie? I have to know. Did he? Did he say my name?" And she is all at once pleading, pressing hard, determined in her conviction that knowing details will somehow lessen her grief, even as it becomes unbearable simply by asking the questions.

"I can't."

"You have to."

"I can't."

"Please, Charlie, I have to know—*I have to know*."

"No, Cat," he says lifting his palms in an unspoken plea. "I just can't—"

Cat stands, turns toward the door. "Don't come back here, Charlie. Just please—don't come back."

He doesn't leave immediately, stands alone on the porch for a while longer, as if he understands this is his last chance. That once he goes, he will not come back. But he doesn't know what else he might say or do to make her see how necessary this is. That he is trying his best to help her because Gray would want her to do this. He might have lied—made an attempt to compose whatever it is she believes she needs to hear, but how can he? Not when there is still a chance of having to repeat the truth before a judge. If not for that technicality, he thinks he may well have invented something for her. He could have said, *Yes, Gray never felt a thing.* Never knew he was too badly broken for hope of repair. That he died without pain, swiftly—but not before speaking a final word—her name. Charlie is not above telling lies, particularly when they are told for noble purpose. And he would do that now, if not for concerns of having it all come undone.

Cat sits on the bed in the upstairs bedroom overlooking the driveway, clutching a pillow against her chest, hot tears leaking unchecked as she waits for the sound of Charlie leaving; tires crunching over gravel in an assurance he is heading back out toward the road.

The population of Lost River is not alone in thinking Catherine Barnett has lost all capability for rational thought. She recognizes this herself and it is a verdict she fully welcomes; seeing no particular rationale in attempting to keep from plummeting into the very deepest depths of hopelessness. To simply fall apart feels the only antidote for alleviating the constant ache, especially when the alternative is the thoroughly impossible endeavor of gathering herself up, pulling together, and continuing as though believing it possible to survive and somehow remain intact.

Twenty Two

She remembers it had been a day ripe with summer. They'd been on a walk going nowhere, deep into the woods pressing up against the back yard, when they first made the discovery of the long abandoned railroad bed all but hidden beneath generations of unhindered vegetation swallowing the tracks in a dense thatch of low lying carpet.

They'd followed the tracks for a considerable distance, curious where the forgotten ties would lead, though the eventual destination ranked a distant second to the actual pleasure of getting there.

They talked and laughed and sang silly theme songs remembered from old television shows as they tramped a path through the pines. And she can't recall who spied it first, only that they'd been equally awed and delighted as they rounded a thick stand of trees and found themselves staring into the deep well of a magnificent ravine carved out between twin hillsides and held in place by the imposing framework of an ancient rusting trestle spanning the narrow valley on thick spreading legs.

The abandoned behemoth proved to be a monument of immediate and endless fascination. Something admirable—defiant even—in the stark ugliness of its graceless steel construction.

"Do you think it's safe?" Cat asked, though she'd already started across, knowing whatever Gray's assessment might be, it was highly unlikely she would stop or turn back as she headed toward the center of the foreboding structure.

"I don't think I'd want to be here during a lightning storm—and I wouldn't really want to be a passenger on a train crossing over—but I think it's probably alright otherwise," he said, as they continued across.

"Wow, that's some incredible view," Gray said in an echo of Cat's unspoken thoughts once they reached the mid-way point of the steel creature and paused to stare out over the valley.

"Have you ever seen anything like this in your life? It's spectacular," Cat breathed, drinking in the scene below. Her gaze swept along the plump green quilt of variegated tree tops spilling out along the opposing hillsides rising up on either side of the valley. She moved to sit, taking in the slowly moving river sliced through the valley below.

"What are you doing?" Gray said, glancing at Cat from behind an expression thoughtful and decidedly far away, indicating that, like Cat, he too had been instantly awed by the majestic breadth of their surroundings.

"I just want to sit here a few minutes," she replied, perching carefully on the heavy rail and allowing her legs to dangle over the edge; respectably frightened by the height and immense spread of airspace separating bridge from land, while at the same time, wildly exhilarated by it.

"What do you think?"

"Pretty amazing is what I think," she smiled at him across her shoulder. "The sky looks close enough to grab a handful."

Gray dropped down beside her and they sat for a long while without speaking; swallowed into the scene from their roost suspended above the earth, thoroughly hypnotized by familiar things made altogether different when viewed from a height simulating flight.

As always, it arrived with the sobering jolt of something unexpectedly remembered—and for just a moment Cat allowed her mood to race along the lines of fear, mourning, horror—a triplicate threat sprinting ahead to a place of distant memory—the passing mummer of sad regret, and yet it wasn't quite strong enough to hold firm.

She imagined running her hands along the tufted green florets of the treetops; her fingers fluffing the leafy heads as her thoughts spun off; gracefully gliding and swooping between the lofty curve of the sky and the rolling mound of the earth.

She felt the pull of Gray's eyes watching her, and she'd turned her head. His expression turned serious as he reached for her, one arm linked through the railing as he placing his other hand against the side of her face. And he'd drawn her to him, kissing her in that way no one else ever had—with the intensity of an eternal promise.

"I love you like crazy, my Cat," he breathed the words against her cheek.

She felt the accelerated tempo of her heartbeat knocking steadily behind her ribs, a reaction to his touch so accustomed she oftentimes didn't note the quickened gait within her chest until she was forced to pause and swallow breath.

His arm tightened, holding her head there against his shoulder as they stared out over the valley.

"I remember reading this terrible story in the newspaper when I was a kid—it was about a woman running alone on the railroad tracks in the middle of the night," Cat says in a quiet careful voice. "She was hit by the train. No one knew why she was out there or where she was headed. They said she never would've felt it, but I've always wondered how anyone could've known that. I think maybe that's just something people say so it wouldn't seem so awful." She wasn't quite sure, even as she spoke them, if she'd intended to say the words out loud.

"No, it's probably true. It seems the worst part would've been those few seconds of terror when she realized what was coming at her—but then it's over. It's a sad story either way. And no one ever figured out what she was doing on the tracks that time of night?"

"I don't know—some people said she was fighting with her husband. Apparently they were both drunks and always fighting. I couldn't get the image out of my head for the longest time, and every now and again I still think about it—how it was such a terrible way for someone to die," Cat said feeling her tongue falter, all at once struggling to hold her voice steady against a surge of emotion threatening to spill.

It was the first time she'd ever offered Gray a portion of the truth. A piece of something that hadn't first been varnished and polished with a protective coating of lies. And although it was only a fragment, right then it felt like a beginning.

Cat felt his arm tighten around her shoulders. "Do you think anyone's really allowed to be this happy, Cat?" he asked, although the satisfaction in his tone assured it wasn't really a question, because he fully believed it—that, yes, some people are.

But she hadn't answered, instead remained quiet in the safe circle of his arm, fighting against the wash of chilling fear flooded to the surface and rushing out after his words. Was it possible? Was it truly possible to hold something as elusive as happiness and keep it safely protected? To hold on tight enough to keep it from ever being wretched away?

And she'd tried to believe as deeply as he did—had never stopped trying to absorb Gray's confidence into her own needy psyche. For a time she'd even succeeded; refusing to surrender to the ever-present uncertainties threatening to topple the improbable concept of a forever brand of joy.

But she'd never truly ceased the struggle. Had never lost sight of those things she knew to exist just on the other side of bliss.

It feels as if the span of decades has spun past since Cat last cared to make the hike out to the trestle. In the final months before Gray's death, their habit of regular pilgrimages had fallen off, having simply become too busy and increasingly occupied with a wealth of other things—all of which appear roundly unimportant when Cat looks back from the distance of now.

But it is an altogether differing sense of reasoning that keeps her away at present, when journeying out to the trestle is an endeavor she doesn't—can't and won't—consider without Gray. His absence marks it as an expedition as unthinkable as it feels traitorous.

It is a conviction so dutifully ingrained in her mind, when the first quavering outline of a suggestion begins to form, coaxing her to return to the trestle one last time, Cat doesn't directly recognize it for what it truly is—the quintessential solution to ending what has become her unbearable pain.

For the first time in over a year, Cat opens her eyes to the murky light of dawn, anxious to jump start the day. She's spent the entire past week cleaning the house and still hasn't finished what she's set out to do; clearing away the piled evidences of neglect which have commenced to accumulate from the very moment Gray was snatched away from her world.

There is much to accomplish, and each day opens and closes with a marathon intended to reclaim order of what has been long ignored. She lavishes the bathroom sinks with a thorough and determined scrubbing, surrendering only once she's forced to concede the aged porcelain bowls are destined to remain "as is" regardless of abundant doses of cleanser and the force applied by diligent fingers.

Next, she polishes furniture turned dull and grainy white under a film of ghostly talc; corrals colossal dust balls a year in the making, sucking them away with the prehistoric vacuum residing in a downstairs closet; washes floors and launders curtains—checking off each task from the list of essential obligations once she arrives at the decision to finalize her life. Duties eternally unappealing, but which she now carries out with the peculiar sense of satisfaction that comes from knowing they will never require her doing again.

Suicide. Cat dislikes the word. She doesn't care for the sound of it any more than she fails to appreciate what this single word is intended to imply. How arrogant that anyone would deign to title so complex a resolution with this single, hard-sounding, seven-letter word. That this impersonal, catch-all terminology will be linked to her own death annoys her far more than it should. And her thoughts continually bristle over the question perched foremost in her thoughts as she moves with steady resolution to complete her preparations: Can it rightfully be termed suicide when a person is already long dead even before they follow through? Isn't the deliberate finish of a living corpse merely a formality?

She sees little validity in leaving behind a note attempting to explain her reasoning or the irreparably damaged state of her mind. Because there are no words. Anyone who knows something of Cat, or has been a friend to Gray, does not require black and white clarification of her decision or subsequent actions. And those who don't aren't likely to care. At least no further than beyond the length of time it takes to pass a curious exchange over a cup of coffee at the diner. *"Did you hear about Grayson Barnett's widow? Sad. Poor thing. But, you know, she was never right in the mind after what happened …"*

Still, there is Leafie. Should she ever reappear and learn the truth, will she somehow come to understand there can be no alternative ending? That none of it has anything to do with old things, past guilt, or failings—nothing to do with Leafie herself. It is wholly about Gray being gone and Cat's inability to function without him.

She knows such questions are pointless, recognizes how foolish it is to think there is any real possibility of Leafie ever choosing to emerge from the shadows she has so effectively tucked in around herself. And even on the chance her sister does one day return to the world she's left behind, there is nothing left in Memphis or Columbia that might serve to steer her all the way up here to Lost River, a place so removed from the world it hardly feels part of it.

Poor sweet Leafie. Cat has handled everything so badly. Has always handled everything so badly. And though her failings toward her sister climbed to a fever pitch on that terrible night when everything teetering on the fragile edge of a broken world came crashing down—it was only the start of her misgivings and not the end.

Leafie is not yet two—sleeping in a three-legged crib propped against the wall, a chair substituting for its missing limb—when Cat leaves her behind the first time. Five years old and stagnant with fear, her only thought is to hide someplace where Henry and Reva will not see her.

The two have battled before—countless times. Fought wars that raged for days. But those times are nothing like this one. Even before it is finished, it feels like the end. Cat holds herself as still as she is able, her cheek pressed against a stained wall molting ancient plaster; terror building pressure like steam in a kettle, waiting for the night to blow apart.

And then the explosive crack that serves to break loose Leafie's high-pitched shriek. Her startled wail tearing apart the echo of dead calm punctuating the shot, and spilling out over the fractured scene strewn around them.

Even as she hears the baby's shattering screams, Cat doesn't—can't—move to offer comfort. She snaps her eyes shut, squeezes tight to keep the outlines of horror from settling.

She is afraid to open her eyes, afraid to keep them shut. When she dares to crack open her lids, one brief slice at a time, she knows at once that something is changed. An essential ingredient shifted out of place.

Leafie continues to wail—harder, stronger, as if she's witnessed a ghost. And Cat understands that indeed she has. Because Reva is no longer there, heaped on the floor where Henry has left her, but gone. A corpse impossibly vanished.

And Leafie cries from her broken cage. But still Cat cannot make herself go to her.

Maybe now, with this final plan, maybe this is the one thing Cat will finally get right.

Twenty Three

Cat hears the telephone ringing downstairs, but she thinks at first the sound must be coming from somewhere inside her head. It's been weeks since she ended the phone service—or is it? Has she only thought of turning it off, but never followed through?

Either way, she leaves it to ring unanswered. The sound scratches like a dozen sharp splinters inside her brain, raking painful lines behind her eyes until the noise at last ceases and blessed silence returns.

Why is it so impossible for anyone to understand she wants to ache and weep and mourn alone?

For the same reason she cannot conceive of listing the shattered components of her soul on paper in some final melodramatic missive, Cat is just as certain there is no one she owes an explanation of her decision to melt away from this life. There is nothing she feels compelled to say or otherwise declare by expounding on her resolution to forgo continuing to live without Gray, other than the truth that her imminent self-destruction doesn't seem so much a choice as it simply feels inevitable.

In this final week Cat completes her attentions on the house; cleaning, scrubbing, and polishing, until satisfied that everything is in place, thoroughly prepped and ready for the next cast to settle here. A sterile house, the only fair compensation she can think to leave behind for whomever it is that will eventually pass this way.

It is deep into the hours of her last afternoon when Cat finds herself pulling out everything from the downstairs closet. Despite its narrow confines, the crowded space holds a surprisingly abundant assortment—things she's purposely left alone in wait of the necessary fortitude to see and smell and touch the intimate collection of Gray's belongings without breaking apart. She watches her hands collect his things: the red-and-black-checked wool jacket, two pairs of work boots, a rather odd looking hat he's brought with him from Columbus but she'd never seen him wear.

She decides the most sensible thing is to pack everything together and set it aside for the women's club in Lost River, certain they will not only welcome such a donation, but unlike Cat, they will know what to do with it.

But she is only just folding Gray's jacket into a brown paper shopping bag when the fragrance of memory comes slamming up hard, sending her brain reeling. She closes her eyes and presses her face into the scratchy wool fabric. And she knows even now, so near to her own date with finality, when it should no longer matter, she is incapable of separating his belongings from the space they occupy intermingled with hers.

She returns each item to the closet and shuts the door, presses her forehead against the doorjamb.

How is it possible her lungs continue to empty and fill beneath the profound weight of this terrible pain—to breathe past this burden of sorrow growing heavier with every passing instant? How is it the components necessary for taking in air have not simply ceased to operate within the clenched fist of her unceasing grief? That a body can continue to function without its owner's cooperation or consent?

She climbs the stairs to their bedroom, determined to finish one final task.

Her own sparse wardrobe hangs in the closet untouched since the accident, choosing instead to wear Gray's oversize shirts, sweaters, and T-shirts over her steadily winnowing frame; striving to reclaim as much of his lingering essence as the soft worn fabric rubbing against her skin will offer.

Her growing fear is that just as Gray's departure from her life has been horrifying and immediate, so, too, will be the swift erosion of details holding together the waning embers of his lost existence; these final remnants whisked away before she can firmly cement each precious component into remembrance. That she's done little other than recall, rekindle, and remember, is of little consequence to her inability to hold on.

She simply exists. Nothing changes. Nothing moves. Nothing evolves across days as unaltered as they are unending; hours melded together with a similarity that makes it all but impossible to differentiate one from another. She sits silent and empty, waiting through afternoons crawling wearily into twilight, lacking the strength to push away from the suffocating cloak of loneliness when it drops. And with the elongating shadows comes the constantly weeping sense of melancholy and loss, pulling all things missing into full view.

She closes her eyes against the never-ceasing pain, wraps her arms around her chest in an effort to still the hollow ache. Presses her mind to reclaim a remembrance of the man whose broad-shouldered wardrobe she now wears like thin ghosts of him. Caressing the fabric between her fingers as she winds her way back through memory, remembering ... remembering ... remembering ...

Now, Cat neatly aligns the shoes jumbled together on the closet floor, heel to matching heel in sharp military rows. Satisfied, she stands and patiently straightens each garment on its respective hanger; shirts and blouses neatly buttoned and conscientiously positioned shoulder to shoulder on the rod, plackets facing right; trousers—parallel seams aligned; sweaters resettled to discourage the potential of pointed shoulders.

She reaches to pull down an assortment of boxes from an upper shelf with the intention of restacking them neatly in accordance of size, but an expected blink of sound reason stirs up from nowhere and she instead shoves the pile back in the same careless manner she's found them.

She passes the remainder of the afternoon immersed in the task of sorting through a collection of mementos Gray has apparently considered meaningful enough to keep. There is an assortment of maps and travel brochures; a handful of postcards sent to Gray at an address in Rhode Island and signed by someone named Rance—a name she wonders if she's heard before, but no, she doesn't think so; odd-sized scraps of paper covered with simple sketches and intricate doodles.

There is a yearbook embossed with the name of a high school in New Hampshire and she flips through the glossy pages until she finds Gray's sophomore portrait; a younger version of the man she loves, the same boyish features, but with a serious mouth, and eyes that hold a certain determination touched by a hint of dubiety. A visage painfully familiar in a way that forces her to look away or further risk losing herself.

Pressed between the pages is a blue ribbon from field day. Her lips curve into a smile as she lifts it with careful fingers. First place. So appropriate for Gray—her champion. Several pages past she discovers another ribbon prize—this one red—and she immediately questions the validity of an event that Gray could possibly have placed second.

It is as she returns his treasures to the closet when Cat spies the rolled tube of paper abutting the wall along the back of the shelf. She knows what it is even before she stretches onto her toes to retrieve and unroll the two sheets of paper curled together.

The echoing whispers of her empty world fall silent, time no longer ticking past as she stares at the sketches they've drawn of each other shortly before they married—a lifetime ago.

Funny, although she's occasionally wondered whatever became of these portraits, she'd never thought to ask Gray. She simply assumed they must've been lost in the move from Georgia to Lost River, never once suspecting they might be right here within arm's reach on a shelf in the closet.

She studies Gray's face as she interpreted him all those years earlier, her eyes combing the cherished features. She clearly recalls the day she sketched him, how she'd considered it such an extraordinary effort at the time. How proud she'd been to so well capture the study of masculine beauty defining Grayson Barnett.

But now, in the cruel light of his vacancy, Cat sees only a likeness painfully flawed when aligned against the true portrait incised into the sheer rock face spanning the width and breadth of her memory.

She re-rolls the single sheet and sets it aside.

There is nothing familiar or even distantly recognizable in the charcoal-shaded eyes staring back at Cat from the drawing Gray has sketched of her. It is the visage of a stranger, altogether disconnected from the person she feels withering to dust and ashes beneath her skin.

When have her lips ever looked so warm and ready to smile? Her eyes so reflective of the rich shadings of love? Had there ever truly been a time when she's been so alive? The likelihood of such a faraway notion feels impossible. The cruelest sort of lie.

And the only thing she can see when she stares back at the steadily clouding face of their shared past, is an image nearly imperceptible in its rapidly lengthening distance from the present.

It is the sound of a raw unintelligible scream that wakes her.

Cat lies perfectly still in the hot dark, her eyes pressed wide against the surrounding gloom, heart scrambling in her chest as tears run warm and slow into her ears. The acrid taste of a nightmare clings heavy and thick against the walls of her throat and she knows that once again the awakening cry is her own.

It is over the routine course of the painfully slow transition from darkness to light when Cat misses Gray beyond the point of bearable; torturous periods which seem to exist for the sole purpose of reminding Cat of the emptiness pressing in around her.

There is no escape from the outline of dread edging the oncoming hours; long cast shadows broad and threatening as evening grows dimmer—an ugly mouth stretching wide to accommodate a greedy swallow. And then is the drag of hours; the sense of an impossible weight holding firm, no place to flee beyond the winding void of passing dark. And only once the night mercifully rounds the corner into the swirly pink tint of dawn, does her clenched jaw slacken, loosening its hold on her tightly held agonies.

The horrifying nightmare stop-start jerks inside her head on an agonizing loop; Gray—his body torn, bloodied, and broken—a wildly spinning saw blade slicing into his chest, severing an arm and ripping across his torso. The features of his beautiful face splintered into an irreparable collage of blood and tissue. *Help me … Why won't you help me, Cat? Please. Do something,* he says over and over, though the place where his mouth should be never moves.

It is a hideous vision holding no true detail of the actual crime that has taken him from her, and yet it nevertheless holds fast within the deepest chambers of her mind, far enough removed from reach that she cannot wrench it away. A perpetually rolling film unceasing in its tortured replay, until the release of her own anguished scream awakens her to the forever-living nightmare of being without him.

A brilliant slash of lightning outlines the deep shadows and furnishings in her bedroom for the pulse of an instant before a shattering crash of thunder slams the night back into darkness.

The air is still in a way that leaves her wishing for rain, or even just the sound of it. The past several weeks have carried a stretch of increasingly thirsty days strung together by high summer heat. And although the brittle days are sporadically accompanied by superficial displays of dry lightning, these teasing electric charges have yet to produce anything other than light and sound.

Cat closes her eyes, willing the sharpened pinpoints of her still-quaking thoughts back toward sleep. She attempts to console herself with the logic that in a few more hours this will all be over. This room, this house, this nothingness. All of this will lie empty. Finished. The unbearable heartache and pain gone.

But even this resolution fails to bring necessary comfort as Cat struggles to unwind the tangle in her mind; the same doubts and questions continuing to twist to the surface. Is such extinction truly possible? Can there honestly be an end to this terrible life right here within her grasp? Because if she genuinely believes this, then why is she still here lying in the dark waiting for dawn to claim her release?

Hours earlier as she is getting ready for bed, Cat selects the clothes she will wear for her life's final event, arranging them neatly over the back of a chair. Now, dressing in the dark, the ordinary act of clothing herself takes on the deepest significance; pulling on her jeans, neatly tucking the long tails of Gray's shirt into the waistband—tugging it loose and leaving the garment to hang free when the bulk of fabric makes it impossible to zip the fly of her pants.

She stares at the grainy visage held within the murky shadows reflected back from the mirror on her dresser as she brushes her hair, acutely aware the effort and result of grooming are of little consequence. It is in performing a familiar ritual in preparation of an utterly foreign event that lends an unexpected sense of calm.

Downstairs in the kitchen, Cat finds her sneakers where she's left them by the back door and pulls them onto her bare feet, her fingers fumbling over the laces.

She pulls the door shut behind her and starts across the yard toward the black cave of woods and the abandoned train tracks which will lead her to the trestle, the maneuvering of her limbs feeling queerly detached from the workings of her mind—as if she is merely the originator of this unfolding drama and not the lone participant.

Twenty Four

She is taking no one with her other than Gray. Not Leafie or Maysel and certainly not Reva. Her mother least of all belongs here, and Cat is full-tilt determined to shut away the nagging hints of old wounds climbing into her head and pinching at the back of her thoughts as she stumbles over the tracks leading her through the dark.

What kind of mother leaves her children alone in the toxic debris of all-out war? What kind of mother abandons her screaming, terrified children in a room awash with unfathomable horror?

They are bitter questions Cat has phrased enough times to defy counting, but now, as she treads her own runaway path to escape what she can no longer bear, she lacks the strength to deny what she has forever pushed away.

They said getting hit by a train happens so fast she never felt a thing. She never would've had so much as a second to think or feel or even recognize the thing hurtling toward her. Gone in an instant—faster than an instant. Quicker than a blink or an intake of breath or a resolved sigh. She never would've known what hit her.

They say this like it's a good thing. A consoling thing. But Cat has only ever understood it one way—as simply one more time when Reva's been caught leaving for someplace else.

Considering her mother's assertion the rail lines are the most dependable route from one place to another, it makes perfect sense why she chose the route she did.

"No dead ends or detours. The tracks go straight through from here to somewhere else. And wherever that is, it's got to be better than here."

Reva's runaway schemes were markedly similar in plot and subsequent failure. She stuffs her only two dresses into a paper shopping bag, followed by a shapeless brown sweater, hairpins, and comb. Cat is watchful and silent, well versed in the ending to a movie she'd already seen a dozen times.

For reasons Cat never understood, Reva's escape route rarely changed, allowing Henry the ease of knowing right where to look as he unleashes a string of ugly curses and climbs into the cab of his truck; tires churning up gritty dust to match his mood as he charges off to retrieve her. And each time, he will catch her well before she gets very far from where she started.

Until that last time—when there's no one to go and fetch her back. No tormentor/savior to retrieve her. Obliterated before she ever has the chance to sober up and consider fixing any of the things she's left broken.

And even now, all this time past, it still leaves Cat more angry than sad. Furious with Reva for letting it happen. For once more standing in place and allowing this last terrible thing to come slamming into her.

Cat's own plunge into the very deepest depths of despair has come long before this night, and it is impossible to believe there is any valley of despondency she has yet to plummet before reaching bottom.

Now, standing on the trestle, swaddled within the blackest night she's ever known, Cat looks out over the edge and knows this is it. The bottom. The eternal abyss—a void holding nothing of hope or promise or even the comfort of finality—the hindmost summit from which to fall.

She feels the night widen and deepen around her, spreading out into the yawning bowels of an emptiness altogether unendurable.

Suffocating. She is suffocating.

Her limbs hang heavy and loose and she can no longer feel where they attach to her torso. She is all at once uncertain what she must do to propel herself to the edge—close enough to slip past the black iron railing. She simply cannot do it. Can neither mentally or physically release her body from its moorings to the earth and sail off into the night-shrouded valley of oblivion.

A jagged splinter of lightning zippers the inky firmament off in the distance. Then nothing. Again full dark.

She stares into the valley below, searching for some focal point in the deep-shadowed expanse. A particular treetop to aim for. A pinpoint in eternity at which to hurl her anguish.

Now—do it now. This is what you want. This is all there is. This is all you have. End this now. Do it now. Step over the edge and have it finished.

A breath of damp air blows softly against her cheek and is quickly gone. The world lies perfectly still and flat around her. Nothing moves. Her lungs stop reaching for breath. Her heart no longer beats out the rhythm of life. And yet impossibly, even as organs cease to function and blood no more pumps through her arteries and veins, she is still here. She continues to exist. Remains stubbornly alive despite her concentrated urgency not to be.

Jump, damn you. Jump! A command and then a plea to a body refusing to comply. Her fingers white-knuckle the cold steel railing—the single physical barrier holding her from release.

She feels a hot trail of tears streaming over her cheeks as she sinks to her knees. "I HATE YOU, GRAY," she screams out, the words painful and raw as they leave her mouth. "I hate you for leaving me here. What am I supposed to do if I can't do this? What am I supposed to do? I can't live—I can't die—help me—help me—help me do this," she cries, rocking back and forth on her heels in an unceasing rhythm of anguish.

She sees herself clearly, plummeting toward the treetops. Falling … falling … never reaching bottom. The air rushes past, lifts her hair in a failed parachute as the final wisps of oxygen sweep from her lungs. She feels every detail—the end she so desperately desires but cannot summon herself to claim. She hears her ragged breathing, raspy and tight, wholly ineffective in drowning away the anguished wails of failure.

How much agony can a body sustain and still fail to collapse under the unbearable weight? How is it possible that her mind and body continue to function so efficiently, insisting on survival, despite her will to surrender? Where is the master switch for disabling the armor strategically placed to deflect every blow she aims against herself?

A tortured, primal howl tears loose from her lungs, "I WANT TO DIE," a broken plea hurtling deep into the valley. "I WANT TO DIE," she screams in enraged defiance of the knowledge that she will not. Not here. Not now. No matter how far she stretches her arm to grasp hold of her ending, she cannot reach it.

And the single death visited upon her in this wrenching moment, is the swift and lethal blow sweeping wide to extinguish the quavering sparks of all that remains alive in the mortally twisted wreckage of her soul.

Twenty Five

The sun has been gone for nearly an hour, yet Cat is unable to summon the necessary effort to pull herself up from the porch rocker and move inside—numb with the same sense of dulled exhaustion that has accompanied her for the entirety of this day. The morning, afternoon, and coming evening meld together large and empty. Herself. Alone and floundering. The second day of the rest of her life. Yesterday the first. Tomorrow the third.

She feels an unexpected sense of calm—not so much comforting as it is settling. She knows precisely what to expect from here on out. There is no secret remedy for repairing the splintered promises of an unfulfilled future, only a dull ache; a void of emptiness stretching out to encompass the stark bare spaces of her deepest anguish. Eternally alone. Irretrievably broken.

Cat knows she will continue to dwell in the null vacuity of her solitary life if for no other reason than the ease of it. There are neither expectations nor demands for anything other than the base requirement she pull herself to standing with the dawn and somehow pass the hours until she has put another day behind her.

It appeals to her as an existence well suited for someone passing through the remainder of a lifetime they don't want.

In time there even feels to be a sense of normalcy winding through days that have little purpose other than to provide a stage for the sun to rise and set. Days wide open and going nowhere.

"But don't you ever just get lonely?" Judy ventures to ask one afternoon when Cat makes a rare trip into town to drop off a bookcase at The Bird's Nest.

"Not unless I'm with other people."

There is the long discomforting pause Cat has come to expect, even anticipate when someone is caught off guard by her colorless answers to unwelcome questions.

"You can't keep living like this and not lose your mind. It's been too long now. You need to open up a door somewhere that leads back into the world," Judy says before Cat sees a chance to escape.

She lifts the glass of iced tea Judy has poured for her, holding the icy sweetness in her mouth for a moment before swallowing. They have already had this conversation a dozen times too many. The content rarely varies; only the diction is occasionally altered.

"Why is it so impossible to understand that I'm fine and this is the way I want things?"

"Because I don't believe you. You've been dealt a rotten hand, nobody denies that, but people recover. They have to. Otherwise they risk doing precisely what you're doing—drifting through life waiting to grow old and die."

"You don't intend to grow old and die?"

"It's actually on my to-do list. I'm just not in hot pursuit of getting there," Judy drops her gaze, swiping a forefinger across the ring of condensation left on the wood counter from the bottom of Cat's glass.

"Look, I know it's hard. I lost my husband fifteen years ago. It takes a long time to sort yourself out. I know. Believe me. I do. But, Cat, what you're doing isn't normal. It isn't healthy," Judy says, pausing to sort through her words with the caution that comes from knowing Cat will immediately turn on her heel and head for the door should she push a fraction of an inch too far in any wrong direction, even as she is aware that in all likelihood she already has.

"I understand how you feel … I know what it's like. My God, when I lost Tom, I just about—"

"If you understand how I feel, we wouldn't be having this conversation. Especially not for the two-hundredth time."

"It's been five years."

"Has it really?" Cat says, the sting in the words leaving her mouth sounding no less sharp than they feel crossing her tongue. "Is there an expiration date on mourning? I wasn't aware. Nobody told me."

"Damn it, come on, Cat. You know exactly what I'm saying."

"You're right, I do. So how about we just leave it alone now and let me deal with my own life."

"That's not an easy thing to do when I can see how—"

"It'll get easier once you've done it for a while," Cat says, setting the glass down on the counter a little too hard. "Thanks for the tea."

Regardless of how quiet or uneventful or dangerous her life may appear to anyone looking in, it's the only way Cat can fathom doing this. Setting Gray on a shelf to gather dust while she spins across the years in a whirlwind of activity pretending she isn't lost and crumbling is a scheme no less impossible than it is inconceivable.

"Some company now and again. A conversation. That's all. Maybe share a meal or go to a movie. Just something to keep you connected to the world. You'd be surprised. People do it all the time without dangerous repercussions."

"I should have something else finished in a few weeks," Cat says, purposely detouring Judy's words.

"Cat—"

But Cat is already turned and striding away; the sound of her own name working to quicken her pace.

From the moment Cat spies the smoky gray thunderheads heaped and boiling in a heavy iron bank massing on the horizon, she mentally prepares for imminent catastrophe.

And she waits.

Throughout the night the rain falls like stones. And although the force of the storm diminishes sometime after midnight, it continues to pound in a steady rhythm carrying well into late morning.

She is in the kitchen measuring coffee into the top of the electric percolator when her gaze lands on the network of ugly brown scribbles staining the ceiling over her head. She stares at the ugly roadmap with a fixed scowl.

"Great."

It's true she's known about the leak sprung in the bedroom ceiling upstairs for quite some time, but her habit is to pretend it away during incoming storms and then promptly forget it exists until the next reminder washes through.

She returns her attentions to the task of preparing coffee as if the potential for worsening damage will be lessened in absence of her interest.

Several months earlier she's taken the precaution of moving the furniture clear of the newly appeared dribble—extending the extra effort to push-pull her bed clear across the room to the wall opposite where it's easier to ignore the telltale indications of the leak's existence. But now, as Cat reluctantly considers the immediate situation, she can no longer turn her cheek to the obvious suggestion the ugly brown arteries and veins stretching out over her head, are in fact, several feet distant from the original leak.

Still, she knows the deceitful nature of leaks, and how incoming water can easily travel a remarkable distance from original point of entry before making an appearance, thereby lending to the impression the situation is far worse than it may actually be. It makes just as much sense to cross her fingers and hope the solution may be as simple as moving the bed again. After all, there are four walls in every room.

But once upstairs, she sees the first leak is still there where it's always been, only now joined by a newly sprouted vein in the hall which links to another smaller tributary in the bathroom. All of which verify what she already suspects—that the entire roof is dying a slow death—only now, not so slowly.

The state of the shingles has been a lingering concern from the day Gray spun her over the threshold, but in the process of weighing dilemmas, the roof had all too easily slipped to the bottom of the pile in favor of essential comforts like heat and plumbing. A roof on the verge of leaking felt only of minor importance all those years ago, but now, with each passing storm dripping down a threat directly into Cat's field of vision, she knows she many very well need to consider a remedy, and not merely every time it rains.

Her immediate inclination is to continue ignoring it, even when logic steps in to remind her that a perpetually leaky roof isn't a condition to be left festering for the remainder of a lifetime. Not unless she intends to watch the entire house decompose around her.

And this isn't even the whole of it. There are other cancers here which have taken advantage of her neglect, spreading a steady trail of damage while she declines to care. There is the section of tile on the bathroom wall that has broken loose and fallen inside the shower; several soft and decaying clapboards on the back of the house; a suspicious hole in the foundation indicating wildlife in residence—likely the family of opossums she occasionally spots wandering in the back yard late at night.

As often as she assures herself she doesn't really care—not even if the walls collapse around her like a rotting peach sinking into the earth—Cat realizes her disinterest is not sufficient reason to continue doing nothing at all. If only because this has been Gray's house, too. Can she truly let it fall away into ruin simply because he isn't here?

And still she pretends not to recognize this isn't simply about leaks and her determined denial of their existence. She's well succeeded in persuading herself that leak is not a red flag—it is only a leak. Just one more segment of her life fraying at the edges and in need of repair. She will eventually get around to doing something. But only when she must.

Now, staring up at the damp brown spot staining the ceiling over her head, Cat can't avoid noticing the shape of the watermark distinctly resembles an outline of Rhode Island. And she thinks maybe she can hold off worrying over this problem a little while longer—or at least until the spot has swelled to the proportions of Wyoming.

"You should just sell this old place," Cat says out loud to the emptiness that is her constant companion.

"But, my memories are here."

"Take them with you." Her voice sounds strangely unfamiliar though hers is the only one she's heard for some time. And arriving all at once—the sensation Gray is here with her—reaching out across some great distance to grasp her hand. Holding so tight she feels the bones shift under her skin to accommodate the intensity of his grasp.

"Which is stronger, Gray, the heart, or the mind?" she whispers, afraid of startling him away.

She no longer feels herself breathing as she waits for some precious response. So desperately longing to hold to his presence she doesn't immediately notice when her hand drops empty to her side.

Yet she knows Gray is here—contained in everything around her. It's true her remembrances have drained of color with the passage of time and now stare back gentle and soft through sepia light. He remains—despite the leaking roof and rotting boards.

It's the reason she stays. The reason she will always stay.

Twenty Six

The first time Cat notices it is on a stingingly sweet morning as she drives into town to deliver a painted chest of drawers destined for shipment to one of Judy's newfound customers on the West Coast.

The air holds the taste of things crisp and new; a freshly laundered garment smelling of pine. Cat rolls down the windows in the truck, liking the feel of the warm breeze whipping her ponytail against the back of her head like a cantering filly. And just like that it is there—the subtle flash of life rekindled, sparking somewhere deep inside and rolling upward. It is a sensation so long extinct as to be thoroughly exhilarating. And she laughs out loud for no reason other than she likes the way it feels right then.

Despite Cat's reluctance to embrace or otherwise recognize it, the business of painting furniture with her fanciful designs has in many ways sustained her, even in the darkest days when her desire has been to do nothing. It is simply a duty she performs. Her creations hold nothing suggestive of the aspirations of artistic prosperity once courted, because there is no connection to Gray. Her dreams have packed up and left for good. Thoughts of accomplishment are no more anticipated or considered than brushing her teeth or combing her hair; tasks she performs out of habit and not of care.

As with everything else shakily holding together the fragmented pieces of her life, being without Gray has brought the entire scope of Cat's earlier accomplishments slamming to a halt. Now is the persistent challenge to coax her imaginings away from the distorted and blackened images of ruin crowding her head in order to compose designs of enchantment and beauty.

She makes little effort to pretend interest when Judy calls with a suggestion or request, simply waits for her to pause long enough to allow Cat an opportunity to decline.

And yet, while it's long been Cat's inclination to disregard a goodly portion of Judy's not-so-gentle prodding, some quiet inner yearning for her abandoned creativity stubbornly holds on. Sheltered deep, tucked into a place where Cat cannot so easily sweep it away with the splintered remains of her other lost dreams, it is here—poised in wait of an opening to begin the long, slow push to the surface.

It's been nearly a year since Cat agreed to Judy's request for a chest of drawers painted in meticulous detail to resemble a medieval castle. A project which ordinarily would require a few weeks for Cat to complete, she has only just finished it now after several months of grudging false starts.

Once she makes the long overdue delivery to The Bird's Nest, the chest is quickly gone, purchased by a vacationer from California. "That's how they are out on the west coast," Judy says. "Just wait and see how many orders come in now."

Cat can't help but smile at Judy's proclamation, wondering how she can possibly claim such knowledge, when by Judy's own admission the furthest she's ever been away from Lost River—the state of Maine for that matter—is a onetime weekend trip to Boston which ended badly—though Judy has never elaborated on the particulars.

"They all want what their friends have. That's their idea of decorating—they just copy each other."

Cat reminds herself how she's actually wanted this at one time—a niche with her name on the door—an ambition to conjoin her yearnings with the tastes of people searching for the unusual. And in this she has mostly prospered. Her whimsical pieces have moved slowly, but well, garnering the intrigue of occasional travelers tickled to acquire a unique and colorful furnishing for a summer home or city apartment hosting accents of the eclectic.

"If I didn't know better I'd think you were under the assumption I have a furniture warehouse out at my place." What she does have are a few random pieces and then the cupboard is bare.

Judy waves away Cat's objections with the confidence of someone who's already wrestled past potential dilemmas and arrived at a solution. "I've checked into a few places and nailed down a source down south where we can buy unpainted furniture direct from the wholesaler. I'm still waiting for this fellow to get back to me, but I'm pretty sure this will be perfect. We'll just raise the prices on your finished pieces to compensate for the additional costs," Judy says, presenting her ready solution conveniently bundled and tied with a bow, purposely oblivious to Cat's reluctance as her own runaway enthusiasm bounds forward undeterred.

She is hesitant to see or otherwise feel the gradual shifting of those things suggestive of change; the sense the long-deadened outer layers are slowly beginning to open and peel away. For the first time since Gray's been gone, Cat feels nearly anxious, maybe even excited, to take her first tentative steps beyond the dull outlines of uncreative obedience she's held to in the absence of her own ideas. Now, rather than a factory mind tuned to automation, painting only what is requested or comes easiest, Cat hears the whispered urgings to compose the more complicated designs originating from the depths of her own imaginings.

Nevertheless, it remains a fragile transition and Cat senses that the rebirth of her stagnant thoughts is in some ways a deception. A restoration skimming the surface, but not sunk deep enough to effectively settle the restless pacing of her grimly fractured mind.

Old things return to taunt her. Rekindled wounds holding fast with the resilience of unsettled hurts and lingering anger; injuries diligently pacing in search of the tiniest crack to push their way back out into the light; ugly and threatening as they have ever been.

Resurrected images return to flavor her dreams with the horror of fresh loss and her memories lift and churn like brackish surf to recall the seedling stages of her life; a childhood where the only promise is the assurance of an unformed future. And she is once again an uncombed child living in a swamp town with the unsavory name of Mudlick. Surrounded by water the color of strong tea—a murky liquid dense with reedy grasses and thick, massing plants jutting from the slow-moving water fringing the edges of the darkly evil place she was born to.

Her thoughts work against her to reclaim every detail and odor; aromas strong enough to sting her senses and roil her insides. A smell impossible to clear from her nostrils—the awful stink of heavy old earth rotting in the fetid humidity of a dead swamp.

She is unable to quiet the voice pacing back and forth in her head, and she frantically searches for an immediate place to hide from her thoughts when she hears the strange mocking laugh riding on the wind, hollow and deep, just as it howled on that blackest night when her childhood was abruptly ended. The eerie whine—a sound nearly human—throbbing cords winding through the stringy webs of moss-dripped trees.

Ugly things waking from a suspended sleep. Nightmares thick and heavy as they'd been in the years before Gray materialized to grab hold and hurl the hideous beast back into darkness. Gray, her white knight.

And now, the roadblock is gone, allowing an avalanche of haunting episodes to come crashing through despite Cat's direct refusal to accept delivery. Angry taunts louder and sharper now than they've ever been previously, if only because Gray himself has disappeared into the horrible, yawning abyss of deepest darkness.

Even now as her life slowly rekindles and she can feel the heft of her endless grief shifting its load and alleviating the pressure on her soul, she fears it is not a redistribution of permanence, but merely a momentary breath to be taken. Because regardless of how any particular day should unfold, how hopeful or promising it may appear, Cat knows that the twilight leading into night will inevitably return.

And she watches the sunset. Waits. Senses the darkness moving closer long before she sees it—heavy and deep in such a way to make it impossible not to hear it breathing. A sound working to unravel her at every seam.

She feels her heart skidding sickly just before her eyes fly open, confusion crashing into consciousness with the uncertainly as to whether the scene unfurled across her mind is real or imagined.

A stripe of white moonlight lays heavy across the width of the bed, holding her pinned beneath its weight. "Gray?" she says to the shadows crowded in, though she is fully awake now and knows there will be no response from what is only the fogged outline of a rapidly evaporating dream.

She lies perfectly still in the dark, aware that to move will all too painfully amplify the emptiness of the bed stretched out beside her. Her dreaming vision of Gray has been so real, so vivid, even now Cat can feel the lingering ghost of his fingers trailing over her skin. She holds her eyes tightly shut, struggling to reclaim even a fleeting spark of an instant where she might again feel his warm breath whispering soft words—the heat of his arms and bare chest melting against her skin where he presses his face into the soft hollow between her neck and shoulders.

But there is nothing. The last fragments of her imaginings carry away like drifting motes of fine dust—then thoroughly gone. Cat rolls onto her side and pushes her face into his vacant pillow, listening to the swell of her breathing as it gradually returns to the quiet pulse of normal rhythm.

The night presses in around her like a scream, stabbing away at the soft tissue behind her eyes. She shoves away the tangle of sheets and drops her feet to the floor, knowing it will be several hours yet before her mind dulls to a state allowing a return to sleep.

It is something of a ritual now, the bottomless void of hollow nights where she wanders the shivery rooms and hallways of the house like a perpetually un-rested spirit, infinitely seeking some lingering particle of what once resided here, wholly unprepared to acknowledge that it no longer exists.

They are hours of nearly unfathomable aloneness and pain, made all the more unbearable by the certainty of their assured permanence over the remaining course of her life. And she can think of nothing to do other than cry out into the vacuity enshrouding her, alternately demanding and pleading for an antidote. Some essential cure for dislodging the tragic renderings settled in her head and transporting them to some other place where they might exist without her.

Cat has been searching all morning for the half dozen screens she replaced with storm windows back in the fall, but without success. It is nearly mid-July and although she should have located and installed them months earlier, it has taken until now for her to kindle the necessary motivation to complete the task. Considering the difficult-to-overlook size of the missing objects, it would seem wholly unlikely, if not impossible, for her to mislay the entire collection, and yet she has.

As with every other chore vying for her attention, Cat sees nothing particularly alarming in procrastination. What does it matter? Who is here to care? If anything, considerations such as unchanged storm windows are simply another symptom indicative of the direction her life has taken, where routine tasks are seldom begun or finished in a timely manner and with little or no consequence.

She climbs the steps to the attic.

The door opens with a whining complaint and Cat pauses for a moment before stepping into the shroud of dim light draping the spacious room. Her gaze moves across the untouched accumulation of time. Aside from the few pieces of furniture she's taken down and painted years earlier, the collection remains equally intact and forlorn beneath the gritty wardrobe of dust draped across the decades and quietly left to cumulate.

Several times in their early years here, Cat had suggested tackling the cardboard pyramids and unknown assortment in order to discover precisely what's been gifted to them. But Gray's response is always a disinterested shrug followed by a suggestion of some other activity of greater appeal; a trek to the trestle; catching the Saturday afternoon matinee at the movie theatre in nearby Lansford—the promise of an ice cream soda afterward; a drive out to the lake on the other side of town.

But standing here now, any interest that once existed over the prospect of sifting through another's castoffs and mementos is thoroughly dead and vanished. And just as well. Cat has already had enough experience with this particular family's brand of keepsakes, still clearly recalling the near ruinous effect a tin of old photos has once had upon her.

While the gloom of an overcast sky serves to further deaden the gauzy shading of murky shadows, the weak strands of daylight spilling in from the high-placed windows in opposing eaves is at least sufficient to allow Cat a shallow survey of the space.

It strikes her how markedly different this room is from the dark cramped attic of the Carper's house in Memphis, where Cat oftentimes snuck away to hide from yet another of Maysel's dangerous rants. Dark and close, the air heavy with the taste of dust, she'd never disclosed the existence of her secret lair to anyone, not even Leafie who would have needed such a hideaway herself.

Now, encapsulated in the attic of her own house, Cat feels a distinct sense of calming solace wrapping close arms around her; a consolation markedly similar to the solitary comfort she'd coveted all those years earlier when trapped in the bowels of another life.

She moves to sit on a large cardboard box, the interlocked flaps sinking slightly under her weight, the missing window screens already forgotten. Outside, the first pings of water spit against the windows and for a long time she remains where she is, sifting through her thoughts, staring up at the cobwebs laced between thick-cut rafters, listening to the rain tapping the glass like needle points.

And she is still here wrapped within her dim cocoon when the clouds all at once break open, no longer teasing sprinkles, but a deluge that slaps like flattened palms against the shingles and rattles the uninsulated eaves like machinegun fire.

Despite the fact she is utterly alone in this place, has been so for years and will continue to be, Cat feels a distinct sense of solace hidden away at the top of the house; sheltered from the silently screaming threats of those things she knows to exist in the rooms below—the lingering essence of vanished life and unanswered prayers lying in wait at the bottom of the stairs. She is safe here. Protected even from herself.

For the remainder of summer, early in the morning, before the heat rises to bake the attic space to combustible temperatures, Cat ascends to the room at the top of the house where she moves boxes, rearranges clutter, and sweeps away the dust and grit birthed in ages past and multiplied over decades.

She never pauses from her determined labors or extends a great deal of thought to the details. There is no need. She is fully attuned to the subconscious import of her preparations; focused in her purpose as she drags unopened trunks and boxes away from the stretch of wall most favorably touched by natural light. Preparing the canvas where she will unleash the twisted images and tortured details of her blackest memories—an impossible tableau she will unfurl across walls stained dark with regret and long-time abandonment.

As Cat has come to expect in this far-northern climate, summer departs without preamble and is one day simply gone. The mornings now hold a chill that carries into afternoons never completely warmed by the sun.

Thoroughly absorbed as she is with her daily expeditions to the attic, Cat falls even further behind on finishing a special order for Judy's store. Despite repeated calls from Judy—her tone at first anxious, now spilling into a place of barely suppressed panic—Cat's resolution to finish this thing she's started is sunk too deep to postpone even temporarily. Least of all for a task so minimal in comparison—painting a coffee table versus emptying her soul.

She sketches crude outlines on the unfinished walls with white chalk, at once exhilarated by the familiar process. It's been a lifetime since she's worked on anything of such magnitude or importance—the unfolding scene feeling more necessary than anything she's ever produced—a live and breathing thing beneath her hands.

There is nothing here to distract her from the peaceful solace secreted in the cloistered space of this eternally quiet house. Nothing reminiscent of Gray to stir her pain. Nothing she needs to think about beyond the images she extricates from the shuttered rooms of memory and spills across the ancient wall.

Despite the drop in temperatures as autumn surrenders to the steady pull of oncoming winter, Cat persists in her daily retreats to the attic, only now layered with a thick wool sweater, Gray's heavy jacket, and worn leather work gloves with the fingertips cut off to allow for ease in holding a paintbrush.

It's becoming too cold for the paint to cure properly and yet it is impossible for Cat to consider leaving the mural unfinished over the long stretch of months necessary to pass before warmth returns.

It is late November when Cat concedes the painting finished. But not until she steps away from her monster, allows her eyes to settle and her mind to fully drink, does she comprehend precisely what she's created—images as horrifying as they are strangely tranquilizing.

The swamp as she best remembers it—only here, on the dark, oily wood in this murky space, it takes on the aura of a place far more sinister. The deep-shadowed fullness of the water lends an eerie suggestion of some strange, thick soup—newly alive and threatening.

Her gaze settles on the image of her childhood home, satisfied that she's effectively captured remembered details; a beaten down structure of rotting wood all but enshrouded by the webs of moss weeping from the twining arms of painfully contorted swamp living trees. A dismal shack with windows blackened to symbolize the absence of life within. And running along the edge of the swamp, a small girl, hair uncombed, dress as outgrown and shapeless as it is nondescript. Her mouth opened wide in a silent scream. Cat, as she best remembers herself.

Later, when warm days return, there will be more. Hideous, macabre scenes released from the deepest, darkest recesses of her brain. Recollections of blood, and death, and horror.

His tears are what startled her most. She has never seen her father cry. He hurts Reva, he breaks things, slams heavy fists through brittle walls, but there is never a tear. Not his own. Not ever. Cat's paralyzed stare holds to his face, not wanting to see, but refusing to leave; watches his features contort into something wholly unrecognizable. A mask peeled away to reveal a visage that on someone other than Henry Baldwin would signify unfathomable pain and grief, but which on him doesn't fit as much as it doesn't belong.

And the expression is still there poured over his face like a finishing glaze when he lifts the handgun from the clutter scattered across the top of the chiffarobe.

She watches him stick the gun's smooth barrel into the black cave of his mouth, and she doesn't understand until it's too late—that the worst possible thing is when she doesn't look away.

As the poisonous memories break loose from the long-sealed vault and spill out across the attic wall, the once-barren expanse melds into a detailed stretch of images resembling the sobering procession of a funeral line. Startling as it is frightening—a surreal collage of pain.

And despite her passionate obsession to compose it, and the long months of living inside it, once finished, Cat cannot bear to see it.

Twenty Seven

She's been teetering on the edge of something dangerous for so long, when Cat finally takes a step back, she doesn't immediately realize that she has.

There is the unmistakable sense of something blinking open, gently stirring in such a way she no longer spends the stretch of cloudy, blue hours between midnight and dawn praying for death.

On her infrequent trips into Lost River, Cat is appreciative as she is relieved that the intervals when anyone approaches to extend pleasantries or inquire how she is doing have become widely spaced. She senses it isn't the brand of ignoring which comes from disinterest. Rather, it's the variety of avoidance that comes with acceptance; understanding or resolved tolerance that Cat has shut herself off from the world in some sadly misguided effort to survive it.

The first definite indication her footing has shifted to stand on a place reminiscent of steady ground, arrives with the impact of a train wreck—stark recognition the house has not only been steadily sliding into decay for years, but is now in desperate need of immediate repairs.

Most imperative is the roof, which has deteriorated to a state of injury requiring Cat to scurry through the house at the onset of every storm, arms filled with an eclectic assortment of pots, empty jars, soup bowls, roasting pans, gelatin molds—anything holding the potential of collecting the drips and occasional streams of rainwater weeping steady tears from ceilings throughout the house.

The understanding of just how dilapidated the house has become as a result of her regrettable negligence makes it nothing less than a supreme act of humiliation for Cat to call someone out to survey the damage and request an estimate for repairs.

The fact Don Peabody is Judy's cousin is reason enough to hire him, considering Judy's personal connection assures she will clue him to the particular aspects of Cat's intensely private nature and established idiosyncrasies well before they actually meet.

That he impresses Cat as a man both fair minded and knowledgeable cements his appeal, as does her assumption he understands and will adhere to the objectives outlined in her unspoken plan. He will come to the house. Do the work. Cat will pay him. He will leave. In that way tampering with her isolation for only the briefest period of necessary inconvenience.

He is a big man, well over six feet, built like a redwood on the way up. It is difficult for Cat to even imagine him climbing a ladder, let alone walking around on her roof—any roof—particularly one in as sorry a state as hers. Nevertheless, she defers judgment, leaning toward the confidence his twenty years of experience carries more weight than his sizable frame does.

"You've already got two layers of shingles up there so we'll need to pull all the old stuff off first," Don says, standing in the yard and staring up at the roof, the massive trunks of his arms crossed over his chest.

Cat nods, feigning only the minimum required of polite interest. She doesn't so much care how it's done, only that it is.

"I can't say a hundred percent until we get everything off whether you've got structural damage. If you do, well then you're lookin' at a whole other set of figures."

"Fine. I understand," Cat says. "When can you start?"

He swings his gaze to look at her, heavy eyebrows lifting ever so slightly. "Most folks like to get a couple estimates on a job like this. It's not a problem, if that's what you're thinking."

"Judy says you're the best around," Cat says, though in truth Judy's opinion is secondary to the fact that should he accept the job, the unpleasant process of further calls and interviews will cease and desist even before it gets started.

Don offers a brief smile at the compliment.

"How long will it take?"

"Well, if I get all four of my guys over here we'll have it done in a few days."

"Perfect," Cat says, shaking his hand.

One more day of dry weather and it would have been finished. Possibly even a few hours would've been enough. But the rain doesn't wait. And it not only comes, it stays for two weeks.

Anticipating the storm's imminent arrival, Don and his crew spend the bulk of the last dry day on the roof nailing heavy plastic tarps over the exposed sections of bare wood they have yet to shingle.

For several days the plastic sheeting holds secure against the gusting forces of wind and rain. But the unrelenting determination of the pounding nor'easter eventually succeeds in tearing loose a large section of the tarp to emit a steady stream of rainwater sluicing in along one attic wall and continuing in an uninterrupted path to the downstairs hall.

But even more alarming than the flood spilling through to inside walls is later when Cat stands out in the yard shivering beneath an umbrella, watching anxiously as two of the men from Don's crew climb the slippery rungs of a ladder rising to the roof in order to reinforce the wildly flapping tarp.

It is still raining days later when Cat finds herself sitting in a booth at the Coffee Spot diner on Main Street, staring out at the slick grey streets while her neglected cup of coffee cools from tepid to cold.

The diner is unusually quiet for a Saturday afternoon—the only reason she's ventured inside to sit. Aside from Cat, there are three other customers planted amongst the red vinyl seats—a man on a stool at the counter and two women earnestly whispering in a corner booth.

The man at the counter clears his throat with a hacking bark, causing Cat to glance up. She looks away swiftly when he catches her eye and stares out the window pretending rapt interest in the bus pulling up at the curb across the street.

An elderly woman struggling with an oversized shopping bag is the first passenger to alight. She takes a teetering step off the curb and for a breathless instant it appears her next awkward movement will send both body and bulging cargo spilling onto the wet pavement. Remarkably, she manages to remain upright as she steps onto the road and weeble-waddles across the street.

A spot of bright color appears at the edge of her vision and Cat shifts her gaze back toward a young woman cloaked in a yellow rain slicker striving to keep hold of a small boy fiercely intent on re-boarding the bus. She watches the brief drama, commiserating with the woman and her obvious frustration as the child furiously tugs to free his hand from her grasp, even as she roots for the child in his determination to escape.

And then they are gone, the boy still stubbornly tugging to extract himself from the woman's hold as they turn the corner at the drugstore and blink from sight.

Cat lifts the coffee cup to her lips, setting it down unsipped when she recalls it has gone cold.

Just for a moment, she allows herself the preposterous fantasy Leafie will be one of the passengers alighting onto the curb. Newly arrived, standing in the silvery gray downpour, uncertain of where to go now that she is here, much as Cat has envisioned her innumerous times in countless destinations over the years she's been missing.

Where are you Leafie? Where have you gone? Where have you been all this time?

Cat returns her stare to the window and the dull stretch of watery light beyond the pane. The bus belches rudely and rumbles to life, and it is then she notices a man standing alone. The last of the handful of passengers to alight, he stands in the drizzly mist with a large canvas bag clutched in one hand. He hesitates on the curb, turning his gaze in a slow moving sweep up one side of the empty street and down the other.

Sometime earlier the rain has slackened, but now signals its return with a steady peck against the glass. Cat holds her gaze on the man, unwittingly curious what direction he means to take. Unable to access details of his countenance at a distance, she searches for something recognizable in his stance and posture but discerns nothing familiar.

He takes a step off the curb, pauses. Cat wonders if he is a onetime acquaintance of Lost River or simply a hapless stranger who plucked down bus fare in some far city only to land in the wrong destination.

She looks away, any fleeting spark of curiosity already gone. It isn't her habit to notice the movements of people around her. There is a certain safety at a distance, and quite frankly, she isn't all that interested.

Cat ducks her head as she steps out from beneath the awning extended in a half circle above the doorway. Over the past half hour, the drizzly spit misting on and off from morning into afternoon is steadily picking up and Cat keeps her head tipped downward as she darts from the sheltered doorway to Gray's truck parked at the curb. She jerks the door open and bounds up into the truck's cab seconds before the heavens split open to unleash a deluge.

And she doesn't notice in her haste to outrun the rain that the man from the bus is now crossing the street and approaching the Coffee Spot. He pulls open the door and steps inside.

Twenty Eight

She hears it only once. A sound so brief it's easy enough to convince herself she hasn't heard anything at all.

Until she hears it again.

She cocks her head.

Knocking? Is someone knocking at the door?

As ordinary and unexceptional as it may be to anyone else, in Cat's world a knock at the door is enough of a foreign occurrence that she instantly freezes—her limbs hanging perfectly still in suspended uncertainty.

The potato she's been peeling to add to the pot of stew simmering on the stove lays half stripped in one hand, the vegetable peeler clattering to the floor as her fingers loosen, forgetting their purpose. She listens, her breathing still. Her last swallow of air caught tight against the wall of her chest by the heavy press of her vanished heartbeat.

Silence. Nothing beyond the sound of gale wind buffeting the windows high and wild.

She waits, tension easing with the returning flow of oxygen leaking back into her lungs. Nothing. Of course, nothing. No one is here. No one ever comes here. Obviously what she's heard is just the wind chasing some unsecured object across the porch.

Cat bends to pick up the peeler, offering herself a weak little smile as she thinks of how proficient she's become at spooking herself.

What she really needs is a radio, something to take the edge off the silence; the sound of something other than her own breathing to drown out the persistent noise of runaround thoughts forever volleying back and forth in her head.

She releases a deep exaggerated sigh and returns her attentions to the potato, cubing it and adding it to the pot.

Rap. Rap.

Louder. A knock. Definitely a knock.

She lays the knife on the counter. Who would come out here? No one ever does anymore. Never. If there's any one intention she's succeeded at better than anything she's ever done, it's her claim of solitude. She's not only demanded, perfected, and polished it, she's received it in abundance.

Maybe someone's broken down out on the road. Run out of gas, gotten a flat and has no spare. She stands for a moment rationalizing, rapidly working through a dozen different possibilities before passing into the long hallway connecting kitchen to entrance foyer.

Again—rap, rap.

She halts, rooted to the floor midway between the safety of the kitchen and the impossible shock poised for admittance there on the other side of the closed door. Because suddenly she knows. With every cell of certainty. She knows of course it is Leafie who is here standing on her porch. Her mind scrambles to grasp the words she will say, the questions she will ask beginning with how Leafie has found her after all this time—why it's taken her so long to arrive.

And now she is moving again, eager steps winging her to the door. Her fingers touch the deadbolt—the briefest pause before turning—unaware until now how violently her hand is shaking. She grasps the knob, cracks the door wide enough to peer out into the grainy light of late afternoon, heart lifting in a forward leap to receive the vision of her sister—standing there like a long lost treasure retrieved from the Lost and Found.

"Catherine Barnett?" A deep male voice says, unknown, and yet oddly familiar.

Not Leafie. Her heart slips down her throat, slides back into her chest in one swift motion.

"Yes …?" she hears her voice pushing up small and weak from beneath a crushing avalanche of immediate disappointment as she stares into the face of the dark-haired stranger who has spoken her name.

She skims her gaze past his shoulder, noting the absence of any vehicle that might have brought him here.

He doesn't immediately answer and it suddenly occurs to Cat that, yes, of course, he is one of the men from Don's crew, here to check on the state of the troublesome tarp. While the rain has stopped some days earlier, it is now the wind that keeps the roofers from finishing up. And although Cat can't say she necessarily recognizes him as being one of the men she's watched climbing up and down the ladders propped against the back wall of the house, from the way he is now silently returning her stare, she is certain she should have.

She scrambles to regroup her senses. "Oh, right—I'm sorry. You're here to check on the roof. I've been keeping an eye on the tarp like Don told me. It looks all right. There haven't been any new leaks since—"

Her words halt mid-speak, tripping up against the amused smile that flits across his lips and just as quickly disappears. It's clear she's guessed wrongly, and she feels the hand of something cold and frightening pass over her. She takes a step backward.

"My name is Rance Barnett," he says quietly. "Gray was my brother."

And just like that, she forgets how to breathe.

Twenty Nine

"I was hoping maybe we could talk," he says, interrupting the uncomfortable stretch of gaping silence leaning in to swallow them both.

"Gray's dead."

"I know."

Her hard stare rakes the man's features for traces of Gray, a thousand accusation-laced questions jockeying to the surface. She finds nothing of the familiar here in the man's dark eyes and roughly chiseled features.

Who is he really? Can this even be true?

"I … don't know if … I, all right, fine. Come in," her spiraling thoughts trip along a line of unlinked words rushing past in an effort to grasp something of rationality; reason and civility making a shaky return.

"Thank you," he says, stepping inside.

Is he several inches taller than Gray? Broader in the shoulders? Or does it only seem so because he is standing here now and Gray is not?

"This is difficult—I understand. I've been in town all week. It's taken me that long to get up the courage to even come out here." He pulls a hand across his eyes as though attempting to remove some unwelcome image settled there.

"I got as far as Portland before my truck broke down and I caught the bus … I didn't have much of a plan what to do once I got here, I just felt it was time I came."

Cat watches his face, wanting to pull her eyes away, but finding it impossible.

"I haven't seen Gray since he was nine years old. I expected things between us would be awkward with me just showing up and I …" He waits a full ten seconds before he completes his sentence. "I wasn't so sure how he'd feel about seeing me."

"How did you find out about—about what happened?"

"I stopped in the diner for a cup of coffee thinking I would either fortify my nerves or talk myself out of coming here. I'd gone through quite a few refills before I finally asked the waitress if she knew him. I got the idea something was wrong even before she told me. The look on her face … then she mentioned you and how I'd just missed seeing you."

Cat listens, offering nothing herself, feeling distant and strangely removed from this man and everything he is saying. It takes a moment for her to perceive that he's fallen silent and is now watching her awaiting some response.

There is a silence that develops into a discomforting stare. "Come in the kitchen," she says at length. "I'll make coffee."

"I would've told you about the accident if I'd known there was actually someone to tell," Cat says, keeping her back to him as she measures coffee into the pot. She hears the accusation in her voice, and although she doesn't intend it, she doesn't otherwise regret it.

"Gray never told you he had a brother?" Rance says, sounding neither hurt nor especially surprised.

"Yes—but he said you were dead," she says, setting an empty mug on the table in front of him, striving for normal even as she grapples with the facts of everything Gray once told her. The tragic loss of his entire family—including the brother who is right now sitting at her kitchen table.

"*Dead?*" His dark eyebrows lift in a suggestion of genuine surprise.

Cat feels a rush of heat spilling out under her skin. "I'm sorry. I really don't know what else to say. That's what he told me."

"Do you mind if I ask how I died?" Rance tries a smile, but there is nothing of amusement in it. She catches a glimpse of something pointed and sharp in his dark stare, and quickly shifts her gaze.

"A house fire."

"Just me?"

"No, everyone. Even the dog."

"We never had a dog," he says, then, "I guess that's what happens when you stay out of touch for too many years."

No. That isn't what happens. And she pretends not to feel it, but it's there—immediate, crushing disappointment that Gray has apparently lied to her. She doesn't mention the pet raccoon.

"Out of touch how?"

"I left home when I was fifteen. It was the last I saw him." He lifts a hand, touches his brow as if all at once recalling something. "Maybe it's more accurate to say we just stopped knowing each other."

Cat unplugs the coffee pot. She hopes he doesn't notice how her hand continues to shake as she pours the steaming brew into the mugs she's set on the table, unwilling he should realize how unsettled she is by his appearance.

"It isn't that he never talked about you. He just said he'd lost his family—that you were all gone. It wasn't like he didn't care—it was clearly upsetting to him," Cat says, compelled now to lessen the damage of what she's already shared. For all the lies she's told with such fluency over the course of her life, she regrets going in the direction of honesty now, when it serves no purpose other than to heap additional conflict onto a long-fractured relationship. "I can't remember his exact words. It was a long time ago."

Rance Barnett wraps his large hands around the mug but fails to lift it to his lips. "He believed I deserted him. Did he tell you that?"

"No." *He said you were dead, remember?*

"Well, I didn't. Not on purpose. I wandered around for a few years. Going anyplace I might find work until I was old enough to enlist in the Navy. All of which turned out to be for nothing—I was turned down anyway because of my leg."

Cat lifts her brows in a feigned suggestion she hasn't noticed anything unusual in his stance. And yet she has. When he passed through the front door and into the hall she'd been quick to jot a mental note. It is an imperfection not so much discernible as it is unmistakably present. Not simply because she's detected something unnatural in the movement of the limb and his markedly rigid carriage, it is something else. The sense of a handicap he makes an effort to conceal, so it is especially surprising when he mentions it now.

Cat feels a flush of heat licking quick flames over her face, all at once aware that she is in fact staring at him and he is staring back. And she is all at once certain she has in fact seen him once before; on a rainy afternoon a week earlier. As she sat in the Coffee Spot nursing a cup grown cold, watching passengers disembark from the out-of-town bus across the street. Certainly it was Rance Barnett who she'd seen hesitate at the curb, surveying the street as he stood in the rain.

If Rance detects anything of the madly spinning thoughts sprinting through her head, he gives no indication as he shifts his gaze and continues. "When I finally got around to admitting it was long past time to try and get in touch with Gray and our sister, it was several years too late. By then they'd both left home and gone off in opposite directions."

"What about your parents?"

"Anne told me they're both dead … though to be honest, I hadn't asked."

Cat drops her gaze, stares at her hands clasped in her lap on the chance they contain the necessary instructions for launching the flux of questions rapidly germinating in her head.

She waits for Rance to continue, sitting in silence until an instant becomes a minute. And then several. She lifts her head. Levels her vision. Struggles to steady her madly racing thoughts as she searches for an exact word or phrase within the still and somber air hovering along the surface of the table.

"I never would've believed he'd ever come back here, though. I just figured he must've felt the same way I did about this place."

Her spine instantly stiffens—her breathing tumbling over the edge, falling away through space. Her stare is heavy and full, hardening across the short distance of chipped Formica tabletop separating them. She watches his eyes survey the kitchen, his expression reminiscent of someone assessing a memory.

"It's weird how little it's changed."

A knotted fist of apprehension presses forcefully against her temples, her mind clearly sensing the threat of some unknown something bearing down hard.

"What?"

"This house ... this kitchen," he says, returning his gaze to her face, a disjointed question blinking awake in the depths of his eyes.

"You're saying you think you've been here before—in this house?"

"Well, sure it's been over twenty years, but it's still the same wallpaper—the same linoleum on the floor. I'm pretty sure that's even the same stove and refrigerator—none of which surprises me. Progress and change never rated very high on their list," he says, the dryness of his tone conveying everything his countenance does not, clearly misinterpreting the look of crashing emotions tangled inside Cat's expression.

"That's impossible," Cat breathes the words low and quiet, even as she comprehends that Rance Barnett's very presence here assures it isn't.

"Strange, yes, but not impossible. This house has been in my mother's family for generations. We spent every summer here when we were kids," he says, and his eyes cloud with the heft of some instantly arrived remembrance. "Change it hasn't."

He drops his gaze, moving his hand to trace a finger along a triangle of missing Formica. "I did this when I was seven or eight—chipped it out with a pocket knife I'd taken from my stepfather Otto's dresser," Rance says, his tone devoid of inflection, and Cat is unable to decipher the quality of sentiment behind the recollection.

She doesn't respond, continues to watch him, stares at his words lying around her like the unveiled mysteries of a foreign tongue—impossible to read or otherwise comprehend. She scrambles to recover the necessary evidence to refute his statements; a bulletproof argument to prove him ridiculous and his assertions wholly invented.

The air lies motionless between them as she strives to reclaim her voice. A thousand syllables crashing together inside her head with the effort. And when the words finally come Cat makes no attempt to settle the awakened anger climbing into her mouth.

"Okay, so you're Gray's brother. I really don't know what you want or why you came, but if you need to spend a few days here to figure out what to do about your truck, or your life, or whatever it is you feel you need to do—that's fine. You're welcome to stay.

"But if you came here with some intention of trying to lay claim to this house, think again. It belongs to me—Gray and me. It's ours. We paid for it and I intend to keep it. Just make sure you understand that," Cat says, her throat clenching so hard on the words it is difficult to draw breath at the same time she speaks them.

"And he might not be here to explain it, but I can only assume if Gray killed you off in a fire, you must've been dead to him for a damn good reason."

Thirty

The bed frame groans a sharp complaint as Cat flings herself back onto the mattress and glares at the bedroom ceiling, furiously searching across the deep-shadowed expanse for a target at which to hurl her indignation.

"There's only one reason I came here and that's to ask you about my brother. Nothing more," is what he'd said, the bite in his tone a clear indication he's been sorely stung by her accusation. "Any other conclusion you've reached is purely imagined."

Maybe if she didn't feel so thoroughly blindsided. Stunned. All out pummeled by the load of impossible charges he's dumped on the center of her life. Maybe then she'd actually be able to think straight; to pause, take a breath, clear her head and examine things logically. To somehow gauge the degree of durable weight in his out-of-the-blue, left-field, inside-out revelations, and somehow see a light of reason or explanation.

Regardless of anything Rance Barnett says, whether now or later, Cat knows to keep focus on what is unequivocally black and white. On the side of Rance Barnett—unsupported claims and a missing chip of Formica are the sole extent of his evidence. Where in Cat's defensive corner there are her years with Gray—well-lived seasons twined throughout with the bonds of love and trust. Black and white. Simple logical truth.

But why then does she feel like someone trailing somewhere off in the distance, staggering through the smoking debris of a devastating explosion?

What purpose would Gray have in lying to her about this house? What would be the intent of such a colossal omission? Alright, so *maybe* he did come here as a boy. So what? Suppose it is possible. Possible, yes—and yet still remains the question of what would qualify something as unexceptional as a summer house in Maine as motivation for secrecy and lies?

There are questions. Entire armies of 'whys' amassing in preparation of war. And while they continue to breed and multiply with every instant that ticks past, there is no reasonable place for Cat to take them. Nowhere other than back to the man who has planted them.

But how many questions or accusations can Rance Barnett possibly field? By his own admission, he hasn't laid eyes on Gray for over twenty years. A span which by her calculations, leaves them more resembling of strangers than of brothers.

And why is she suddenly so angry with Gray? Because she is. And she tries to press it down and pretend it away, because it feels so horribly wrong to be angry with the dead—with her beloved Gray. But it holds firm. Crowding her thoughts into a corner so tight it feels impossible to move, or think, or see beyond to anything else.

It is still early when Cat creeps downstairs the next morning. Just after six o'clock. She pauses for a moment in the hallway outside the living room, swallowing hard in a bid to drown her nerves before throwing a quick glance toward the couch were Rance Barnett has elected to sleep the night. Vacant. Blanket neatly folded and stacked with the pillow she's lent him centered on top.

She feels something plummet below her ribs and drop to the floor of her stomach. *Disappointment*? Has he simply gotten up and gone? She knows this shouldn't surprise her. Not after the onslaught of ugly insults layered with accusations she's hurled at him from behind her barricade of stunned confusion.

But there are so many things she needs to ask him yet. Questions sprouted and grown in her mind over the endless span of a sleepless night. She'd been terribly wrong to say the things she had—or at least wrong in the way she'd elected to say them. Her words have been unnecessarily harsh. Maybe if she had—

"I've never seen anything like this—it's pretty remarkable."

Her heart and several other organs leap directly into her throat at the sound of Rance's voice coming up behind her. She spins around as though yanked by a length of invisible rope.

"Sorry. I didn't mean to startle you," he says smiling, thought the curve of it only crosses his lips halfway. "I didn't realize when I saw this yesterday that there were more."

"We wanted to paint a mural in every room, but … well I don't expect I'll ever finish them myself."

"You did these?"

"Gray and me. Mostly Gray."

"Gray was an artist?" His expression is one of genuine surprise and something else—pride? tenderness?—she doesn't know him well enough to guess with any certainly, but whatever it is she sees, Cat finds herself unexpectedly warmed by it.

She nods.

"They look so … alive or something … incredible."

"I guess you didn't know then that he graduated from the Art Institute in Savannah. He had an incredible gift. I just wish—" she turns abruptly, heading down the hall toward the kitchen, working to push down everything she all at once feels rushing to the surface.

For the first time in recent memory, Cat finds herself entangled in emotions other than the press of grief and all-encompassing emptiness which have constituted the whole of her existence since losing Gray. Now, running parallel, are the sharp-edged blades of uncertainty and confusion; a startling awareness that the precious image of the man she forever loves and profoundly mourns is subtly shifting to allow for the swelling proportions of a larger more complex picture.

And for no absolute reasoning other than a perceived recognition reflected back from the depths of his dark eyes, Cat believes that Rance Barnett is thinking this very same thing. Or at least, something very close to it.

"I told you it's not a problem if you need to stay until it's fixed," Cat says after Rance makes the call to Sal's Garage in distant Green Oaks to inquire over the prognosis of his disabled truck.

"I know, and I appreciate it. But now this guy's telling me it could be several days before he even gets around to looking at it," Rance says, tapping the butt of his unlit cigarette against the kitchen counter in a distinct tempo of irritation.

"This is a big house. I'm sure we can manage to stay out of each other's way," Cat says despite her uncertainty as to whether she actually means or even believes it. Rance's presence here feels huge. Enormous. Ineludible.

"Look, I know you have your doubts and I don't blame you, but I honestly didn't come here with the intent of crashing into your life like a meteor," he says with a sheepish blend of sincerity that causes Cat to smile, if only briefly.

She thinks maybe she believes him. But she can't really say for sure.

It is several days after the rain stops before Don's crew finally returns to finish shingling the roof, and Cat is several degrees beyond grateful to have them here. While before her sole focus rests on having an essential repair completed and her solitary corner of the world returned to quiet, she now embraces the workmen's presence as an assured distraction to what would otherwise be a discomforting aloneness with Rance Barnett.

And it isn't simply the man himself and the tornado winds he's stirred awake here—raining debris that pierces her thoughts with a thousand burning points—nearly as significant, is the ten-ton presence of the canvas bag he finally concedes to carry upstairs to a spare bedroom. The single bag holding his personal possessions that somehow makes his being here, and every startling revelation he's delivered, all the more indisputable.

Their conversations are odd exchanges. Spotty and incomplete dialogues representative of two strangers improbably linked by things each knows from separate experiences with the same person, and their mutual need to somehow connect these ill-fitting pieces in order to form something of a recognizable whole.

It is a strange, silent dance. Cat feels Rance standing beside her on the edge of something—uncertain what it is, only knowing it exists. She senses him watching her, and when he isn't, she is watching him, increasingly convinced there is some definite purpose in his being here. And while she doesn't yet understand what it is, she is determined to uncover it despite the tightening bands of caution squeezing her insides.

When she thinks she can do so unobserved, Cat studies him for resemblances of Gray. And she can't say if she is disappointed or relieved that aside from an occasional fleeting expression—a particular flicker of something around the eyes, the slightest curve at the corners of his lips—there is little about Rance Barnett that rings familiar to her heart. He is taller, broader, darker, than his brother. So unlike Gray, who Cat has forever viewed as a man perpetually moving through strands of shimmery light. Easy to smile and laugh, warm and affectionately loving. Altogether dissimilar to Rance, who carries no such aura of illumination or ease.

She thinks maybe it is the discernable stiffness of his imperfect leg that so easily lends to his decidedly sad and damaged air. And although he smiles often enough to prove himself amicable, it is an expression which only just touches his lips, never quite reaches his eyes, reflecting a distinct hint of somberness Gray never carried himself.

In an odd and frightening way, he reminds Cat something of herself.

"We have different fathers," Rance says when she ventures to remark over the dissimilarity of his looks in comparison to Gray.

"Oh … Gray never told me."

"It seems there's a lot he didn't tell you," Rance comments dryly.

A racing current of heat flames over her face, stung not only by his words, but by the undeniable truth holding them together. She bites down hard on the sharp edge of an indignant response, swallowing her annoyance in exchange of a purposely dignified rebuttal.

"Apparently it wasn't all that important to him," she says.

He offers no reply other than a briefly landed smile. Not so much an expression of pleasure or amusement, as a suggestion of yet another unexplained something she can't possibly begin to understand the meaning of.

The roofers have been gone for nearly an hour. And while it is an event she's anticipated from the very commencement of their labors weeks earlier, now that it has arrived and the work is finished, Cat is just as earnestly wishing for their return.

Her anxiety over the presence of a noisy crew traipsing back and forth across the space customarily inhabited only by herself has all but evaporated with Rance Barnett's appearance on her doorstep. His arrival instantly tilting her world off kilter, spilling a palpable load of uncertainties and impossibilities spreading in a deepening threat.

She passes the afternoon on the porch striving to force her attentions back onto the bench she's been painting for days; half listening to the men's banter as they finish up, glancing up occasionally to watch as they pack tools and ladders back into the bruised and dented vehicles that have brought them here.

Ordinarily, such uninspired activity would hold little interest, but today it is a welcome distraction from the influx of determined thoughts steering toward places and things Cat prefers not visit.

She hasn't seen much of Rance all day. The only tangible evidence that he's passed through is the jacket left draped over the porch railing sometime earlier. And while she is unwillingly curious of his whereabouts, she holds her immediate questions unasked when he at last materializes around the corner of the house and ascends the steps.

She drops her gaze, pretending not to notice or otherwise care when Rance leans his shoulder against a porch post and silently watches her work.

The press of quiet rapidly takes on weight, piling higher with every second it goes unused. Cat shifts her position, leans forward on her haunches, stirs the saucer of paint, inattentively dabs green loaded bristles where blue is intended.

She drops the brush and lifts her face, "I can only assume he had his reasons for keeping certain things to himself," she says, picking up the dangling threads of their earlier conversation as if there has been no intermission.

"Maybe."

"And of course you claim to know what those reasons are, right?" she says, a brittle accusation she doesn't intend any more than she aims for the sarcastic tone bringing it forth. And yet how else to cloak her increasingly desperate need to have him reveal something—answers or imperative revelations to settle the screaming questions Gray has left at her feet like scattered bones.

Rance doesn't immediately answer. He taps a cigarette from the partially crushed pack in his shirt pocket, places it between tight lips and lights it, blowing out a sharp stream of smoke before replying. "No, actually I don't. But like you said, 'if he kept it to himself he must've had a reason.' So if you're asking me to pour out his past—and I think you are," the penetrating pinpoint of his gaze resting on her face, "then I respectfully decline."

Her spine stiffens though his tone has not been unkind; her chin lifting a fraction in receipt of what feels to be a distinct reprimand. The sharp blow inflicted on her pride running parallel with her embarrassment that he has so easily read her.

A biting retort rolls up into her mouth, but she manages to hold the words unsaid, reminding herself a heated response is least likely to reward her with something of what she is hoping for.

"You and Gray never had children?"

The question is unexpected in a way that leaves Cat feeling at once vulnerable. *An opportunity missed. A road not taken. A purpose unfulfilled.* She recovers quickly. "I'm sure if Gray had wanted you to know he would've told you. And since he didn't, he must've had his reasons," she answers, nearly grinning in appreciation of the prompt opening to deliver his words back to him.

"Touché," he answers, and Cat is certain she's caught the fleeting ghost of a smile cross his lips. "Okay, point taken. I probably deserved that, but I didn't mean it the way it apparently came out. It's just … I don't know … this whole thing is just so hard. So damned impossible," he says turning his head to stare out across the yard.

He doesn't speak. Smokes awhile in thoughtful silence. Then, "We shared a history, Gray and I."

"So did we," Cat replies with quiet firmness.

"Ours was painfully imperfect," he says, and his smile of the moment previous, if indeed there has been one, is now thoroughly vanished.

"So was ours. He died, remember?"

He shifts his head, staring out at something Cat doesn't see, though maybe he is simply watching the safety of empty space. He turns back a moment later. "I've never seen a point in retelling old stories. Nothing changes. It's always the same ending."

They stare at each other, the silence going on and on until it sounds like noise.

He looks away.

"I want to know—I deserve to know. That's purpose enough," she says, ignoring the sting of tears lining up behind her eyes and slowly dripping into her voice.

Rance shakes his head, keeping his eyes from Cat, but then unexpectedly turns to face her. He smiles in a way which makes his expression all the more undecipherable. "It's more my story than it is Gray's. Maybe that's why he kept it to himself. It's just one of those things better left unsaid."

If this is true, if it is Rance's story, then what is Gray's? Doesn't he have one of his own? And suddenly Cat is biting down hard to keep from laughing. Laughing long and bitter and hard at what is looking more and more to be a foolish delusion—namely the untarnished life she's always believed she shared with Gray.

Thirty-one

She doesn't know how to stop being alone.

Not until Rance Barnett's emergence from nowhere has there been even a single distraction successful at coaxing her away from her chosen life of solitary oblivion.

Cat finds herself unwillingly intrigued by him. Not because of his similarities to Gray, of which there are few recognizable, but rather it is the force of his differences that most prod and stir at her curiosity. The smiles that rarely come. His words that suggest a dozen possible meanings, but which tell her nothing absolute. Statements that serve only to breed more unanswerable questions. The stark contrast of dark hair and even darker eyes, when everything about Gray has held a suggestion of light. The brooding look customarily settled over his features—a deep-rooted expression hinting at thoughts perpetually dwelling in some sad and distant place. All of it effecting to draw her ever so subtly toward him.

His are an oddly distorted assemblage of traits that tug at her mind in a way she feels to her roots without benefit of understanding. She only knows that before he leaves here, she fully intends he reveal some significant portion of those things he carries behind his eyes; namely, the missing pieces of Gray he is deliberately holding within.

The wounded flock together. Cat has always believed this though she doesn't comprehend how that's supposed to help anybody. Fragile, broken people commiserating over how lousy their lives are, or have been, and how miserable they feel because of it. It's a brand of logic she avoids as much as she distrusts it.

Even now Cat is loathe to admit either out loud or in the hidden confines of her thoughts, the verity of what she's always known—the truth that she is one of them—the wounded. Just as she is becoming increasingly convinced that Rance Barnett is likewise afflicted.

Cat is out in the barn rummaging through her dwindling supply of paint cans when Rance comes up behind her. She doesn't hear his approach and the unexpected interruption of his voice lands on her rambling thoughts with the force of a dropped boulder. She nearly jumps but doesn't, swings her head sideways to face him with a quizzical brow.

"Sal says my truck should be ready by Friday."

"Oh," Cat replies, looking away quickly, fixing her attentions back on the cans, at once flustered by his announcement. "You called him again?"

"You seemed pretty busy and I didn't think you'd mind if I used the phone. I'll pay for the call."

"No, don't be ridiculous," she says, attempting to distance the confusion of her immediate thoughts from the clear message in his pronouncement.

So, this is all there is. The end of it. He's leaving. Maybe even as early as tomorrow. Going and taking his secrets with him.

She stares at the labels arrayed on the shelf in front of her, suddenly seeing them as if from a distance—trying hard to focus across the span of a mile-long tunnel. Dusty rose, forest green, slate blue ... There is a heaviness in her chest—a load tumbled down from its perch on an upper ledge. A suffocating press of anxiety firmly weighted by something that feels distinctly like dread.

She sets aside the cans she intends to carry back to the house, silently assuring herself it is the ungodly press of summer heat causing her brain to thump crazily against the inside of her skull. It has been oppressive for days. Ever since the rain ended.

"So you're leaving then."

Rance nods. "I know this hasn't been the most pleasurable week for you … having a stranger show up on your doorstep and stirring up things you didn't need to think about. I should've said so before, but I appreciate your hospitality and—"

"Your being here isn't a problem," she interrupts before he can finish, purposeful to keep her face from him as she loads her arms with an assortment of cans, unwilling to relinquish the safe barrier offered by her back. "And we aren't exactly strangers anymore, are we?" she adds, attempting to sound casual and unaffected, even as she hears her own consummate failure to attain the intended tone.

"No, I suppose not," Rance says, then, "I'd like to take you out to dinner before I leave. Give you the night off from being chef," he smiles.

"Dinner?" Cat repeats, turning swiftly, staring at him as if this single word is as incomprehensible as it is foreign.

"Yes, dinner," he says, and he is still smiling at her.

It is a simple invitation that nevertheless brings a surge of unreasonable panic flooding over her. She shakes her head vehemently, watching his cloudless expression turn to something of stunned surprise.

"No. Thanks, but I don't go out. I don't have time," she says, turning brusquely and starting toward the house, intent on denying him an opportunity to reply.

"You don't have time to eat?" he calls after her.

"No, actually I don't."

She feels the threatening weight of his presence moving up behind her like a lead-bearing shadow as she strides across the yard with the awkward load of cans clasped in her arms.

"I can help you with those."

She doesn't respond, her sole objective at this moment, to get across the grass without mishap. The load shifts in her arms as she quickens her stride, but she doesn't pause to rearrange her cargo; altogether focused on gaining immediate distance from him and the ridiculous tide of emotion brought on with his invitation.

Damn it—Damn it to hell. What is wrong with her?

She knows full well she's behaving like an idiot, but aside from recognizing this fact, she is altogether powerless to stop herself. If there is a switch she might flip to reset her emotions, she doesn't see it.

"Cat—"

"I really don't have time for this, okay? I have a lot to get done," she snaps, feeling her mood take a wildly veering curve away from any remaining semblance of control. And it's right at the juncture where her dangerously quavering resolve to retain composure comes up against the steadily crumbling wall, that the cans in her arms tip to an angle of impossible balance—one, then another, dropping from her grasp and landing at her feet.

She leans forward, groping blindly for the runaway containers, and loses several more. One can popping its lid as it hits the ground, splattering a swath of vibrant blue across the top of Cat's sneaker and leaking into the grass.

"Shit," she swears behind gritted teeth, horrified by the flames licking up over her face, lifting her arm to rebuff Rance's attempt of assistance when he stoops beside her to retrieve the cans.

"I don't need you—I don't need your help. Please leave me alone. Just leave me alone."

He pauses, clearly startled, then, "Alright … if that's what you want," he says straightening, watching her for a full minute before he starts to walk away, then stops and turns. "It was only dinner, Cat. That's all."

She doesn't answer, dipping her head in an effort to conceal the lone tear running down her nose. A single droplet lingering for an instant before falling onto her hand.

"Go to hell, Rance Barnett," she says quietly to the rigid line of his back as he strides toward the house, the telltale stiffening along his spine assuring that he's heard.

The worst of it is that she doesn't altogether understand what has happened. There's no question the entire span of days since his arrival have been strange—complicated and unsettled. But even so, Cat has no ready explanation for the origin or purpose of her outburst other than what feels to be a case of stark lunacy.

All he's done is announce what she's wanted to hear all along—that he's leaving.

It's an episode so regrettable on her part as to still be sitting squarely in the center of her mind hours later. The awareness of having gone too far in the wrong direction and now desperately anxious to make an immediate u-turn in order to double back to the place where she's so carelessly veered off course.

She forces her concentration onto painting the blanket chest she's been working on sporadically since Rance's arrival, sensing the necessary importance in being occupied and busy. A farm scene. Bucolic. Comforting.

As early as this morning she's had a dozen vibrant ideas for the project. But now, crouched before the chest, balancing her weight on her heels, she stares at the unfinished surface, her mind's eye staring back in a blank reflection of empty space. It is as if she's never seen a farm in her life; has lost all inkling as to what ingredients comprise such a customary and well-versed landscape. Every calendar glossy of home, field, and livestock she's ever retained in memory, cleared away in a single, obliterating sweep.

She harbors no illusions that he isn't already gone. Understandably he's been so thoroughly repulsed and disgusted by her insane outburst he's simply packed up and left. And while she hasn't actually eye-witnessed his departure, she can easily envision his route away from here as clearly as if she has.

The weary canvas bag carrying his possessions slung over his back—or maybe gripped firmly in his hand—as he makes the long trek back to town where he'll catch the very same bus that brought him to Lost River a week earlier. Only now he'll be heading back to Portland, or Green Oaks, or whatever town it is where his truck now waits at Sal's Garage. Gone. Simple as that. The last of Rance Barnett. The last of him and the cache of memories he's carried here—split wide open—then refused to share.

It's a wholly disappointing conclusion lying thick and heavy as a stone wedged into the pit of her stomach. And try as she does, Cat can neither ignore it or shake it loose.

So, this then is the price she is required to pay for all the years of self-imposed exile. All because she's succeeded so well in turning herself into some perverse variety of recluse, incapable even of navigating uncomplicated friendships or casual acquaintances. Just how far removed from normal has she drifted that a simple invitation to dinner extended by her dead husband's brother has so recklessly set her into a mortal tailspin?

She drops her brush on the lid of an open can, aware the paint-laden bristles will harden quickly in the heat. But the fact it will be ruined makes little difference. Really, no difference at all.

Thirty-two

Cat opens her eyes, the slant of sunlight coming through the window indicating the onset of late afternoon. She rolls onto her back and stares up at the ceiling, closes her eyes against the immediately rekindled recollection of the morning's events; an unfurling reel of images flickering behind her eyelids, mercilessly replaying the humiliating scene through to conclusion before abruptly restarting.

If she'd been gracious and accepted Rance's invitation as any normal person would've done, she would right now be dressing for dinner, rather than here, limp and contrite on a bed of remorse, donned in the same uniform she's worn for years: blue jeans and shirt faded to the point of nondescript. A wardrobe well matched to a life comprised of painting and perpetual mourning.

She pulls herself upright, limbs sluggish and heavy as she shifts her legs over the edge of the bed. A strand of sleep-twined hair falls across her eyes, but she makes no move to push it away. For a long while she sits without moving, unsure even how to go about forcing herself to rise to her feet.

It's likely she would remain right here, weighted to the mattress, drowning beneath the incoming waves of emptiness, if not for the fact it is several shades more depressing than going downstairs and returning to her accustomed routine of solitary suppers.

Why is it so impossible to admit, even within the safe harbor of her unseen thoughts, that it has been nice, comforting even, having Rance here under this roof? Not only for his presence down the hall at night—another body in residence to temporarily alleviate the hollow press of vacancy—but there is his undeniable link to Gray. A precious, fragile ligament she has callously severed.

She stands at the kitchen sink absently rinsing lettuce leaves for the salad she's decided to prepare but is unlikely to eat; lifting her gaze to the window just as Rance emerges from the dark fringe of woods hemming the back yard.

Her heartbeat skips forward, high stepping past its accustomed tempo. She watches as he walks slowly across the grass toward the house, her attentions caught and held by the stiff, uneven movements of his damaged leg.

He's still here. He hasn't gone after all. Not yet.

She wonders if maybe he's gone to the trestle. A simple enough consideration that lingers only a moment before swiftly accelerating and crashing head on with the sobering realization that, of course, Gray would've known about the trestle long before they unexpectedly happened upon it. *Gray had known.* Had been acquainted with the steel monster and every other thing erroneously deemed a mutual discovery or intriguing mystery.

And it isn't anger or even bitterness she feels falling inside with the force of colliding timbers, but rather, the impossible recognition she hasn't known Gray as fully and completely she's always believed. She wishes more than anything to pretend away the sobering heft of things distinctly changed—shifted off center, spiraled out of reach—but it is impossible. Her life with Gray is no longer a perfect thing in her memory.

Rance is gone now, abruptly leaving her field of vision as he rounds the back corner of the house.

She doesn't know what her precise words will be when he comes through the door, she only knows they will compose a necessary apology.

The lettuce rinsed, Cat washes tomatoes, cucumbers, and peppers, cutting each into neatly uniform slices she arranges in a clear glass bowl—an effort she would never extend solely for herself—but which now offers something of a distraction from the angst piling up around her as she contemplates her intended regrets.

She takes a moment from her efforts of vegetable collage to flip the potato wedges browning in a skillet on the stove. The hamburgers sizzling beneath the broiler are nearly done, and she slides the rack out just far enough to dress each plump patty with a slice of cheese.

Hopefully Rance will interpret the aroma of supper cooking as something of a peace treaty, drawing him into the house, where she will promptly—and sincerely—offer her apologies for the morning's regrettable scene.

Yet, just as she's done from the start, Cat has unequivocally misread Rance Barnett. She listens, but fails to hear his footsteps moving across the porch or the sound of the screen door opening and slapping shut. Instead, the house lays quiet and painfully bare beneath the pangs of expectation. Vacant beyond the hiss of meat juices popping under the broiler flame, and the empty whine of self-inflicted reprimands spinning on a loop inside her head.

For a long time afterward, as the yellow afternoon light turns watery blue on a steady slide into twilight, Cat paces the confines of the kitchen. She sits at the table … rises to stare out the window overlooking the backyard … sorts through the weeks of unread mail accumulated in a pile on the counter … all the while her senses tuned to waiting. And still, despite the focused determination of her efforts, no amount or degree of telepathic coaxing proves successful at drawing him in.

In the end she leaves a neatly arranged place setting on the kitchen table and the uneaten meal on the stove. (Minus the portion she serves herself, but is unable to eat—moving the food around on her plate in a play at eating before finally putting the meal out of its misery and scraping the long-cold contents into the kitchen wastebasket.)

His is as clear a message as she's ever received. That Rance is several layers more offended than Cat has hoped, is no less obvious than the truth he has no intention of offering her an opening toward redemption. No potential route exposed or flagged by arrows which might serve to detour her around the mess she's made.

For lack of any other plan or option, Cat takes a bath and climbs into bed, full well knowing she is hours away from any possibility of claiming sleep. Her mind has been running at full throttle since before sunrise, and it is altogether futile to expect the howling menagerie clamoring inside her mind to simply quiet once she lays down and closes her eyes.

She listens to the slow tick of minutes crawling past, staring wide eyed into the descending gloom as she accesses potential truths she hasn't been willing or ready to see before now.

From the start she has expected Rance to deliver answers he doesn't necessarily possess. Because if anything, the questions he's carried here share more than a passing resemblance to the ones Cat has amassed and piled up herself.

So why then can't he give her something of value? There must be something from his shared history with Gray that will help in her efforts to understand the nature and reasoning behind her husband's omissions and purposely veiled secrets.

What's more, he is leaving, so why does it matter what he tells her? What purpose is there in shutting the very door he's thrown wide open without first offering her a look inside? Why carry away a burden which so clearly belongs here within the mystery of its origins?

It is an unchanging ritual perfected over years of unhealed vacancy. Nights where sleep is as far removed as the dawn. Restless passages when Cat drifts through the house like a haunted whisper, roaming the gloom-draped hours in wait of the dull heft of weariness to eventually fall; enwrapping deadened mind and weary limbs and sinking her into a waning state of dreamless sleep.

Now, slipping quietly from her room, Cat hesitates in the upstairs hall, momentarily held motionless by the strangely sobering recognition that although he is soon to be gone, Rance is still here now—two doors away. Two doors away, roughly ten or eleven steps from where she stands, bare soles pressed against the cool wood floor, her breath soft and steady despite the disorderly rhythm tapping inside her chest like a flawed Morse code.

The darkness presses up against her like an audience of unseen hands, a crush of palms pushing harder with every instant tripping past; taunting Cat as she attempts to elbow past whatever is here hovering so close she can feel its breath licking hot across her shoulders.

She stares at the closed door of Rance's room, sensing the pull of something … something she refuses to recognize. With a deliberate yank, she pulls free, turns on her heel and hurries beyond reach of the dangerous thoughts forming in her head.

The air trapped within the walls feels unbearably oppressive, discomfortingly close and solid even once she descends the stairs to the yawning stretch of rooms below.

She passes into the front hall, pushes open the screen door carefully in an effort to minimize the squeak of long-ungreased hinges as she slips out onto the porch. The ancient floorboards, long worn of paint, feel cool as stones against the soles of her feet.

She breathes deeply with the effort to steady her raging senses.

How impossible it is to believe or even contemplate the avalanche that has come crashing down, changing everything. All these things Rance has come here with—those spoken and not—feel potentially shattering. Pivotal in a way that leaves this barren house feeling several degrees colder. Colder even than the eternally frigid world butting up against it.

A light breath of air stirs, drifting across the night, brushing the light fabric of her cotton nightgown against her legs in a slow, dancing rhythm.

"It's a nice night," Rance says, his voice curling out from the darkness.

Cat clamps a hand over her mouth, holding back the scream otherwise certain to awaken the house, the dead, and anything at rest for miles.

"Rance ..." she manages weakly, reaching to recover her voice, turning her head to see him sitting in one of the metal porch chairs.

"I couldn't sleep."

"Me neither."

His face is shrouded in shadow. Cat lifts her chin, feels his eyes watching her as if waiting for her to sit, or leave, or speak. When she remains where she is—holding still as several discomforting moments tick past—he makes a move as if to stand.

"Wait a minute," she says with quiet firmness, her courage wavering even as she says the words, then floundering miserably as she wrestles to untangle the knot lodged in her throat.

Finally, "I just wanted to say I'm sorry about this morning. I handled things badly. You didn't deserve that."

He doesn't immediately answer, and the all too obvious vacancy left by his lack of response stands between them loud and screaming.

"You don't like me much, do you, Cat?" he says finally. "And it's not just because we don't really know each other. It's something a good deal more complicated than that."

Cat sits in the chair opposite Rance—close, yet far enough removed to allow her to hold to the protective cloak of night separating them.

"You remind me of Gray, but in a painful way." For no reason other than it is dark and he is leaving, Cat doesn't rush to hide behind the curtain when she feels it slipping, leaving her exposed. There is little point in offering him anything other than straight-forward honesty now. "I can't exactly say why because you're both so different. But you do."

She pulls her legs up and hugs her knees under her chin, releasing a brief trembling breath as she fortifies her mind to surrender her thoughts. "I don't understand why you even came here, Rance. You claim you want to know things about Gray—about the kind of man he was—but you've never really asked me anything—at least nothing of depth. Nothing that makes me believe you honestly want to know.

"And now you're leaving and I can't figure out what I'm supposed to think. I don't understand what any of this was even about. It can't be that you wanted the truth, because the truth takes time, and I believe you know that."

She falls silent, waiting for him to say something. Moments pile into minutes. The night is no longer breathing around them, but lies still. She waits.

"I told you why I came," he says in a voice filled with thoughts. "I came here looking for Gray, wanting … hoping … I don't know, hoping we might be friends. Given enough time, maybe even brothers again.

"I never considered the possibility he wouldn't be here—that he'd be gone. I can't really tell you what I expected from you because I don't actually know. Just … I guess I was hoping you could tell me something. That you'd have an answer. You'd know what I needed to hear even when I don't know what it is myself. Maybe I just wanted to know everything turned out okay for him, despite … well, despite everything.

"And you're right, Cat, I realize it was more than a little foolish to expect someone to reconstruct another person like that—so simply. With a handful of words and the re-telling of a few shared memories. Gray was my brother, but I didn't know him. He might just as well have been some nameless person I passed on the street once or sat next to in a movie theatre. It's what I find hardest to admit to myself, but there's been too many years spanned out between us to pretend otherwise," he says, and she hears the sound of something lost and broken in his voice.

"When I asked the waitress at the diner if she knew Gray I could see she was completely thunderstruck—the way anyone would be when they're stuck having to tell someone that kind of news. Except the truth is, when she finally said it, I didn't feel what I know I should've. At least not the profound sort of grief you'd expect to feel over losing a brother. Sad, yes. But more the kind of sad you feel when you hear any tragic story. There's no emotional depth because it doesn't feel close enough to require mourning." He pauses, searching for the necessary words to clothe his thoughts.

"I guess what I'm trying to say is the reason I came out here to talk to you looked like the truth at the time, but maybe it was really only a lie I was telling myself. It seemed easier and a lot less painful than having to face the fact I'm twenty-five years too late in wanting to know him."

Cat slides her feet to the floor and leans forward ever so slightly; attempting to focus on the murky outline of his face, anxious to decipher in the occasional glimmer reflected back from his eyes, everything she believes she recognizes in his voice.

"I wish I had what you're asking for. I wish I could tell you what you need to know. But you've made it painfully clear that the Gray I was married to and the Gray who was your brother were not the same person."

"Yes, and I'm sorry. It was never my intent to trash your memories. That's why I don't blame you for this morning. I had it coming. I mean, I just showed up and dumped all this stuff on you when you weren't asking for it and that was pretty lousy. I'm sorry," he says again.

"Well, sorry isn't enough," she says, crossing her arms over her chest, grasping her shoulders in a bid to hold herself steady.

"There's nothing unreasonable in assuming Gray would've told me the truth about this house," she says, making every attempt to level her tone beneath the heavy press of unanswered questions piling and ready to fall.

"But what I can't understand—what I can't accept—is your insistence on secrecy. It makes me wonder who this is really about. Just who it is you think you need to shield?" she says, feeling the rise in her voice even before she hears it.

"Why can't you just tell me—tell me something—anything. What difference does it make to you either way? What could possibly change now, after all this time?"

"My point exactly," he says with clear finality, deliberately misinterpreted her words. The tiny opening momentarily uncovered between them snapping shut.

For a smoldering instant she envisions her hands reaching out and grasping his wide shoulders, shaking him hard enough to loosen his trove of buried secrets.

"Gray's past doesn't belong only to you. If he was sitting here, I'd ask him myself, but he's not and you are," she says slow and deliberate to keep from choking over the oncoming turbulence of surging emotion. "You say it wasn't your intention to stir all this up, but you have. You have, and now you owe me something. Even if it's just a piece of something."

Again the silence; a deliberate void turning the night several degrees colder in the span of a blinking eye.

He offers no response, lending Cat to believe he is gathering the words to most effectively rebuff her.

But when at last he speaks, it is nothing of what she is expecting.

"I feel nothing and everything being in this house again," his voice comes through the darkness low and quiet, devoid of emphasis which might otherwise suggest the profundity of his statement. "Maybe it's why I felt I had to go out to the trestle this afternoon—to prove to myself it no longer has a hold on me. I expected … well, I'm not sure what I expected. That damned ugly thing felt like an anchor holding me to this place when every part of me was fighting to get away from it. I never thought I'd ever …"

Cat slows her breathing, waits for him to continue, careful not to stir so much as the air between them—anything that might prove to remind him she is here on the other side of his words. Fully aware that, while he is at last giving her something of what she is asking for, it does not come easily or without sacrifice.

"I used to go out there all the time when I was a kid. Gray wasn't born yet and Anne was just a baby. It was the perfect place to daydream—safe from everything else. I never told anyone where I was going, I just snuck away every chance I got." He hesitates. Continues.

"My mother rarely went anywhere by herself after she married Otto. She believed he was a buffer against all the gossip—if he was with her, the whispers couldn't touch her. So it was pretty unusual when she went off alone one Saturday morning with Anne—shopping or maybe to visit someone—I don't know. They weren't gone ten minutes before Otto announced he wanted me to walk out to the trestle with him—just him and me. I wasn't surprised he knew about the trestle being there, everyone did, but I had this sick feeling there was something else going on in his mind. Otto never wanted me to do anything besides stay out of his way. To say he wanted to go for a walk was like declaring he was taking me to the moon.

"He never said a word the whole way out there, and it was his weird, smug silence that scared me more than anything else. By the time we reached the trestle, I was literally shaking in my shoes. He started across and motioned for me to follow. We were about halfway over when he just all of a sudden turned around and said, 'Here, right here—this is where you get off. Do it you little bastard. Do it—jump—you little shit.' He just kept repeating it. Screaming at me to jump. Angry, then furious when I just stood there."

"He didn't really expect—"

"He told me if I didn't jump he'd throw me off himself. I grabbed onto a support with both hands. I was so terrified I couldn't even scream when he pried my fingers loose—not even when he lifted me by the ankles and dangled me over the side," Rance continues, then halting, as if his own words have surprised or confused him.

"I can still remember what it was like staring down at the treetops, terrified that the pressure of blood rushing to my head would make my eyes pop out and I wouldn't be able to see myself falling when he dropped me—hoping there was something down there that might break my fall, so I might survive at least long enough to tell someone what he'd done.

"I tried saying a prayer in my head, knowing I only had a few seconds before he let go, but I couldn't think of any. And that scared me as much as him dangling me over the side of that damned bridge—the fear I'd go to hell because I didn't know a single prayer," he says, and then, for the first time since Cat has known him, he laughs; an oddly fragile sound fully devoid of amusement, but nevertheless a laugh.

"To this day I can't say with any real conviction if I think he honestly intended to drop me, or whether it was simply the thrill he got from instilling terror in another person that provoked him into doing it."

"Dear God," Cat whispers, so softly she isn't certain if she's said the words out loud. And suddenly she remembers the tin of photographs discovered years earlier, knowing without needing to ask whose pain she'd seen etched across those faded portraits.

"That's the kind of monster he was—terrifying enough to make an eight-year-old boy fear hell even more than the immediate prospect of having his brains splattered across the valley."

"But what about your mother? She must've known what he was like? Didn't she try and do something?" Cat says, gathering up the pieces of his revelation for a closer look, because it is so far beyond anything she's expected. And she understands without him needing to say it outright that he isn't simply detailing an isolated incident, but is in fact revealing an abbreviated portion of things infinitely deep rooted and complicated.

All at once, hurtling through the dark tunnel of a painfully sprung memory—spilling into a deep-laid swath leaving a visible stain across her thoughts—is the forceful recollection of her own mother's inadequate defenses against her father's torments.

"She was devoted to him," he states simply. "Not because he was a loving husband—far from it. It was more about him filling a vacancy. She had a hard time enduring the shame of being an unwed mother—especially at a time when such things were still considered a top-tier sin," Rance says, tapping out a cigarette from the pack lying on the table beside him, rolling it in his fingers, but declining to light it.

"I can't honestly say what her true feelings for Otto might've been. But I do know she was crazy about my father—her and apparently a half dozen other woman around here. For whatever reasons, she had herself convinced she was *the one* and she firmly believed he'd get around to marrying her once she had his child. Except he never did. Maybe he thought there was too much he'd have to give up. People said what he lacked in morals he more than made up for with charm," Rance says, turning his face toward Cat, allowing her to catch the briefest glimmer of light reflected in his eyes.

"But I wouldn't know. I didn't see all that much of him. When he did show up, he always had something for me—a little model airplane, or a piece of candy, some plastic army men, stuff like that. Just a few cheap toys I used to keep in an empty cigar box he'd given me. Somehow I knew it was all I'd ever have of him. That box and a couple of pictures. He died young. Apparently run off the road by a jealous husband.

"I was very careful to keep that box hidden in the back of my closet and out of sight of Otto's radar. But one day I slipped up and left it on the floor next to my bed when my mother called me outside to take in the washing. When I came back inside it was gone. It was the first and last time he ever won his game at trying to make me cry. I pleaded with him to give the box back, even while knowing full well the unlikelihood of such a thing. After a week or so of him taunting me with it, I forced myself to pretend I didn't care about it anymore, hoping he would lose interest and I could somehow get it back. But things with Otto were never that easy. It was like he could see into my head and knew exactly what I was planning.

"I understood what was coming when he hauled me out to the backyard and made me sit on the ground while he lit a fire in the burning barrel. He took his time about it and made sure I was watching as he tossed each toy into the flames one by one."

Cat drops her gaze, swallows against the tight knot hardening at the back of her throat, all too familiar with this particular brand of cruelty. Having no clearer understanding of it when applied to Rance's life than she has when reflecting on her own—this sadistic penchant to cause deliberate suffering upon another human being.

"My mother couldn't handle being an unmarried woman with a child. Especially in a place like Lost River, where even a neighbor's grocery list is cause for discussion. She considered not having a husband more of a curse than a self-inflicted circumstance. She was convinced everyone was talking about her—though to be fair, they probably were. I figure it was easier for her to rationalize Otto's abuses by agreeing I must've had it coming than it would've been to admit she was sleeping with the devil."

"But what about Gray? Your sister?"

"Anne has no interest in talking except to say 'they're both dead, the past is the past, leave it alone.' And when it comes to Gray, I can only guess. Otto made no secret of his resentment toward me because I wasn't his son, but I always hoped their status as his blood offspring provided them with some sort of armament against his cruelty."

Cat feels his eyes, full and close, watching her.

"But, now, seeing what he's done here—the paintings—I have to wonder if maybe they're the answer to that question."

"Gray's murals?"

"My very first thought when you said Gray had done them was that he'd gotten even."

"Even for what?"

"He was never a bad kid—pretty much my polar opposite considering I always seemed to be doing something wrong—but he had an obsession for drawing on the walls with crayons. It earned him a few spankings, but it wasn't enough to make him stop. When Otto threw away the crayons, Gray switched to colored pencils. When those got tossed, it was chalk he smuggled home from school in his lunchbox. If not for Otto getting so worked up over it, the fact the kid couldn't be deterred might've been almost funny. That Gray turned out to be an artist couldn't be more perfect," Rance says, his voice holding the sound of a hidden smile.

"But I don't know. I can't say what their lives were like. I left home a week before my fifteenth birthday and it's the last time we ever saw each other. I sent Gray a couple postcards once, but that's it. I didn't really know how to reconnect once so much time had passed.

"That he came back here says a lot. It's hard to believe he'd be able to live in this house if his life here had been anything like mine. Unless maybe his purpose had something to do with *conquering the beast*—something like that. Still, it doesn't explain why he kept any of this from you, does it? I can only assure you I'm telling you the truth when I say I don't know that part of it. I honestly don't know."

She senses there are entire chapters he might add, but won't. Just as she understands the horrific remembrance he's given her is hard earned and the retelling difficult. And right now, at least for this moment, it feels as if he's said all that is necessary.

For the first time Cat finds herself wanting to share her own past with another person. To reveal the unspeakable horrors that have carved out her early life and set the mold for everything engrained across her future. She longs to tell him everything. To unburden the entirety of her own living nightmare. Certain he will understand what no one else possibly can, for the simple fact Rance himself has endured a history of pain.

In opening his wounds and allowing her a glimpse inside, Rance has struck the deadened place cached deep within Cat's own rocky soil, the tightly secured binding all but undone by his words.

But just like that, in the flash of an instant, it is over. Cat reaches to grasp the moment before it passes, but it is already gone; the distance spanning their separate torments at once returned when the unidentified something moving between them sweeps out of reach, shutting the door as it leaves.

"I'll need to head out pretty early tomorrow if I hope to catch the bus. Sal said he'll be at the garage most of the day so …" he doesn't finish, pushes himself up from the chair. Cat feels the weight of his stare slipping across the darkness to rest on her.

"I'm glad I met you, Cat," he says quietly. "I'm just sorry that … I wish it had been different for you."

She wants to reach out and hold him there. Make him stay until she's told him everything he's churned to the surface. But she doesn't. She doesn't move. She doesn't say anything at all.

The night presses in, screaming loud and shrill, and Cat nearly misses his final words.

"Take care of yourself, okay?" The screen door whines shut behind him and he is gone. Dissolving into the black shadows crowding the silent house as though he's never been here at all.

Thirty-three

For a long while after he goes inside, Cat remains on the porch, her thoughts pulsing behind her forehead and radiating into her temples in an erratic race toward an unreachable finish line.

Is it true Gray too has lived a life shadowed by fear and abuse? Is their deepest connection one they have never shared? It seems so unlikely. Impossible even. It is all so far removed from the person she's known—the caring, gentle man she's loved with the certain assurance of believing he is so unlike herself.

It's true there have been questions passing through—fleeting enough not to settle, but nevertheless apparent. Quiet, yet tangible indicators she's misread certain essential clues: the vanished tin of photographs, his sporadic episodes of restless nighttime wanderings marked by frenetic painting, his too-easy willingness to leave their separate histories unspoken and questions unasked. If only they'd shared those ugliest parts of their lives. If only they'd delved that deep and gone that far.

A light flicks on in an upstairs window and Cat stares transfixed at the weak square of yellow light cast out onto a patch of lawn.

He is right now gathering together his things, readying for an early departure.

The morning lies in wait only a few hours away.

In the watery light of dawn, Rance will descend the stairs carrying the single canvas bag he arrived with gripped in one hand, his jacket in the other.

Maybe Cat will plan to be up herself, showered and dressed, ready with an offer to drive him into town. She doesn't expect they will talk much as she drives, both feeling shy with each other after the distinctly personal revelations left unclothed and glaring in the light of this night's conversation.

When they arrive at the bus stop there will be an awkward exchange of goodbyes—the simple, generic variety extended between casual acquaintances who never expect to lay eyes on each other again. Then she'll pull away, briefly glancing back through the rearview mirror where she'll see him standing on the curb, watching her leave. Her eyes holding to his reflection in the glass until she turns the corner at Peabody's Hardware Store and loses sight of him forever.

And she will return here to this house and the stagnant life she's been living up until his crash-landing interruption a week ago, where she will pass the remainder of the day right here on this very porch, thinking about everything, thinking about nothing, painting the same insignificant piece of furniture she's been attempting to finish for the past several days; brushing several gazing cows onto the hillside, a silo beside a barn, fence circumscribing a pasture, a few scattered trees...

She'll reheat one of the cheeseburgers left untouched from tonight's supper and she'll sit down for a solitary meal, attempting all the while to pretend away the heartache of her isolation and the tangled confusion of newly revealed truths.

A state of aloneness made all the more poignant in the face of these past days when she's had something more. Someone here besides the dull echo of herself.

Cat pushes up from her chair and moves to the edge of the porch, glancing up to see that Rance has finally turned off the light and gone to bed. The night returns to full dark.

The bedroom door yawns slightly ajar in an uncertain cue. Her heart knocks heavy and loud inside her chest, the very sensation of it reminding her to breathe. Her mind feels feathery light and faraway, her body tingly and jittery all at once, as if her skin is being pricked by a thousand sharp needles.

For a long moment she holds herself still, just on the other side of his door, knowing that to enter is in every sense to never return.

He is awake but says nothing. She can see the faint glimmer of his eyes watching in the dark as her steps carry her toward him, deliberate, as she is uncertain. She feels something as yet unrecognizable drawing her closer, the clear lines of his features now swimming into focus.

"Cat …" he says quietly as she sits carefully on the edge of the bed, touching her hand to his bare chest exposed above the pale sheet gathered at his waist. "I can't be Gray for you."

She doesn't answer, flattening her palm—absorbing the heat of his skin—her fingers quivering as his warmth races up along the length of her arm. He doesn't move—lies still beneath her hand.

"I know," she says, barely above a whisper, unwilling to hear the distraction of her own voice. "I couldn't … I would never ask for that."

She leans forward haltingly. Careful. Touches her mouth to his face. His cheek … his lips.

His response is slow in coming, as someone abruptly stirred to unfamiliar surroundings, gaining wakefulness as Cat unfolds against the length of him.

He lifts his arms, encircling her back, pulling her against his chest in a way that causes her insides to scramble madly behind her ribs.

The taste and smell of him press in around her. The fabric of his skin like warm liquid melting in through her open pores. She feels herself falling like sunlight through glass—lost to him in an instant—wholly unwilling to pull herself back, even as she feels the world tumbling away. The only sound beyond the rhythm of breathing is the rush of blood in her ears, rapidly pumping through veins and arteries linking body and brain.

"Cat," Rance whispers thickly against her mouth, cradling the back of her head in one of his hands. His lips trail along her cheek as he speaks her name, then returning to her lips, drawing her in with the fervor of his kiss.

His breath is warm in her hair and she reaches around him as his touch moves to erase the dust of time, returning her sweetly to that distant season when she was last alive. And she holds to the wide expanse of his shoulders, afraid of falling away from this moment and back into the hollow shell of her existence.

He kisses her … holds her … strokes her … loves her with a thoroughness she's all but forgotten, as if he too comprehends that this fleeting interlude passing between them requires a certain potency to endure over the continuing stretch of solitary years.

She doesn't speak when Rance slides one hand along the curve of her back, gently shifting her in his arms and easing her back, her hair spilling out behind her in a golden cloak.

Her breath catches sharply at the back of her throat when he lifts his head to stare at her. And in his face—a visage long accustomed to masking emotion rather than displayed it, a face customarily composed and insular—Cat sees something changed.

"You're so beautiful," he says with eyes that seem to swallow her, drawing her into the deepening intensity of some raw emotion. And when he pulls her against the length of him—the single sheet separating them somehow gone—she comprehends with every molecule of being that she must sustain the entirety of this night in her mind intact. Every breath, every touch, every whisper.

And her eyes never leave him, trying hard to remember everything.

Thirty-four

Cat knows even before she opens her eyes that he is gone. She can feel his vacancy stretched out beside her, a barren field too broad and screamingly desolate to pretend away.

Even so, when she rolls over and opens her eyes against the white morning light, it is with the desperate hope her instincts are blessedly wrong and his dark, gold-flecked eyes will be right there staring back at her.

But no, of course. She is alone. Nothing redolent of Rance other than an indent in the pillow where his head has been. She has known to expect this. She understands the hours with Rance have been something … a gift maybe. But not a promise.

She is a body tumbling through space, hurtling a million miles away from her very self—heading toward a bottomless vacancy. The urge to cry, to retch, to react in some way, hovers thick and moist in air too full to swallow. She reminds herself she has come to his bed without expectation. She understands it is merely some crazy sense of aching that has brought her here. Loneliness, yearning, or something like it. She's wanted nothing more than to have him touch and hold and love her before he leaves. To pretend it actually means something. And he's done that. Responded like a lover. Only now it feels altogether unbearable because it is over and he is gone.

Yet there's no question he's done the right thing. The only thing. There is no other option but the one he's taken, which is to simply leave. She understands this.

Cat pulls on jeans and a sleeveless blouse stained with paint from the previous day, intent on smoothing the ragged edges of her thoughts with a tonic of reasoning she doesn't feel.

Goodbyes are foolish. Awkward. Particularly in the bright light of morning when the memories of a previous night are still too fresh and there is nothing to hide behind.

She carelessly drags a brush through her hair; continues raking the bristles through tangled strands as she silently coaxes the troubled reflection staring back from the bathroom mirror to believe it would've been an experience worse than awful had she been challenged to face him. Dreadful. Humiliating. And yet even as she piles up her convictions in an essential alibi—assures herself she believes them—the words feel like a hideous lie inside her head.

Why has she let this happen? Why has she done this to herself? Why, when she knows the only possible outcome even before the onset?

She swings her gaze away from the unblinking eyes of grief watching her, reaches for her shoes and heads downstairs to put on coffee.

The safest thing, the only thing, is to pick up the severed strands of her life where she's dropped them. Blink awake from this mirage and refocus if she hopes to recover the fragments scattered in every direction like dandelion seeds from the instant of Rance's disturbing appearance. It is in reconstructing her familiar routine of ordinary and uninspired days that she will forget him. Forget that he was ever here.

This juncture with Rance is altogether distant from the love and passion she's had with Gray. There are no promises. No future. No intended durability. A week from now she will find herself questioning if it was even real.

And yet, as Cat stands in the kitchen—filling the pot with water, measuring coffee into the filter—she presses her hipbone into the counter, instinctively bracing against the incoming waves of emptiness all at once rolling over her in a suffocating tide.

"Damn it … damn it … how will I do this …" she cries in a choked whisper, the words tearing something loose inside. She grasps the edge of the sink; regaining her balance even as she feels the waiting arms of melancholy reaching out to enfold her in its embrace.

And she knows she'll do it simply because she has to. Because there is no alternate plan.

Nothing moves in the bright white sun spanning out beyond the cool shadows of the porch. Cat stares across the yard, seeing nothing in particular, the familiarity of the landscape having long turned it nondescript.

How impossible that he's already been gone one full day. Nearly twenty-four hours.

And though she understands it will only deepen the hollow core of vacancy yawning wide to swallow every other sensation she holds inside, Cat closes her eyes, remembering what it had felt like to be loved again after such a long, deep absence. Her heart, mind, and flesh gently coaxed to life with the sweet pain of recollection. And she hates herself for her weakness, for remembering so well. For wanting him back here.

Not even a goodbye. Why not even a goodbye?

It is a morning no different than the two previous. Cat sits on the porch with her shoes in her lap, her mind racing behind closed eyes, chasing after an image that is already beginning to lose its essence with every minute ticking past.

Enough. She has to shift her mind away from him … leave him behind and begin the process of forgetting ... force him to fade into the hazy place of distant dreams.

Doesn't she deserve this agony after succeeding so well in orchestrating her own betrayal? For so effortlessly convincing herself one night is only that—an arrangement of hours to be experienced without the promise of resounding consequence. Somehow it feels like the worst thing she's ever done—allowing herself to believe living with the memory of a moment will be enough when she so well knows the hideous lie in this. It is a misstep made all the more grievous for the fact neither fate nor circumstance is to blame. She has done this to herself. Inflicted the crippling blow with her own hand.

Her eyes snap open to the sound of tires rolling over hard-packed earth. Her shoes, forgotten in her lap, smack against the floorboards with a dull thwack when she stands and moves to the edge of the porch, staring hard at the vehicle cautiously creeping along the driveway.

She stays there rooted at the top of the porch steps even once the truck breaks to a stop in the dooryard, watching as Rance opens the door and steps down from the cab. He glances up and sees her, pauses, burns her insides with a look. And then he is all at once smiling, coming on.

She feels her legs carry her down the porch steps when she is unable to issue the command herself, moving toward him warily, her bare feet stirring the dust. She lifts a hand and touches a finger against her lips to keep them from quivering. And while she doesn't right away sense it, her eyes are wet and threatening to spill in the brief seconds it takes to reach him.

He pulls her against him without speaking, gently holding her where she presses her face into his shoulder.

"I thought you'd gone—" she says, the sob in her voice muffled against his shirt.

He cradles the back of her head with one hand, breathing his words softly against her hair. "I just went to get my truck and clear my head a little. I suddenly found myself with a lot to think about," he says, pausing, then, "But you knew I was coming back, didn't you, Cat?"

She can hear the shy uncertainty of a smile in his voice and her heart takes a wild lurch around a sharp curve.

"I'll leave if you want me to, but you'll have to say it. Because I won't otherwise. You'll have to tell me to go."

"Please stay," is all she says.

There is not so much as a semblance of doubt creeping in along the edges of her mind to dispel the conviction what she feels for Rance is something of love. But it is the sort that comes without pledge or assurance. It is simply there, quiet and filling and vibrantly alive in the present, while at the same time pointedly distanced from the future.

Because Gray is here—will always be here. Regardless of passing years, he is unmistakably present, his very essence melded into the walls and fibers of this house; wafting through quiet rooms on an unsettled current weighty with motes of ancient dust and long-past things, never having left this place where she now lives and sleeps beside his brother.

And yet ever so subtly, the soft and gentle image of Gray she has carefully held for all these years, gently wrapped and tucked within her heart, is gradually slipping, shifting in ways she is not prepared to see.

Increasingly what she feels is anger. Whether fair or not, deserved or unwarranted, rational trails at a distance. It's true she is likewise guilty of gross omission, but her purpose in sheltering certain truths has always felt honest and necessary, where in comparison, Gray's unraveling secrets distinctly appear as something else. Deception. Betrayal.

Never mind that her logic is questionable and not altogether reasonable, the raging of emotion easily shouts past the quieter efforts of reason.

How have they succeeded so well at being dishonest? So gifted at turning their mountains to molehills?

Cat makes something of an effort to dissuade Rance when he suggests having a look at the assortment of failing bandages and impending surgeries requiring attention if she hopes to keep the house alive through another winter.

"Of course I appreciate the offer, Rance, but it's not your responsibility. And besides, where would you even start? It's a mess."

"I'll start with dire and work my way to imperative."

"And ignore disastrous?"

"All in due time, my dear," he grins, sealing the deal.

With Rance here taking on the weight of necessary things, Cat is left free to reclaim her unfinished projects and abandoned pursuits where she's left them piled to grow dust. There is nothing to divert her from picking up a paint brush and getting back to work on pieces she started months ago in the hope of rekindling Judy's enthusiasm for her creations.

If only she can make herself ignore Rance and the concentrated urge to watch everything he is doing. Whether hammering, sawing, plastering … it is all but impossible to keep her focus trained on her own endeavors and away from wondering what he is right now thinking. What he is right now remembering.

Cat raises her hand in a brief wave as she heads into town, the blanket chest she's finally finished after weeks of false starts, anchored protectively in the truck bed. She glances back at Rance standing in the yard and something rolls up inside her chest—tips, spills warm and thick behind her ribs—her stare holding fast until the only thing visible in the rearview mirror is the spiraling dust stirring up from the truck's tires.

And as swiftly as a sigh, her enthusiasm is all but vanished, washed away by the sick taste of fear flooding into the back of her throat, assuring that despite his promise, Rance will be gone when she returns.

It is a sense of doom that never quite settles; rides shotgun all the way into town. An uninvited sidekick she is unable to shake loose well enough to toss it out into the ditch at the side of the road.

And it isn't until later, once she speeds back home and finds him not far removed from where she's left him replacing a rotted clapboard—only now, re-glazing a window—that the heavy weight of dread settles, her anxiety tumbling away as effortlessly as it initially arrives.

Cat finds it remarkably easy to overlook, even forget for a time, that they've only known each other for a handful of weeks, and for the most part, their separate histories remain largely unspoken. She has no intention of repeating the pattern of omission so regrettably constituted with Gray. And yet she senses with Rance, while the truth must and will come, it will be a gradual, careful thing, as it is with a certain brand of stories requiring unfolding in their own way, at their own time.

But for now there is a certain comfort in knowing that while the telling of some things may very well prove painful or imperfect or infinitely damaging, none of it need come until later. At present there is a purposeful ignorance screening the deepest components of their respective lives. Past things quietly obscure and contained, aside from occasional glimpses when a brittle piece of something breaks loose and rises to the surface.

It is late afternoon when Rance comes into the kitchen, moving to the sink to wash his hands while Cat busies herself setting the table.

"Would you like a cold beer with your supper?" she asks, glancing up from the task of aligning cutlery on carefully folded napkins. The past week has been discomfortingly hot, one blistering day piled onto the next with no traces of relief in between, and so Cat has thought to stop at the liquor store in town after picking up a few essentials at the market, acting on the impulse that like Gray, Rance will appreciate a frosty can on this inferno of a day.

He doesn't immediately answer and Cat is on the verge of repeating the question since his mind is clearly off in some other direction and her words have passed unheard.

"No thanks. Water's fine," he says a moment later.

She feels ridiculously disappointed by his refusal, as if she's failed miserably at a simple test of assuming his taste.

"Are you sure?" She says to his back. "It's ice cold."

He turns, eyes her levelly as he dries his hands on the dishtowel she's left draped over the handle of the stove. "I don't drink, but you go ahead and have one," he says kindly.

"Oh," Cat says. And later she will wonder whether it is a glimmer of childish disappointment registering on her face that causes him to elaborate.

"Actually, I'd love a beer. The colder the better. But I can't," he says, trying a smile that doesn't quite reach completion. "One of the stricter rules at AA."

"Oh … I'm sorry."

Now, when his grin emerges it easily reaches the proportions of genuine. "Sorry I went? Or sorry you can't get me drunk and have your way with me?"

"Sorry you had to go," she says, feeling a pang of regret for whatever it is that has sent him off in such a direction; returning his smile before the weight of awkward discomfort has an opportunity to drop and settle.

"Though I'm willing to bet I can still have my way with you," she says, steering back to safer ground.

She crosses to where he is still standing at the sink and lifts her face to kiss him … long … lazy … and warm. And even as he grasps her waist and lifts her to sit on the counter in front of him, she is thinking she will discretely pour the contents of the offending cans down the drain after supper while she is washing up the dishes.

"Rance … what happened to your leg?" It's a question that's piqued her curiosity for some time, yet she's lacked the courage or gumption to mention it. His stiff, unnatural stride is an imperfection he appears especially adept at pretending away—the assurance of which is clearly apparent in the way he carries himself—proud? defiant? though maybe neither of those things. And now, when she at last ventures to speak the question out loud, she immediately fears she's made a mistake in prying too soon.

They've spent the entire morning in the garden tearing away thick handfuls of weeds threatening to choke the rows of fledgling tomato plants and golf ball sized lettuce heads. Because although Cat has long given up on the prospect of successfully growing a garden, Rance has easily convinced her otherwise.

"You've obviously never experienced the exquisite taste sensation of a green bean direct from the vine or pulled up a carrot, wiped the dirt on your pants leg, and eaten it on the spot," he grins.

"No," Cat smiles. "I can't say I have, but if the woodchucks around here could talk, they'd likely agree with you."

As impossible as it would seem, considering the years she'd been indentured to tend the Carper's garden with Leafie—required to plant, water, and weed—the sisters had never been allowed to sample the fruits of their labors or otherwise savor the harvest.

"Once you do, you'll never be without a garden. Just wait until everything starts growing by the bushel basket. You'll be smitten."

Now, she waits for him to answer her question, but his response is slow in coming. The obvious stiffening along the line of his back assures he's heard the question, and she knows she will not repeat what has clearly unnerved him. She well understands the need to discard things serving no purpose other than to rekindle painful experiences, and she's immediately sorry for bringing it up.

"I had polio when I was a kid."

"Polio … how frightening. Just you? What about Gray and Anne?" she asks, at once recognizing it is the first time she's spoken Gray's name out loud in weeks. Not because she has so easily ceased thinking of him, but because she is ever conscientious to the fact he is here—is always here—firmly established in such a way even the briefest mention of his name holds the potential for erecting a monument within the space tentatively occupied by herself and Rance. And she is not ready to leap this hurtle. So very far from ready.

"No. Just me. My mother was careful to keep me isolated for the duration."

Cat nods, but offers nothing further, sensing his reluctance to elaborate. She returns her attentions to the business of weeds even as she carefully squirrels away this newly acquired fragment with all the others collected thus far. Satisfied she is yet one step closer to composing the picture Gray has failed to paint for her.

Thirty-five

On occasion, when she stumbles over a hairline crack or detects the faintest glimpse of an opening, Cat allows herself either a simple inquiry or full-on question with the belief each acquired morsel will in time allow her to understand something of Rance the man and his complicated history in this house.

The one thing she doesn't ask—the question she shoulders like a patient tensed in wait of a grim diagnosis—simply because she isn't prepared to hear his answer: Where does he intend to go once the time comes for leaving?

She knows that to lend voice to her fears is to likewise acknowledge an entire world of imperfection and complication continues to exist beyond the protective boarder circumscribing the sanctuary of their days here. And while she understands there will be a conclusion to their affair someday, she refuses to consider the inevitable moment before its time.

For now there are other things she wants to know, random curiosities that skim across her thoughts in quick flashes. They are unexceptional inquiries anyone might ask, but which feel monumental to Cat, if only for the fact she knows so little about Rance.

"Have you ever been married?" she asks, keeping her gaze on the single band of tangerine light sinking low behind the trees as if the question is not so much deliberate as it is an afterthought.

She's left the supper dishes to soak in the sink, anxious to join Rance when he heads outside. For a long while they sit side by side in a pair of metal porch chairs, hands joined and resting on Rance's thigh as they stare out into the yard, watching evening come.

As far as questions go, this one is culled from the file marked Relatively Uncomplicated. Not especially personal or prying. Just a question. Simple. Or at least this is her assumption until he finally responds and she knows from his tone she's tumbled into something of depth.

"I came close once … but no, I haven't," he says, and the lack of inflection in his voice speaks volumes.

"Oh … do you think you ever might?" she presses past the immediate warning sense to leave this alone, if only because his answer suddenly feels very important and altogether necessary.

"I don't know. I've never been very good at relationships," he says, and she feels something shift inside—then sharply swerve. "I guess maybe I come with too much baggage."

What does he mean? How much is *too much*? Who doesn't have something unpleasant, possibly devastating, they carry around inside their head, under their skin, sunk to the floor of their stomach, dragging from their ankles?

For a swollen stretch of airless minutes Cat ponders asking him to elaborate on his meaning, but doesn't. Because now there is something of greater importance weighed between them like a dropped anchor. Something she hardly dares think about, if only because she lacks the necessary fortitude to see it.

She waits for the last sapphire strands of twilight to sink below the edge of sky and surrender to full darkness before slipping her fingers from Rance's easy clasp, deliberately placing her hand in her lap. She turns away from the voice traipsing back and forth in her mind with the insistence she stop now and swallow the words before they chance to leave her tongue. Because once they are said, there will be no retrieving them or otherwise pretending they haven't been spoken.

"You haven't told me how you feel, Rance … how you feel about me," she says and her voice sounds very small and faraway as it tumbles out into the space between them.

The night dims several shades. The air stretches thick and unyielding into the broad eternity passing before he finally speaks.

"It's because of Gray—because of you and Gray," he says slowly, carefully. "It doesn't make enough of a difference how little I really knew him, he was still my brother ... and you've never made it a secret how much you loved him."

Rance reaches into her lap reclaiming her hand, holding it tight to keep her from pulling away. She feels his eyes seeking connection across the darkness, but she cannot turn her head to meet his gaze.

"Sometimes I get the feeling you're looking at me, but really seeing him," he says. And his words run through her, sharp and burning.

"If you really believe that then why do you stay? How can you stay?" Cat says, stung by his admission.

He releases her hand and pulls himself up, moves away and leans his shoulder against a porch post. He remains facing her, but his gaze moves past to some safer distance.

"I hoped I'd learn to accept it—that you'd never fully care for me the same way you did for Gray. I figured it was a fair trade if it meant having even a small part of you."

She hears something in his tone. Something that pushes her heart up into her throat.

There are discernible threads of painful things in his voice. A subtle inflection she's heard before and again recognizes.

He turns his face to take in the night and Cat rises, crossing to where he stands. She feels his back stiffen as she wraps her arms around him and rests her cheek against his shoulder blade.

"It's because you're not Gray that I can love you. I thought you understood that," Cat speaks softly, nearly a whisper. "And I do, Rance. I do love you," she promises, speaking the words she hasn't considered saying until now.

Thirty-six

Somewhere downstairs Rance is whistling, and hearing him makes Cat smile. She rolls over in bed, tucking the sheet under her chin, still warm and sweetly sated from the lingering essence of his body heat.

The mornings have all at once turned chilly. There is nothing gradual in days leaning toward autumn, and it is becoming increasingly difficult to leave the comfort of flannel sheets and wool blankets in exchange of goose-pimpled flesh and cold wood floors beneath bare soles.

She turns her gaze toward the window, disappointed to see the smoky white sky framed in the sash; a day much like the one previous, when the sun hadn't seen to trouble itself with coming out.

The coffee is already made and warming in the pot when Cat finally treads downstairs, showered and dressed, mentally listing her intended projects for the day.

The house is quiet. Apparently Rance has already gone outside to tinker with something he's started and mentioned to her the day before but which she now can't recall the specifics of.

He is growing restless, his unease becoming increasingly obvious as summer gradually slides to a close. And as often as Cat has warned herself over the inevitability of this juncture, now when she can see its actual approach, she has no way of knowing how she will either counter or accept it, and so she simply works to pretend it away.

She understands that one day, possibly soon, Rance will tell her he is leaving. It is a forthcoming hour she's known to expect from the beginning—feels looming like a stormy threat in the distance. And yet she possesses no secret stores of necessary strength or stamina she might draw forth to survive it, other than to continue pushing the determined force of an oncoming future back into the deepest, darkest corner and out of sight for as long as she can.

Cat passes the morning sketching a small chest of drawers, outlining a gathering of fairies in the midst of a meadow tea party.

Shortly before noon she takes a break to prepare a sandwich for Rance's lunch and pour herself a glass of iced tea. While she's long fallen out of the habit of pausing from her work to eat a meal, she now anticipates her mid-day intermissions with Rance.

"I was thinking I'd start putting in some of the storm windows for you. There won't be many warm days left before winter."

"If you really want to," she shrugs, trying not to see the apparent suggestion in his choice of tasks.

Is he conscientiously preparing the house for a winter she will be spending alone?

"There's quite a few that haven't been changed since Gray … in years. I fully admit I'm not the most responsible home owner."

"Don't pick on yourself. You do okay. There's a lot to look after in a house this size. It can be overwhelming," he says, pushing his chair back and rising to set his empty plate in the sink.

"That looks nice," he says now, turning his attention to the chest she is painting. "Those cherubs are cute."

"Fairies."

"Oh … they're not the same thing?"

"Nope."

He watches her for a quiet moment, then, "I seem to remember the windows being stored in the basement. Do you still keep them down there?"

"Um hum … most of them should be there," she answers absently over her shoulder, her attentions returning to her task.

She could just as easily admit how she never descends to the basement unless absolutely necessary—to reset a blown fuse or relight the pilot light in the furnace—but she sees no point in stirring up anything which might require elaboration. There is a certain density in the air beneath the house she finds difficult to breathe. Something unpleasantly probing in the stark, white light glaring from the single bare bulb dangling from the ceiling at the foot of the stairs. The chilling suggestion of unseen things—musty and damp with ancient odors—that carry her to a place beyond shivery. It is an awful place Cat has disliked from first glance. And while she knows there are surely windows stored there, she never has and never will care enough to venture down and claim them.

Rance leans down to kiss the top of her head; the screen door twang thudding shut a moment later as he goes out.

The background is more or less as she envisions it; wild flowers interspersed amongst feathery threads of pale green meadow grass. But it is the creation of the fairies proving to be the greatest frustration, flatly refusing to materialize from paint and brush in the same proportions Cat has composed in her mind. Rance's observation is in fact spot on. They actually are far more resembling of plump, round-cheeked cherubs than they are of slight, delicate fairies.

Somewhere in the idle space tucked behind her immediate thoughts, Cat registers the sound of Rance in the living room banging on a stuck screen. From his diligent rapping she knows it is the window facing the side yard. She hasn't bothered with it in years for precisely this reason.

Oh hell—she's really making a mess of this. Not only do her fairies not look like fairies, they no longer look like cherubs either. In her ill-conceived attempts at transition, the once tiny bodies now bear a distinct resemblance to squat potato dumplings sprouting arms and legs. Unredeemable casualties of too much tampering. It would've been best to leave them alone to be fat and happy cherubs—back when they were still recognizable as such.

"The storms from the front room aren't with the others. Did you put them somewhere else?" Rance asks, coming into the kitchen.

"The front room?" she repeats, considering his question as she straightens her spine and leans back on her heels. "Umm … actually, those have been missing for years. Maybe they got broken at one time or another and were never replaced."

There's no way around it. She'll have to paint over the entire scene and start over. Still, she hates to lose the background. It has come out quite well. Particularly the tree stump table set with acorn cups and green leaf saucers. Well maybe if she is extremely careful—

"I guess I'll check the attic. They might've gotten mixed up with the ones for the bedrooms."

Cat nods without answering, thoroughly immersed in the dilemma of how best to rework the scene with minimal ruin.

Somewhere in the back of her mind she registers the sound of Rance's heavy footsteps ascending the stairs to the second floor—then further removed, but still discernable—his tread thudding up the final flight to the attic.

She opens a can of dark green paint, stirring it absently as she glares at the hideous non-fairies, then dips the brush, beginning the altogether frustrating process of relinquishing nearly an entire day's work.

More than any other thing, it is the too-long stretch of quiet following his ascent to the top of the house that brings the horrible realization slamming head on. So swift and unexpected, for a pulsing span of airless minutes she stays where she is without moving, anchored to the floor, heart madly bouncing between opposing poles of nausea and all out terror.

He's gone to the attic.

He told her. He told her where he was going and she wasn't listening. She heard what he said, but she wasn't paying attention. He told her and she didn't do a single thing to divert him. And it is the ever-widening span of time he's been gone which most assures he's found it—her awful, hideous monster.

He is descending the stairs now; each step landing like a cinder block dropped square onto her chest. And when he appears in the doorway, staring at her with an expression dark and terrible, there is no question of what he has seen or how much he has absorbed. The hideous panorama spanning the attic wall all right there in his face turned to stone.

Her hands begin to tremble, though it is just as likely they have been quaking all along, and she wraps her arms tight across her chest to keep her madly slamming heart from splintering out through skin and bone. The flesh of her face and neck feel both hot and cold at the same time, exposed like a tree stripped of bark.

"Why didn't you tell me? Why didn't you tell me that was up there?" he demands, his tone dark with accusation. "All this time I'm thinking the reason he never told you anything was because nothing happened. That it was only me. But you've known all along. You've known everything. How can you tell me you care about me and still lie to my face? Don't you understand how important this is—what it means?"

His words blast up into her head and she tries not to hear. Tries not to listen, but receives everything. His eyes are dark, wholly absent of light; twin storms shadowing his face. She shrinks back as if expecting him to strike her. Flinches from a blow that is not delivered.

"When did he do it? You can at least tell me that."

She doesn't answer.

"When? When? Cat?" he repeats, his voice coming to a full stop after each word.

"Who?" she says dumbly, because all at once it is impossible to think any way other than stupidly.

"Damn it, Cat. I want the truth."

She knows there is still time to lie. She can, and he will never know any different. She can. But she doesn't.

"He didn't … he didn't paint it," she answers in a whisper, nearly choking on the oncoming waves of humiliation and horror sweeping in on the coattails of his discovery. Her words splitting apart like breaking limbs as she forces each syllable to the surface.

His eyes bore into her as if he is right now seeing the flecks of blood and brains stippling her hair and skin. Can see the stain on her dress where she wet herself sometime during the early morning hours because she is afraid to move away from the wall holding her intact. Trying to make herself believe

Reva is coming back and hasn't truly left her alone with a howling baby and her father's ruined body.

"It's not Gray's." She turns her face away, unable to meet his eyes.

"My God …" His breath whooshes out with the force of immediate comprehension. "Cat—"

She hears him say her name and she cannot answer.

Again, "Cat …"

But already she is on her feet, propelled by the immediate urgency to escape the unbearable press of his astonished stare.

Thirty-seven

He catches her before she reaches the door; wrapping his arms around her tight enough to keep her there. She thrashes wildly—twisting like a snared animal struggling for life—and still she cannot wretch free. Not until her strength is thoroughly exhausted does she crumble against the steady wall of his chest, gulping the air in great leaky breaths.

The agony of her breathing achingly settles, ragged swallows welling up from her insides, her tears soaking a wide wet patch into the front of his shirt. She feels everything inside her slipping to the floor like melting wax.

When Rance finally speaks his voice is quiet and soft against the top of her head.

"I never had polio. When I was ten my stepfather threw me down the basement stairs because I'd forgotten to roll up the garden hose. The fall broke my leg in three places.

"The pain was beyond anything I can describe. I thought I was dying, but Otto wasn't about to let my mother take me to the doctor. He knew there'd be questions and they'd already run out of believable answers by then. My mother lived in fear, not just of him, but of gossip. She knew people were starting to talk and that was a hard thing for her to take.

"I remember having a high fever and going in and out of consciousness. I couldn't feel it when he tried to set the bones—I mean, I did, but how do you separate agony from the unendurable? Needless to say, it never healed right."

She holds still, her forehead resting against his chest, soothed by the steady beating of his heart as he unwraps his tortured lullaby.

"It doesn't matter that it happened over thirty years ago. Not when I'm back here in this house. It still feels like yesterday and all those things I promised myself I'd never think about come rushing back. The injuries—but mostly the shame. That's why I didn't tell you the truth when you asked about my leg. In a way I've always felt like the author of my own disgrace—like I must've done something to mark myself a victim from the start because I wasn't good enough or clever enough to be anything else.

"Gray and Anne saw everything, but it didn't matter, what could they do? We were helpless as mice in a cage. So I took on the job of protecting myself as best I could. I even went so far as to take Otto's shotgun and bury it in the garden because I couldn't trust that his constant threats to use it were just words. I knew he'd be enraged when it turned up missing, but it felt worth the risk. Gray knew what I'd done, but he never told on me. He was like that as a kid, always watching, but never a tattletale. I was always so grateful to him for that.

"My mother gave me up the day she married Otto. I used to think she considered me something of a dirty smudge from her past. The only thing standing between her and respectability. Maybe I still think that. It's a hard thing to get rid of."

Cat's frantic desperation to be away from him—to protect herself from seeing the stark ugliness of who she is reflected in his eyes—has broken loose at some point and crumbled to dust within the circle of his arms.

"I tell myself it doesn't matter now. It's been a long time and the key players have left the stage. But I've never stopped wondering about my brother and sister. Whether Otto eventually turned on them, or if it was only me he hated. When I look at these walls you painted with Gray it makes me think my brother was clearly a sensitive man. And I can't help but think Otto would've hated such a flaw in his son."

He falls silent even as he continues to hold Cat securely against him, as if to protect them both from the far-reaching shadows of their separate memories. And when his voice comes again, his are the words that might have been her own had she only possessed the fortitude to speak them.

"I think he never told you, Cat, because he must've been as sick with it as I was. There are some stories none of us know how to tell. A life like that makes you feel like you're nothing. You tell yourself that if other people know, they'll think you're nothing too. And it's easy enough for us to believe because it's the only thing that truly makes sense.

"When I saw those pictures up there … I just … I thought … this is what I've been looking for. This is what I needed to know. This is Gray. And I felt the most incredible sense of relief thinking he'd understood after all—that it wasn't just my shitty story anymore."

He takes a step back, grips her arms, stares hard into her face, his eyes large and deep with everything he's said and what he hasn't.

"I never would've imagined it was really you I was looking at," he says, placing a hand on either side of her face, tenderly stroking away her rekindled tears with his thumbs. "What happened to you, Cat? Tell me what happened."

Thirty-eight

The wind sighs deep and moaning through branches stripped of leaves. Winter, or nearly. Everything is so cold. Broken and brittle. Lifeless and echoing in a way that leaves this ghostly dwelling feeling more bleak and ungiving than it has ever been. Making it all the more difficult for Cat to believe she has chosen this over Rance.

Increasingly as the days crawl past, she lends herself to tending the illusion he isn't really gone. That he is still here, somewhere in these rooms, holding her hand over the kitchen table as they sip their morning coffee in comfortable silence. Exchanging a warm glance or gentle touch, helping each other forget, as only the wounded can.

There is little satisfaction in her delusions. Always present is an undercurrent of the truth winding through her imaginings, marking her fantasies as the foolish and nonsensical things they are. But still she allows herself the indulgence, succumbing to hours of useless daydreams, if for no other purpose than passing the ever-widening stretches of time.

She's failed miserably in her attempts to explain to Rance why she can't go with him. It has been a hopeless endeavor—struggling to grasp the necessary words to clothe her conviction of the impossibility of leaving here. Because to lock the door and walk away is to surrender the lingering echoes and too-fast fading remembrances of Gray. And while she hasn't said these words precisely, she believes Rance recognizes all she fails to offer, if for no other reason than he feels the same about staying.

On the morning he leaves, Rance pulls Cat against him in a way that makes everything inside her shatter. He burrows his face in her hair. "Please … come with me, Cat."

"I can't," is the only thing she can say. There is nothing that fits the thoroughly impossible notion of words.

Only after a long aching stretch does he finally release her and step away. He doesn't speak, though his eyes say everything.

"Where will you go?" she asks, the question slicing her throat with a dozen sharp blades on the way out. It is a useless inquiry that has no point in being asked, inasmuch as it serves no real purpose to the one left behind.

Incredibly she is able to hold the knot of her emotions tightly within, even while she feels everything inside crumbling to fine ash. There will be time to cry later. Nothing more abundant than time.

"Back out west, probably."

"Still planning on finding a ranch?" she says, trying to smile, but can't.

"I don't know ... I'm not so sure I really even wanted that. I guess I just always feel better when I have something of a dream tucked in my pocket."

She expects to cry for days, but the tears never come. She is too numb. Her senses too dulled and impossibly tangled to complete the process. And despite her determination to forget the final words passed between them, they come back again and again, stabbing away inside her head.

"Come with me."

"I can't—I can't leave here. I … Gray is—"

"Gray is dead, Cat. He's been dead a long time. You need to stop believing you are too. You're allowed to be happy. You're allowed to have something else."

She'd been furious with him for saying what she's fought so hard not to think on her own. So angry it made her teeth hurt and her brain clench tight behind her eyes. And it is at that moment when the fragile thing they hold between them falls, tumbling out of reach beneath the disturbing impact of truth in his words, neither of them making the necessary move to retrieve it.

Her indignation carried her as far as the porch, though it might just as well have been a distance of a thousand miles. Because when she turns around, he's already climbed into the cab of his truck and closed the door.

He doesn't tip his head for a look back, not even briefly, his tires rolling down the driveway in a swirl of rising dust, out toward the highway that will take him a million roads away from here.

And she is alone in just about every way a person can be.

It is a brittle, windswept afternoon in March when Cat treks down the driveway and finds the first letter from Rance waiting in the otherwise empty mailbox. Holding it in her trembling hand, it feels as delicate and fragile as a sparrow's egg.

She hurries back to the house with her treasure clutched against her breast to protect it from the weather, tearing it open it even before she's closed the kitchen door behind her, unable to carry the weight of expectation even one step further.

She isn't especially surprised to find the envelope is empty. Somehow she understands the meaning of his wordless correspondence lies in its existence and not in anything he might say. The entirety of his message is there in the letter's return address—neatly printed in the upper left-hand corner of the envelope—asking her, telling her, inviting her, to find him.

Winter is gone and another summer nearly ended when the empty envelopes stop coming. While Cat has determined early on she will not accept his silent invitation, there has been a comforting sense of security in their continuous arrival. And now there is nothing. She feels like a mote of dust spiraling out to nowhere; helplessly falling through a never-ending string of days she can't recall other than for their sameness.

She spends long hours studying the murals she's painted with Gray, walking through memories, remembering how different life had been in the days when they were first created. How much she'd had to love and cherish when Gray was here with her. When everything turned toward them held out a promise for them to take.

Only now is Cat beginning to see those things which have previously eluded her—how extensively the colors have faded. The centers now as muted as the edges, where once the lines and purpose of these images had been sharp and clearly defined.

Without conscientiously steering herself toward it, Cat finds herself dead-eye focused on all the things Rance has revealed to her—the tragic life he'd lived in this house. She pushes her memory back to the vanished years when Gray had so assiduously planned to paint these walls with his bounding visions of sweeping magnitude. And with a sharply stabbing pang she recalls how he'd designed each tableau even before he *pretend stumbled* into finding this house.

So many of the precious things between them have been lies; a recognition which even now Cat is not wholly prepared to acknowledge anymore than she feels equipped to accept the sobering truth she can no more trust memory than she can rely on dreams.

And it stares back at her hard and unblinking—the very real possibility that it's been Gray's insidious conviction to paint a mask over the ugly truth of what this house had once been to him. Change it into something altogether unrecognizable simply by cloaking it with images of color and beauty. *Conquering the beast,* as Rance once suggested.

She knows there will never be a time when she wouldn't regret not knowing the scope of Gray's childhood injuries or wonder over the unexplained reasoning behind his decision to return here.

They have thoroughly loved each other without ever truly knowing who they are. Too many things have been left unsaid. They had been so easily contented with the little bits of nothing they'd given each other; neither willing to risk the uncertainty inherent in revealing the shame dwelling in their separate truths. Was it because they'd loved each other enough to think all the old things insignificant? Or is the actual verity far less absolute. Cowardice where there should have been trust.

It is these omissions that remain just as they've been left—a slowly turning mobile of unanswered mysteries suspended in murky fog—increasingly dark and eternally unknown.

It arrives like a lightning bolt from the heavens, though Cat suspects she's known for a time far greater—the truth this is no longer enough. Somehow, the memories of Gray she's so carefully nurtured and protected have lost their ability to sustain her. In much the same way the roll of time has drained the paling images on the walls of their former vibrancy and life.

Now, when she stares over the whole of this, accesses it with a heart unveiled and honest, she knows everything here has ceased to be adequate. Is no longer effective in buttressing the crumbling walls of her quietly fading life. Just as she knows no matter how determined she may be to hold on, she will only continue to lose it.

As much as she will always love Gray—will forever love the person she's believed him to be—she finally understands the time has come to leave him.

Cat asks Dolly Stevenson not to hammer the For Sale sign at the end of the driveway until after she's gone. The sole realtor in Lost River, Dolly has no qualms with such a request. A place like this can take years to sell, and a day, a week, or even a month, without a sign stuck into the sadly overgrown lawn isn't likely to have much of an effect on that fact.

For the first time in years Cat rekindles thoughts of once dreamed things and faraway places. Leaving here feels both impossible and necessary. There is the question of where to start, but then, not really. She knows where she's headed. Her destination as purposeful as the promise she's made herself to find it.

It is the most indescribable feeling, driving Gray's old but steady truck along roads she has never before traveled; leaving behind all those things she's never believed herself capable of relinquishing.

The woods and fields lay quiet, held still under the dewy mantel of early morning. Nothing stirs beyond the comforting whine of the engine and the occasional bumping together of the cardboard boxes she's carefully packed into the truck bed. Her cargo in leaving is nearly identical to the one she arrived with, back when she'd been a shiny new bride with a heart full to bursting with a million pinpoints of bright, hopeful light.

Everywhere are the ripe, golden shades of autumn. The air so sharp and clear the simple act of breathing feels nearly like joy. And as her lungs reach for each full and satisfied swallow, her gaze stretches out across the acres of scrub pines rolling out on either side of the road, eager to draw it all in, even as her mind speeds forward, alive and scrambling.

She folds a drifting tendril of hair behind her ear, and with one hand still holding the wheel, she reaches up to re-tuck the neatly creased road map securely in place above the visor.

Over her last days in the house, as she prepared her heart and mind for leaving, Cat had collected the necessary details to fill in the outlines of her future. And she'd studied the red inked path linking the myriad of paved veins and arteries to her destination enough times to constitute it unlikely she'll need to refer to the route now as she drives it. Still, there is something wholly assuring in having the chart there just above her head—one corner exposed in an ironclad promise.

And though she's long memorized the unchanging address neatly printed at the corner of each one of the envelopes she's received from Rance over the vacuous span of months since his leaving, Cat has nevertheless tucked his final mailing into the chest pocket of her jacket. An added assurance maybe, not only that such a place truly exists, but that he's somehow known in his heart not to leave it.

The End

About The Author

Barbara Forte Abate grew up in Millbrook New York, and currently lives in a creaky old house in Pennsylvania, where she makes up lies, doses them with truth, and titles it fiction. She is long time married to a very fine man, the mother of four pretty excellent children, and over-the-moon in love with her perfect baby grandson.

Visit Barbara at her website:
http://www.barbaraforteabate.com
and:blog;
http://www.barbaraforteabate.wordpress.com

www.ingramcontent.com/pod-product-compliance
Lightning Source LLC
LaVergne TN
LVHW051039080426
835508LV00019B/1596
* 9 7 8 0 6 9 2 2 0 9 3 4 9 *